Game in the Garden

George Colpitts

Game in the Garden:
A Human History of Wildlife
in Western Canada to 1940

UBCPress · Vancouver · Toronto

09 08 07 06 05 04 03 02   5 4 3 2 1

Printed in Canada on acid-free paper ∞

National Library of Canada Cataloguing in Publication Data

Colpitts, George, 1964-
  Game in the garden : a human history of wildlife in Western Canada to 1940 / George Colpitts.

  Includes bibliographical references and index.
  ISBN 0-7748-0962-0 (bound); ISBN 0-7748-0963-9 (pbk.)

  1. Animals and civilization – Canada, Western. 2. Animals – Social aspects – Canada, Western. 3. Wildlife utilization – Canada, Western – story. 4. Wildlife conservation – Canada, Western – History. 5. Frontier and pioneer life – Canada, Western. I. Title.

QL85.C64 2002   333.95′4′09712   C2002-911077-7

Canadä

UBC Press gratefully acknowledges the financial support for our publishing program of the Government of Canada through the Book Publishing Industry Development Program (BPIDP), and of the Canada Council for the Arts, and the British Columbia Arts Council.

This book has been published with the help of a grant from the Humanities and Social Sciences Federation of Canada, using funds provided by the Social Sciences and Humanities Research Council of Canada.

UBC Press
The University of British Columbia
2029 West Mall
Vancouver, BC V6T 1Z2
604-822-5959 / Fax: 604-822-6083
www.ubcpress.ca

To Gabriel and Francine

Contents

Illustrations and Tables

Illustrations

Tables

Acknowledgments

I have amassed debts to many people during the research and writing of this book. My first thanks go to Francine Michaud for her companionship and affectionate encouragement while this book was being completed.

Part of this book is based on my master's thesis done at the University of Calgary. Thanks must go to the Department of History there and particularly to Donald B. Smith, who, as my supervisor, taught me a great deal and showed unfailing interest in my work. I wrote other portions of the book later while I was at the University of Alberta undertaking doctoral studies and pursuing a dissertation on a fur trade topic. Many scholars there provided inspiration. My supervisor, Doug Owram, deserves special thanks for our many discussions and his enthusiasm for archival research and his love of ideas. I also greatly appreciated the guidance of the late John E. Foster and the encouragement of Gerhard Ens. The book also benefited from criticism in its earlier stages and from readers of articles published in *Prairie Forum* and *Histoire sociale/Social History*. Chapter 4 is drawn from my article in the *American Review of Canadian Studies*, which benefited from suggestions provided by readers. I also owe a personal and scholarly debt to Stuart Adams. I had the opportunity to work as a recent MA graduate under his direction on an environmental and traditional resource use study at Fort Chipewyan. That work considerably broadened my approach to questions pertaining to humans and their relationship with wildlife.

Many other people have helped me in the "writer's craft." The late Ken Lewis, journalism teacher and great friend, read the first draft of this book before his death. Chris McLean and Mark Curzon deserve special mention for their steadfast encouragement. And, of course, my family – sisters, brother, mother Berna, father Grant (deceased) – has always been supportive.

I thank the archivists and librarians at the Hudson's Bay Company Archives, Winnipeg, for permission to use materials; the National Archives of Canada; the McCord Museum Archives, Montreal; the Canadian Pacific Archives, Montreal; the Royal Ontario Museum, Toronto; and the provincial archives in Manitoba (Winnipeg), Saskatchewan (Saskatoon and Regina), Alberta (Edmonton), and British Columbia (Victoria). I must make special mention of the Glenbow Museum Archives, my home away from home in Calgary, and the courteous and always professional help extended to me by its library and archives staff.

The Alberta Historical Resources Foundation provided funds for the early research and writing of this book.

Game in the Garden

Introduction

Like most Canadian families, mine has a bear story. It was best told by my great-aunt and -uncle Hazel and Lee, longtime residents of Calgary, who in the 1960s frequently drove up to a garbage dump in Banff National Park to watch the bears. The dump was generally known as the best place to see bears. While they were there on one occasion, my aunt sent my uncle out of the car with a bag of marshmallows to entice one bear closer to her window. She had a camera and wanted a good picture.

At family dinners and other social events, Lee used to relate what happened next. The marshmallows that he scattered around the front bumper of the car eventually attracted the attention of a big black bear. Head swaying, the massive animal moved within yards of the car. My aunt, however, was squinting through her camera's wide-angle viewfinder. Unsatisfied with the picture that she was composing, she urged Lee to entice the bear closer. (He would imitate her in the storytelling: "Closer, Lee! Closer!") When he found himself offering a marshmallow to the bear's sniffing nostrils, he realized that the animal was altogether too close. It unexpectedly reared up, teetered forward on hind legs, and grabbed my uncle in what can only be described as a bear hug. Fortunately, the vigilant dump attendant working nearby intervened before anything serious happened. He ran over and hit the bear with a baseball bat.

Our favourite part of the story came at its conclusion. Back inside the car, Lee discovered that Hazel had been so startled during the encounter that she had forgotten to take the picture.

Besides its entertainment value, the story raises questions about why my aunt wanted to photograph a bear in a dump in the first place. The public has less interest now in visiting wildlife in such settings. Wild animals are not ideally viewed, much less photographed, living off human garbage. If they are still allowed to frequent dumps, these garbage-eating bears are generally passed off as too domesticated for photographic preservation. I learned this when I asked a park attendant in Kananaskis Country, Alberta, where I could find a similar garbage dump to watch bears. I was told in frosty tones that such recreation was no longer available in provincial parks, or in Banff National Park for that matter, and that if I wanted to see a bear that way I should go to a zoo.

Evidently, bears and other "wild" animals are appreciated differently according to historical circumstances. Like other aspects of the natural world, wild animals continue to occupy specific but changing places within the modern imagination. In this book, I attempt to identify such places in the history of the Canadian west up to the Second World War. As a "social" history, the book depends on a broad range of intellectual, social, and economic indices to evaluate the subsistence and imaginative purposes of wildlife within communities that happened to be in conflict with the natural world. It will become clear that, when they are followed to their sources, stories, symbols, and rituals surrounding wild animals found meaning in particular settings where expectations and fears accompanied western development. In the case of the Canadian west, frontier and pioneer societies invested wild animals with new symbolic meanings at critical moments of environmental and economic change.

Most European and North American communities have similar histories worth pursuing. This book delimits its geographical boundaries according to outstanding features of western Canadian history. In its earliest conceptualization, the area sprawled west of Lake Superior and beyond the mountains as a wild animal reserve. This expanse of forest, lake, river, and plain tended to form a single geographical reference in European mind-sets as early as the late eighteenth century. By then, it was the most contested beaver-pelt-producing region of Rupert's Land, earlier ceded to the Hudson's Bay Company as the extent of watershed drainage into Hudson Bay. By the early nineteenth century, it extended farther, as did the fur trade, when the British "Indian Territory" that encompassed the Mackenzie region and the western drainage of the Rockies was annexed to Rupert's Land. The centre of the fur trade, western Canada found its first unity in the returns of animal pelts; a far more important economy of wild meat protein, however, gave these regions a common history. This was particularly the case with food sharing between First Nations and newcomers. Such a geographical boundary remained meaningful to early settlers making sense of their new surroundings.

Members of the Historical and Scientific Society of Manitoba, who first met in 1879, for instance, still collected the animals, fishes, birds, historical objects, and fur trade relics found within much of this area. Their interest in preserving the area's wildlife specimens – including the almost extinct buffalo – was no accident. They identified meanings in wildlife that were attached to a particular place, the west. For them, wildlife had long returned tangible benefits to their western communities, social stability being one of them. Subsequent periods of western development, becoming intensive by the late nineteenth century, led westerners to develop common directions of naturalist study, conservation schemes, and even some of the first preservation programs.

This topic can be approached as a regional study for another reason. In many areas of western Canada, common symbolic meanings were attached to wildlife. Westerners joined in the heavy promotion of the west officially undertaken by the federal government's Department of the Interior after 1870. Provincial, territorial, and municipal governments added their own promotional images. Wildlife taxidermy, illustrations, photographs, and peltry communicated certain ideas about vacant homestead lands and resource industries that demanded immigrant workers and outside investment. As might be expected, westerners using animals for such promotional purposes modified significantly the ethics and message of the North American conservation movement gaining ground elsewhere. Westerners indeed often advertised – and exaggerated – regional wealth by describing wild animals, fishes, and birds as superabundant. In doing so, they sharpened contrasts between the Canadian west and the impoverished American (and by implication) central Canadian wildlife populations.[1] Some aspects of environmentalism, indeed, were rejected completely in a region represented as inherently abundant in wildlife and, more evocatively, providing refuge for animals fleeing American overdevelopment, pollution, and industrialization.

The idea of western superabundance conformed to the expectations of visitors and writers who had long imagined the region as a "refuge" for wildlife. In early representations of Rupert's Land and the British "Indian Territory," wild animals ranged in abundance. Animals, indeed, defined the region as wild. When *Saturday Magazine* published a lengthy essay on the fur trade in the 1840s, it conceptualized the region as a natural world separate from civilization;[2] it was, as the article suggested, a place for "privations and trials" where trappers and hunters not only faced hunger, cold, and fatigue but were also "frequently attacked by grizzly bears."[3] In this account and numerous others, wild animals defined certain harsh qualities that thrilled European readers of the time. This wildlife, indeed, gave to Rupert's Land a transcendental nature and inspired romantic writers who hoped that a close encounter with a terrifying natural realm would allow the soul to commune, or find its correspondence, with the natural and the unexplainable. Wildlife remained an essential ingredient in the mixture of geographical, topographical, and climatic features forming contemporary ideals of the British North American wilderness. Overrun by nature's "minions," the territory was viewed as distinct from the artificial and temporal world of fallen humans. The *Saturday Magazine* article turned with great interest toward the fur traders themselves, who lived "in the depths of

wilderness": it was a wonder that men "more or less civilized" would aban-
don comforts at home to "wander through the wildernesses and sterile plain,
the companions of wild beasts, or men almost equally wild."[4]

This was by no means an isolated case in which a narrative describing the
fur trade territories identified animals and men as "companions," living
together in such close proximity that they were equally confused as "wild."
In many of the earliest published accounts, western images blurred distinctions between a wildlife and a human refuge. The region gained an identity from titles such as H.M. Robinson's *Great Fur Land*.[5] The 1885 Achilles
Daunt narrative more blatantly drew the west as a wildlife refuge. The
central characters of *In the Land of Moose, Buffalo, and Bear* (describing
areas of present-day northern Alberta) were wild animals and humans, the
latter rejecting the false promises of civilization to live in wilderness areas.
Sportsmen such as Dr. W.B. Cheadle, Lord Milton, Charles Messiter, and
the Earl of Southesk sold their nineteenth-century narratives to readers
back home fascinated by natural regions abounding in wildlife. The habit
of thinking about the west as a land where wildlife ranged in plenitude
proved to be long-standing. Even in the twentieth century, big-game hunters from abroad described western areas as "unexplored" and drew maps by
hand to show the "wild" state of the land and their quarry. Never missing a
promotional opportunity, Canadian Pacific Railway shipped taxidermy displays to Europe to magnify the western image as an abundant big-game
reserve and a region welcoming homesteaders. A region so well stocked
with wild animals, fishes, and birds offered almost unimaginable natural
wealth. So persuasive was this proposition that, by the early 1900s, British
Columbia's first chief game guardian, Bryan Williams, coined the expression "jumping-off places" to describe the province's many departure points
for hunting and fishing opportunities. The expression suggested some of
the emancipation offered by a visit to the western wildlife refuge.[6]

As the foregoing suggests, such an understanding of the west had a specific meaning. By the early nineteenth century, wild animals were increasingly invested with potent imaginative associations. The rise of Darwinian
understandings of a "web of life" connected animals more closely with human natural history. Natural selection itself was founded on the mechanism and drama of competition between species in nature. It is difficult to
assess the impact of Darwinian science on popular mind-sets in the nineteenth century; however, social Darwinists certainly capitalized on a distorted version of Darwinian theory that in turn heightened lay interest in
animals in nature. By the late nineteenth century, wild animals displayed
natural instincts. They competed with each other according to the amoral
dictate of self-preservation, surviving at all costs. To Europeans, the struggle
between wild animals raised an evocative corollary in urban settings: the
relations of wild animals in nature might parallel a struggle between races,

between rich and poor, between civil and "savage" within human communities. Wild animals, then, gained new currency in writing and philosophical debate. European and American city dwellers, moreover, already perceived a distance between urban and rural environments; many, reviving Arcadian pastoralism, identified the degraded human condition within heavily populated places by pointing to alternative relations between animals in nature. Humanitarian campaigns against cruelty toward animals, the purity movement to cleanse dirt and morals in impoverished city areas, and the public drive to establish parks in cities all gathered momentum when their supporters pointed to the evident lessons of the wild animal kingdom.[7]

Although there were innumerable ideas about animals in the nineteenth century, Romanticism itself likely allowed Europeans and North Americans to view wildlife as essentially different from domesticated animals. Before the Romantics, traditional systems of philosophy ranked life on Earth according to scholastic hierarchies. Medieval thinkers, drawing on Aristotle and other classical writers, placed both wild and domesticated animals in the same category. Animal life was defined not according to its proximity to the human home and the degree of submission to human will but according to the nature of the soul invested in it by God. The popularity in France of René Descartes's writings, as radical as they were in their conception of "animal machines," revived interest among the *philosophes* in recognizing animals – and sometimes even humans – as machines driven by natural instincts. But many eighteenth-century thinkers still believed that humans had a divine intellect breathed into them by God and that their animal counterparts belonged to a lower order. Although that subkingdom gained greater complexity with naturalist study, its members were still separated by equal distance from humans' special place in the divine order.

A new appreciation of nature in the nineteenth century prompted a revolutionary new sensibility toward animate and sentient beings. Now writers more readily separated wild from domesticated animals. The Romantic legacy defined nature as an organic rather than a mechanical entity and invested it with a host of positive qualities. Although the Romantics themselves did not display great interest in wildlife, their literary and artistic adherents subsequently appreciated animals living in nature as inherently different from their domesticated counterparts. This "wild life," as it was first understood, had a mystical nature and an essential purity compared with animals subjugated to human will. As a construct of the imagination, "wildlife" as *indominitus* (i.e., not domesticated by humans) seemed to gain its positive understanding during the post-Romantic period.[8] Thus, as ancient as the notion of wilderness is, as the "nest" or "lair" of wild animals (from the Anglo-Saxon expression *wylder ness*),[9] the nineteenth century was a period when modern values and veneration of wildlife came to the fore. Wild animals lived beyond human control; they offered numerous lessons to and gained didactic usefulness among writers and social critics deeply troubled by growing urban squalor and later by the social and environmental effects of the Industrial Revolution.

Visitors usually applied some aspect of Romantic criteria of landscape to appreciate the geography of Rupert's Land. Wild animals, too, helpfully defined the boundaries of this natural world against those of the civil one thousands of miles away. Even by the beginning of the twentieth century, back-to-nature adherents searched for wildlife so that the regions visited could be validated as truly natural. The same visitors, meanwhile, were chiefly interested in certain types of wildlife. Present-day nature guides list over seventy-five wild mammals in western Canada. They range from wolverines to white-tailed rabbits, golden-mantled ground squirrels to hoary bats. Nature lovers now search for amphibians, reptiles, birds, invertebrates, and fishes in their ramblings through wilderness. In earlier periods, as published accounts suggest, the wildlife species most interesting to visitors were comparatively smaller in number. The beaver and its amazing social and survival habits and the seeming intelligence of voles, gophers, and other animals became interesting according to the degree to which these animals attained self-sufficiency, struggled to survive in nature, and lived apart from human control. Fish and fowl also interested naturalists in the nineteenth century from this perspective, especially when they proved the existence and suggested the complexity of either a design in nature or natural law. But the wild animals that attracted the greatest attention were the larger-framed mammals, which lent themselves to moral storytelling. They later occupied many of the narratives of Canadian nature writers such as Charles G.D. Roberts and Ernest Thompson Seton.[10] Large mammalian quadrupeds – buffalo, elk, deer, bear, antelope, and other animals – shared with humans important morphological similarities. Their mouths could display anger and a range of other emotions. Their eyes could communicate fear, pain, and sometimes pleasure. Newcomers easily switched from thinking of these animals as objects of utilitarian exchange in a subsistence economy to granting them a new place in a Romantic pantheon. Whether in folklore or in a taxidermy hall, these animals suggested aspects of the human condition but were still wild. The Earl of Southesk suggested how such sympathetic traits could be identified after a mountain sheep hunt at Jasper House in 1859. He looked over the dozens of animals he had recklessly shot and wrote, "One thinks little – too little of the killing of small game, but in shooting large game the butchery of the act comes more home, one sees with such vividness the wounds, and the fear, and the suffering."[11]

Since it was believed that such wild animals were inherently different from their tamed counterparts, it is not surprising that the former served didactic purposes. To old-timers, wildlife became important indices of economic and social change. To newcomers, wildlife embodied natural wealth.

Their interest in wild animals, then, barely concealed their expectations, fears, and aspirations in the lands that they were newly occupying. In numerous pioneer settings, wildlife symbolized the obstacles – natural and human – that farmers encountered when they tried to claim and clear land. Charles Dickens's *American Notes* described a Canadian government official who had to dissuade an eastern European immigrant "from investing some of his small capital in firearms and knives to kill the buffalo, wolves and other wild animals which his fellow passengers had persuaded him were to be encountered in the streets of Winnipeg."[12] Most settlers expected a confrontation would take place between themselves as agents of civilization and the wildlife that they would encounter on the prairies. Many of the killing rituals in settler society – the railway platform shooting sprees (before they became illegal), the piles of ducks in town sites, and the strings of fish in postcard photos – find sociological explanation in the dual cosmos that newcomers imaginatively traversed in coming to a wild land.[13]

To analyze such matters, I have divided this book into five chapters. In Chapter 1, I examine fur trade society, its "traditional" uses of wildlife, and the social relations established with the exchange of wild meat. The chapter does not provide a complete treatment of Amerindian hunting and religious traditions concerning wildlife. It does, though, identify elements of Amerindian customs involving the exchange of wild meat that lay the foundation for fur trade society. Sharing food in the fur trade significantly altered the European experience in the west and determined in no small measure the outcome of relations at contact and the outlines of an interdependency between people in the west.

In Chapter 2, I discuss the period when the dominance of the fur trade in western life officially ended, at the time of the transfer of the Hudson's Bay Company lands to Canadian care in 1870. Although many watersheds in western history preceded the transfer, the chapter identifies the imaginative construction of an old order and a new order at the time, when a way of life dependent on wild animals was replaced by one dependent on individuals, merit, and farming improvements. The 1870s were a difficult period for westerners who made the agricultural transition successfully. Moreover, continued dependency on wild meat undermined western promotion. More distressing, however, was the real social crisis that arose when wildlife populations began to disappear by the mid-1870s. The near extermination of the buffalo and the extirpation of many big-game populations in the west led both old-timers and newcomers to assign new symbolism to wild animals. They also kindled some of the first interest in conservation, particularly in wildlife domestication schemes that promised to safeguard features of the old order in a new settler society and thereby to ensure social stability.

Conservation initiatives and domestication schemes quickly disappeared with the first land rushes and the beginnings of the wheat boom. Chapter 3 examines the Laurier era, when rapid homesteading, western promotion, and immigration formed a backdrop of change that affected local understandings of wildlife. Although rapid settlement and city growth brought about an unprecedented demand for wild meat, westerners were anxious to achieve complete self-sufficiency within western nature. A new priority was the revolutionary transubstantiation of a food source into a symbol of western development. To curb subsistence hunting and end settler dependence on provisioning hunters, newspapers showed animals as emblems of western climate, poor soil, and thick forests that inhibited the growth of towns and crops. Charter groups began "safeguarding" local resources, particularly wildlife, from Amerindian subsistence hunts in a period when they hoped to gain control of natural wealth and conserve British-Canadian values. In fact, not only Amerindians but also recent immigrants and marginal groups within communities faced stringent game ordinances while wildlife became closely associated with the natural wealth that pioneers sought.

Meanwhile, as I point out in Chapter 4, local boosters began using wildlife in promotions, natural history museums, postcard photographs, and slaughter rituals to suggest the natural wealth of the region that they were promoting. Rapid demographic changes and competition between towns and cities for people and investors intensified this promotional effort. Pioneers now portrayed the wildlife to be as abundant as the wealth that they advertised in virgin western soils, pristine forests, and unexploited mineral claims.

The close association of wild animals with natural wealth led, in no small measure, to the formal conservation strategies that took shape just before and after the Great War. In Chapter 5, I examine the membership and aims of fish and game protective associations that gathered momentum between 1885 and 1940. These associations seemed to gain their greatest following during acute moments when boosterism, overspeculation in western resources, and demographic explosion wreaked havoc on settler communities. Rising fears of "foreigners" and disagreement over the use of the land and its resources energized early conservation work, often against marginalized outsiders, particularly new immigrants and First Nations. Leading townspeople enacted the first wildlife ordinances to control groups and, conversely, to conserve community values associated with the intended model of charter societies. By the beginning of the Second World War, preservation campaigns had already led to the opening of game preserves. But even these initiatives can be traced to local social concerns. Particularly after the Great War, westerners supported wildlife preserves in part to create areas of abundance to enrich neighbouring settler communities and to replicate a pre-Fall state in nature from which western society would benefit morally, spiritually, and economically.

As a contributor to environmental history, I remain unapologetically anthropocentric. In this book, I seek chiefly to identify early ideas about wild animals and a wider western context of hunting, conservation, and preservation history. My emphasis on local history takes me in a different direction from that of Janet Foster in her examination of the rise of preservationism in the federal civil service. The development of national parks policy had, as she rightly points out, great implications for the west, where many preserves were soon established. I have identified a grassroots movement that Foster did not address. Robert G. McCandless has more recently undertaken a similar analysis in his "social history" of Yukon wildlife, as has Paul-Louis Martin in his analysis of hunting in Quebec. My book, indeed, focuses more on changing definitions of "good" and "bad" animals, new uses for wildlife, and the social backdrop of game ordinances. I follow, in that respect, some of the social analytical approaches in western Canadian history that David Elliston Allen, Harriet Ritvo, Keith Thomas, and James Turner have used in studies of the changing place of animals in English society at critical points in its social, intellectual, and economic development.[14]

In taking this approach, I am attempting to remedy a feature of environmental history that overlooks social explanation to explore attitudes toward wildlife. Most work addressing the place of wildlife in North American thought has investigated the rise of conservation and later preservation policies that occurred after environmental change.[15] Although some writers have assessed the scientific, industrial, and economic backdrops to such matters,[16] historians have mainly been concerned with identifying the emergence of modern sensibilities, chief among them critical pathways to ecological understandings.[17] As valuable as their work has been, this primary interest has generally been directed at Americans who formed sport hunting lobbies or founded a scientific interest in animal preservation.[18] Endangered and extirpated species such as the buffalo have also captured a great deal of attention in this respect. The buffalo's rapid disappearance in the west certainly figured in the march of such ideas. Once the bloody skin trade had begun by the 1870s, predated by environmental and human population changes on the Great Plains, the alarming spectacle of near extinction sparked new sensibilities.[19] By the 1880s, the first conservationists were using the buffalo as a powerful symbol to fortify campaigns against other forms of commercial hunting and the still thriving but environmentally devastating feather industries.[20]

Historians, however, often look to specific groups affected by the disappearance of such animals for intellectual changes,[21] such groups often being the sport hunters who lost their game and turned to conservation work.[22] But there is little work exploring the interplay between social thought and environmental thought, modes of subsistence and attitudes toward wildlife, conservation practices and contemporary economics, and preservation movements and social phenomena such as xenophobia and nativism. Moreover, little research has been directed at what are arguably unique Canadian responses to the environment and local traditions in wildlife hunting, use, and conservation. This last point seems to be all the more important because many western Canadian environmental activities grew out of the belief that settlers had a right to wildlife abundance. The political history of western environmentalism is often marked in fact by a complete disregard of the American conservation movement or by innovations to it.[23] In this book, I look at some western understandings of environmental sensibilities, those established within local settings, by examining wildlife in its social context.[24]

I am reviving more than simply a past drama; I am also indicating some of the problems that the past continues to impose on the present. In light of what are now understood as ecological realities, the Romantic definition of wildlife makes mistaken assumptions about nature and contradicts conservation priorities. Wildlife has been viewed, and continues to be understood, as animate creatures that live beyond the imaginary boundaries of town and city. Although preservationists sometimes benefit from the enduring popularity of this conceptualization, its archaic intellectual foundations continue to influence government policy and public opinion. It is often easy for conservation groups to mobilize public support against measures that affect wildlife in distant park reserves. But when the same animals violate boundaries and enter civilized spaces, they become either virtuously domesticated or hunted as vermin. Wildlife can easily become a nuisance to civilization and a detraction to investment capital. As wildlife biologists and ecologists often point out, the human mind-set that dichotomizes human from wild nature places significant restrictions on real ways of maintaining environmental diversity and initiatives in biodiversity. Reincorporating wildlife into human society will only take place with major intellectual changes and a complete rejection of Romantic conceptions about any animal being "wild" and any life form really being "domesticated." In that regard, a historical lesson drawn from western Canada is that an animal that transcends its nature and is understood by a community as "wildlife" does not, and really cannot, become truly extinct. This chilling thought is best apprehended in the case of the buffalo. This animal still generates the emotional response among westerners that it did in the 1890s, when newcomers saw massive piles of bones along railway lines. That response was likely as striking as the emotions felt by those who saw the original herds in the Saskatchewan River valleys. Perhaps, indeed, ecologists have difficulty trying to preserve the diversity of wild animals when they move against the modernist human mind. Dead or alive, wild animals provide nourishment for the human imagination. John A. Livingston's recent condemnation of the "fallacy" of wildlife conservation is greatly supported by my own findings.[25] The problem is not that wild animals have not been conserved in the past; indeed, much of western Canadian history has been shaped around the conservation of wildlife as food, totems, symbols, and valuable commodities for recreational pursuit. The problem is in trying to move the human mind beyond the dated conception of wildlife as a resource to be "managed," "husbanded," "harvested," or "preserved." I provide an overview of this modernist dilemma as it was played out in the Canadian west when human society underwent change and shared an uneasy history with the wild animals in its midst.

1
Amerindians, Voyageurs, and the Animal Exchange in the Western Fur Trade

In 1774, increasing competition in the North American fur trade forced Hudson's Bay Company (HBC) employees to voyage inland from their Arctic coastline forts. They were intent on re-establishing trade relations with Amerindian middlemen who were being met in the interior by rival traders from Montreal. However, when canoes ran ashore at Pine Island Lake, in present-day Manitoba, brigadesmen eager to build Cumberland House likely wondered how they would feed themselves.

The land itself offered few immediate answers. The chilly waters of the Saskatchewan River briefly slowed there before rushing southwest to the massive Lake Winnipeg basin. Outcrops of Canadian Shield granite were covered in lichen, wild onion, and little else. The men unloading bales of goods would undoubtedly have anticipated the approach of winter, only a few months distant, and noticed the impressive but daunting aspects of northern Manitoba geography. Mirrored in the lake's surface was the scruffy outline of the mixed boreal forest, beyond which rose a Precambrian landmass swept by subarctic winds.

With food supplies dwindling, the men had little hope of returning to Hudson Bay. The tumpline ascent of the Nelson River and the numerous backbreaking portages inland had already mauled most of the brigade's canoes. The HBC employees were physically exhausted from sixteen- to eighteen-hour days spent either paddling or portaging. By now, the men were building their camp to withstand the summer and, particularly, the winter ahead. Beginning to consume the last of their dried goods from York Factory, they found themselves increasingly dependent on Amerindian hunters, who provided them with wild meat.[1]

The exchange between fur traders and provisioning Amerindians forms an opening chapter in a social history of wildlife in western Canadian society. As these HBC employees soon learned, wild meat circulated as the first currency of the northwest. Tacit obligations arose in this exchange, and they learned that the "custom of the country" included reciprocation of the food supply. They recorded the importance of these exchanges long into the nineteenth century. From Cumberland House along a labyrinth of brigade river routes westward, wild meat changed hands and reached disparate areas of Rupert's Land and what became known as the British "Indian Territory." Tracing even local exchanges suggests that shared food resources served to link people during early contact. And the meat exchange, the chief subject of this chapter, determined some of the earliest human relations in what is now the Canadian west.

Clear instructions were given to the first traders who went inland. They were to increase the numbers of furs from Amerindians at the greatest margins of profit. In the case of the Hudson's Bay Company, based in London and supporting the North American fur trade since 1670, the annual packet of letters to Hudson Bay usually included a directive to better the previous year's trade. Even if this basic order was not repeated to each person at each post, company symbolism and the trade's exchange units subtly reminded everyone why Europeans were in North America in the first place. The company motto was *pro pelle cutem*, "skin for skin." The beaver and the stag adorned the company's coat of arms in the monopoly seal appearing on numerous documents and on baggage. As soon as they reached Hudson Bay, employees dealt exclusively in "made beaver" currency (abbreviated in accounts as "MB"), representing the current value of goods exchanged for a prime beaver skin. Meat, fur, skin, tallow, and other animal products were converted into this currency for accounting purposes. Traders were commanded in turn to keep track of the skins and furs collected at a post. Adept at bookkeeping, they carefully enumerated these animal products in thickly bound accounts sent by canoe "inward" – that is, back to York Factory. After being double-checked there, the books went back to London by boat. Crucial to the year-end accounting were these MB units, the "returns" that constituted the number of furs and skins traded from Amerindian middlemen, and the trader's own evaluation of trade goods, also converted to the skin standard, used to procure each post's returns.

This might suggest that the company focused solely on the outward and commercially valuable portions of a wild animal, and the trade did depend on these staples. All HBC employees understood their ultimate responsibility to home investors. Even in remote areas of the New World, Europeans were surprisingly knowledgeable about home market conditions and the commercial capital supporting their work. Andrew Graham, who wrote in the 1760s some of the first and most complete naturalist writings in the north, kept himself well informed about the converted retail value of wildlife. At York Factory, he described the natural history of the caribou and noted that its skin sold for four to six shillings in London. The marten, "well known to the English ladies as it makes them muffs and tippets," sold for six to fifteen shillings each.[2] Whether traders took advantage of profit sharing in an enterprise or simply hoped to hold on to their jobs, they worked diligently to support European demands and zealously dispatched a staggering quantity of furs and skins homeward. When wildlife biologists today attempt to gauge the impact of the trade on animal populations, using company inventories that have survived, they determine that millions of animals were killed during the North American fur trade.[3] Probably, then, it was not only Dogribs and Slaveys who complained about traders being too eager to gather up skins. After offering animal meat to a trader in the subarctic, they observed that he spoke "too strongly for Hair, that Meat has not hair."[4]

This industry, sustained with returns from dead animals, became more voracious as traders travelled farther into the interior. The Napoleonic Wars drove up the prices of goods and shipping charges. Competition between traders further raised prices on goods. Companies therefore urged employees to trade anything cartilaginous, furry, or leathery that might find profitable exchange back home. This meant that, by the early nineteenth century, when hundreds of Europeans found postings in present-day western Canada, the trade gathered the skins of as many as forty-two animals and birds. They included four colours of bear, six colour phases of fox, "panther," "polecat," porcupine, and sea lion. Europeans took the skins of grebes and loons, musk-oxen, and elk. Traders even took bone and sinew. Barrels of bear grease were shipped home by the hundredweight measure. Innumerable bales of bedding down made their way to auction, as did blubber; goose, swan, and eagle feathers; reindeer horns; walrus tusks; tallow; tortoise shells; and whalebone. When prices for certain furs fell, a recurrent problem of European markets by the mid-nineteenth century, the trade seized on alternative species. Red River community members produced buffalo wool in the 1820s to cash in on rising demand in industrializing Europe. Some 600 pounds of the coarse hair were combed from the carcasses of buffalo in 1818, 5,516 pounds by 1822. Buffalo tongues offered other profits. Those not eaten by traders went home in barrels to auctions. Almost 2,200 tongues went to England in 1823, 4,300 in 1845. When numbers dropped to only 370 in 1875, the buffalo disappearing by then from its western ranges, deer tongues became a favoured import. Some animal products simply appealed to tastes for the exotic. No fewer than 230 pairs of elk antlers went to England in 1806. Not to be forgotten were the two massive chests "of quadrupeds and birds" aboard an HBC ship bound for the Royal Society in 1771 and the specimens of "American Panther," "Mountain Deer," and "Albatross" that followed from the Columbia River in 1831.[5]

Traders and Amerindians prepared most of these animal products for the Atlantic sailing. Labourers followed a meticulous regime to avoid having skins spoil during the crossing. Dried lynx skins were rolled with the fur on the outside. Marten claws were carefully clipped before furs were wrapped.

Beaver and bear skins were beaten and dusted before being baled. In the early nineteenth century, fur presses allowed employees to bind large numbers of furs into cubes easy to stack in a ship's hold. Between 250 and 300 marten and fox pelts could be pressed into a single bale. Wrapped over each bale were ten large beaver skins and two bear skins; sometimes bear and beaver skins were placed on the top and bottom of a bale, while deer skins were wrapped around the sides to provide protection. Marten and silver and cross fox skins were shipped in sixty-pound to eighty-four-pound bales protected by dressed leather.[6]

These exports arrived in Europe in what can fairly be described as wind-battered arks. The cargo was transferred to massive warehouses in London, and the bales were opened so that the furs could be separated into lots for sale. Crusty with blood, alive with vermin, unimaginably smelly, these skins underwent their final exchange in crowded auction houses. Although reporting at a later date, a *London Times* article in 1914 caught a glimpse of these auctions. Over a three-week period, "ten to twelve million skins" (undoubtedly an exaggeration) were sold. The reporter visited one warehouse five storeys high, each storey "packed from floor to ceiling with skins." The short-haired species captured his attention, but he also counted 208 grizzlies, 141 black bears and 16 polar bears, and 411 lynxes. Although "scientific deodorants were used upon each skin," the reporter stated, "the aggregate of millions of them together [ensured that] they are far from odorless."[7]

Furs and skins, then, dominated the first large-scale capitalist venture in present-day western Cànada. But the hides of animal carcasses were of less concern to traders than their official accounting suggests – and their overseas directors likely preferred. Although the trader's career developed with the returns of skins, his life depended on the collection and preservation of animal flesh. No activity of the inland fur trade was so critical to his survival. Furthermore, the scarcity of food, high cost of wild meat, and need for Native hunting techniques inevitably separated even the most conscientious trader from the narrow commercial concerns of metropolitan accountants.

Their journals and letters clearly indicate that fur traders fretted about food almost all the time. North West Company traders divided themselves along dietary lines between the "mangeurs de lard" who transported goods from Montreal to the lakehead and still ate salt pork and the "northwesters" who ate wild meat.[8] The northwester built a reputation on and drew some of his identity from a stark dependency on nature inland. This "most wretched state Man can be inflicted with," as one trader described his northwestern service, included the vast consumption of wild meat, which at times was his only food staple.[9] One trader at Lesser Slave Lake lamented being "confined to the courser [sic] foods, and deprived of almost every comfort."[10] The wild meat diet helped to remind traders that they had been completely removed from civilization. Even trade organizers admitted that life inland, with its attendant rigours and discomforts, revolved around a dietary regime that severely tested even the most able recruits. Those dispatching Montreal brigades to areas beyond Lake Superior glumly noted that "those whose stomachs require fresh Beef and Poultry will not suit that country."[11]

Life inland was not only foreign in terms of diet but also notoriously harsh. Enjoying little of the European food supply available even at frigid York Factory,[12] the wild meat eaters of the northwest often went hungry. Posted either on the plains or in parkland belts, traders diverted much of their energy to a perpetual search for meat. They sought fresh venison, for instance, as a possible remedy for scurvy.[13] They anxiously awaited Amerindian visitors not only for social interaction but also because they often brought food. Traders stretched their imaginations to discover similarities between country food and home fare. When big-game flesh was not available, a starving trader could eat porcupine, which, when roasted, tasted like suckling pig. Traders also ate "Albany beef," the euphemism for the sturgeon often boiled in a soup: "delicious," trader John Long stated, "but as it rather increases the appetite for food, as I have experienced, it should not be taken but when there is plenty of meat to be got."[14] Complete reliance on fish, particularly sturgeon, seriously undermined morale, and traders believed that too much fish ruined their health. When nothing else was available, they defied their commercial directives and ate their furs. They claimed that bear skins, shaven and boiled in water, could taste a little like pork; if made into a soup with lichen, known as *tripe de la roche,* bear skin broth could save one's life. But traders also feared the intestinal cramping that often accompanied this last resort.

HBC employees maintained journals separate from a post's accounts that help to clarify the degree to which the search for food dominated day-to-day life in the fur trade. They recorded the first appearance of geese and waterfowl in spring and fall. They noted the success or failure of Amerindians hunting around their posts. Traders almost unfailingly numbered and identified by species the fish caught daily in nearby lakes and streams. They diligently maintained a record of the pheasants shot, rabbits snared, and moose killed. Their quills scratched out the total weight of flesh arriving on a Native's sled or canoe. At Cumberland House, these concerns were prominent in the post's first journals. The writers recorded news offered by Amerindians in 1776 that "no moose are about" and in 1778 that there were "no moose stirring." Within a year of the establishment of Cumberland House, a trader reported that lynx (the "inland cats") were nowhere to be found. This foretold a downturn for rabbit populations in the winter ahead, no trivial matter considering that rabbits and pheasants might be the only protein available to rationed traders in January and February.

As well as lamenting his famine, the European trader celebrated his feast. John Long noted "the joy arising from an unexpected supply, and sitting down to a table in the wilderness."[15] H.M. Robinson praised a plains posting "well stocked with all the delicacies and substantials afforded by the surrounding country." He bragged about his plate being filled with buffalo hump and moose nose, "the finest and most savory waterfowl, and the freshest of fish." Like many traders, this hungry European was also a voracious natural historian. He cited ninety-four different quadrupeds in the west and suggested that he knew how to cook them all. "The list of meats is so extensive," he said, "and each requiring a particular mode of cooking that a long time may elapse without a repetition of dishes."[16]

When possible, those dishes were arranged around a hierarchy of meat preferences. Following Amerindian tastes, northwest traders ranked wildlife according to its palatability. Moose was the tastiest to traders because of its soft fat, particularly when they ate the *dépouille*, the portion of fat three to six inches thick beneath the skin along the moose's back. Stripped from a carcass and dipped in hot grease, this delicacy was hung up to dry and smoked before being eaten. Traders preferred females over males in a species, cow over bull moose, moose over elk and caribou, elk over cow buffalo and deer, and so on. Although yielding little flesh, beaver and muskrat provided valuable and tasty dietary diversions. Fish, ranked low in the hierarchy, was nonetheless a basic and important staple, even on the plains. Red deer (wapiti) were hunted and their flesh traded only when moose and other animals were not available; the fat of wapiti left a bad taste in the mouth.[17]

The uncertain food supply inland was a feature of northern continental ecology and the fur trade's business organization. The lines of trade from both Montreal and Hudson Bay followed the great water routes over subarctic, boreal, mixed boreal, parkland, and plains zones that spread out around the Precambrian shield. Each zone provided different varieties and quantities of game resources. Many features of western Canadian geography were misunderstood in the mid-nineteenth century by outsiders who believed that the area was inherently abundant in game. European settlers imagined these natural regions in Edenic terms and, by implication, human conditions within them in idyllic terms.

The area most populated seasonally with wildlife – the region with the greatest available supply of meat – was likely the wide band of plains, scrublands, and in winter northerly aspen parklands that trailed east to west across much of the present-day prairie provinces. There moose and deer lived in copses along rivers and tributaries, and buffalo moved in massive herds on the plains. In winter, buffalo herds usually moved from the bald plains to the protection of mixed aspen forests. Antelope herds – impressive in their own right – complemented the heavy grazing of buffalo by feeding off brush and forbs. Deer and elk, coexisting with these animals in winter, browsed on aspen buds. In many river environments, forests protected trading posts and provided some moose and deer meat. Indeed, traders living along the Saskatchewan and Peace Rivers occasionally noted abundant populations of elk, deer, and bear.[18]

They knew, however, that their forest food supply could easily be exhausted. Both local hunting pressure and inexplicable natural forces emptied forests of certain game. The farther north from the prairies traders went, the more uncertain their hunting success became. When the fur trade moved into the Mackenzie region and subarctic areas, the hunt often depended on seasonal migrations of caribou and large herds of elk. People living in these regions frequently depended on short-haired animals such as rabbit and wetland species such as muskrat and beaver. When traders moved to postings beyond the Great Divide in the climax forests in the interior of modern-day British Columbia, they were often desperately short of local food. Indeed, most areas where the fur trade took place required backup food supplies. In the subarctic, Europeans encountered Chipewyan, Dene, Dogrib, and other trading peoples who themselves frequently faced starvation. Their hunters often arrived at posts with little food to offer. William Dease in 1825 at Old Fort on Great Bear Lake reported the "poverty" of the lake and the Slaveys who lived nearby: "a Motley Crew they are and overstocked with families and vermin, they are incessantly begging for the few fish we take."[19] McLeod's Lake Post employees, in what is now north-central British Columbia, lived almost exclusively on fish, rotten or fresh, and made up shortfalls with pemmican from the plains.[20] At Fort Resolution, in what is now the Northwest Territories, employees struggled to survive in 1861 on potatoes and fish.[21] During the winter of 1833 at Fraser's Lake, near Great Slave, one trader reported the news of fourteen Amerindians near his post who "paid the debt of Nature from Starvation" because of poor fishing that year.[22]

The patchwork nature of game populations and the periodic, and sometimes chronic, food scarcities inland were not well anticipated by HBC traders who first reached the Saskatchewan River in the 1770s. Back at Hudson Bay, they had heard from visiting Cree middlemen that the plains and forest regions abounded with "buffalow, moose and waskesews (elk)," as Andrew Graham recorded as early as 1767. Those who ventured across barren shield country and reached the inland regions discovered the vagaries of this bounty. Samuel Hearne's men did not get very far across the shield before they faced tight rations. They became almost mutinous in "this scanty way of living, at times, being so different from the sertin good allowance at the Factory" at Hudson Bay. Hearne's men discerned bad omens in their rations and in the unfamiliar preserved meats they got from Amerindians. Their leader eventually gave up trying to "Perswade them from thinking that Entire famine must Ensew."[23]

Provisioning presented enormous challenges because the plains, where the buffalo herds were located, were too distant from the fur-bearing regions. Moreover, in forested areas, moose and deer were often scared off or hunted too intensively to provide a constant source of meat. Traders also lacked the hunting skills to survive on their own in these difficult regions. Men under Robert Longmoore's leadership in 1778 learned this lesson after giving hunting their best effort. Finally, huddled along the Saskatchewan River in early November, they were a shivering, sorry lot. Given extra provisions as a reward for remaining "without any [rebellious] words and always ready to obey," and having "done the best of their endurance" in the chase, they were nevertheless "still in want."[24] Of the apprenticing clerks and Orkney Scotsmen who signed HBC contracts, few were proficient enough to endure an isolated life in a winter hunting camp. Newcomers did well ice fishing in lakes, using nets made of Italian twine to catch runs of goldeye, pike, and pickerel; stronger jack twine nets caught the enormous sturgeon that swam ponderously through eighteenth-century Canadian lakes. Tramping about the sloughs and lakeshores of present-day Manitoba, newcomers used shot and ball well enough to bring down seasonal waterfowl passing in droves in grey skies. But game hunting was a time-consuming and skill-testing affair; even if three men at a post were appointed solely to hunt, the post's meat supply inevitably fell short and had to be replenished from trade with Amerindians.[25]

Not uncommonly, employees who spent their first years inland abandoned the fur trade altogether to acquire meat from Amerindians. Matthew Cocking, one of the first HBC men posted at Cumberland House, admitted in 1777 that he had rejected five canoes of furs because his stock of liquor, a favourite trading item of Amerindians who brought meat to his post, "is so small I am obliged to preserve it for Provisions, for as yet I have but small stock considering the season of the year."[26] Robert Longmoore went farther up the Saskatchewan River and established Lower Hudson House. In the grim, small-pox winter of 1780-81, buffalo herds eluded the Beaver, Stone, and Assiniboine hunters who usually traded meat to Europeans. Longmoore thus used about a third of that season's goods not on furs but on the few highly priced meat supplies available.[27]

The other means of survival traders learned soon after arriving inland: taking refuge in Amerindian societies, at the band level, during the hardest periods of the year. There their meagre skills and dietary shortfalls could be offset by the hunting talents of their host families. Fur traders married Amerindian women not only to secure furs but also to gain links to a coordinated hunting effort among a band's members and to learn skills vital in surviving post life and transporting goods.[28] Particularly in winter, Europeans looked to seasonal Native settlements that formed around their posts, the "plantations," as traders called them, that appeared in late summer. Amerindian families who traded furs sometimes elected to tent nearby for the winter and share their hunting successes with traders in exchange for European goods. Traders themselves actively recruited other hunters by offering them goods at lower rates or on generous terms of credit early in the fall. They had to give good terms. Once winter winds began to howl over the frozen lakes and ice became inches thick on the interior walls of posts, these plantations became the traders' only means of survival if storehouses became empty, which was frequently the case. River transportation ceased. Forest paths became muffled with snow.

Plantations were often kin-linked camps that pooled special hunting skills. By November, they began breaking up so that members could disperse to distant "wooder camps" where they could hunt in smaller numbers with more mobility. Europeans attempted on their own some of these survival measures. HBC traders arriving inland in 1774 noted during the ensuing winter that Montreal "pedlars" were often grouped into six-man companies. They disappeared like phantoms into the forests, carrying supplies of net for fishing, ammunition, and powder. They left little record of their journeys. Many likely ended disastrously. In 1775, Samuel Hearne heard from Nor'Wester Benjamin Frobisher news, "which ware realy shocking," he said, that "one or two of his men dyed for real want and one of them shott by the Indians for Eating human flesh the Corps of one of their deceased friends." Frobisher claimed to have survived only by eating moose skins and furs that he had acquired earlier in the winter and even "a few garden seeds which he proposed to have sown the following Spring." Nor'Westers called this risky survival strategy *cawway* when they broke a company into two parties and decided by lot which one would go into the woods to hunt and fish. The other party would stay behind at the post with the leader. John Long, who himself experienced near starvation inland, heard of men at a winter outpost resorting to cannibalism in *cawway* when even ice fishing yielded nothing.[29]

Far more commonly, traders sent many of a post's personnel to winter with Amerindian bands. Those who remained at the post dispatched barrels of rum, tobacco, and other goods to encourage Native hunters, or they served as couriers to carry to the post whatever meat the "hunter Indians" had procured. As wild meat passed between hands, social obligations inevitably accrued, and the links that connected family-based bands with particular traders were strengthened. And since traders relied on this "hospitality" during the worst months of winter (even if meat was expensive in terms of trade goods), they could not turn away Amerindians in fall, summer, or spring if their own hunt had failed. From the Europeans' condition of perpetual dependency, then, developed an occasional interdependency between Natives and newcomers.

Fur trade journals suggest the degree to which such interdependency transformed post life inland. Native subsistence traditions determined early on the type and quantity of food available to Europeans. Amerindian visitors brought food according to the season, and at Cumberland House and other forts farther inland a dietary cycle overtook the fur trade experience. Traders, after all, depended on bands whose size and mobility were determined by seasonal game and fish resources. The bands hunted big game in forests in winter. In the case of Cree and Assiniboine families, they joined buffalo hunts on the plains in summer. They travelled to bramble and bush areas in spring to pick berries and to rivers and lakes in fall to hunt waterfowl. Abundant fish stocks drew bands from forests to lakes at various times of the year. Plains Natives moved into parkland regions to take advantage of northward bison migrations, and in late winter and spring they headed to rivers full of spawning fish.[30]

Amerindians offered animal flesh in a variety of states to Europeans. It arrived fresh (or "green"), "beat" (pounded between rocks and occasionally mixed with dried fish), dried, and half-dried. Amerindians also traded animal fat transported in bladders. Dried, "beat" meat could be taken a step further and pounded literally to dust, which could be stored for long periods of time.[31] Each commodity had a different trade value. In northern areas, the most expensive trade item was the most favoured fresh meat, as journal entries make clear. Traders made notes such as "30lbs beat" arriving at the post and "Indians traded the flesh of a moose," but they underlined the arrival of "green" meat. The most tasty, fresh meat was understandably celebrated when it arrived at the post. In the south, following good buffalo hunting, fresh meat was actually cheaper than the labour-intensive dried, beat, or pemmican meats.[32] Although accounts were rarely clear about the prices of wild meat, likely because it was exchanged as a gift and went unaccounted for in a post's skin trade, Amerindian and Métis hunters certainly asked higher and lower prices according to the success of their hunts. At Cumberland House, for instance, between 1811 and 1840, pemmican was rated in sterling to improve accounting practices. From such conversions, it is obvious that pemmican, fat, and dried meat prices underwent periods of inflation. For instance, pemmican prices at Cumberland House rose from four pence to five pence per pound in 1814, to six pence in 1815, and then to nine pence in 1822. Prices fell back to four pence for the next nine years. In the 1830s, prices dropped further to between three pence and two pence per pound.[33]

Relations with traders were compromised when Amerindians arrived with rotting, damaged, or suspicious-looking wild meat. However, Europeans rarely turned away consumable meat offered to them. When fresh meat arrived at the post, employees immediately dried and smoked surpluses and placed them in storage. The meat was weighed, inventoried, and stacked carefully in the "victualling shed." This was one of the first structures built when a post was constructed. Its stock became the most carefully guarded secret. Prices of meat rose dramatically if Amerindians discerned a trader in want, one reason why old hands instructed incoming European traders to keep the door to the victual shed closed and locked at all times.[34] Employees continually turned meats throughout winter to stop mildew and rot from ruining their supply. This task was crucial because preserved meats were extremely susceptible to water damage. Cumberland House, for instance, lost 1,190 pounds of pemmican in the 1830 season and, likely because of employee negligence or flooding, 3,400 pounds more in 1832.

One of a trader's most important daily tasks, then, was to undertake a successful victual trade. But gathering food from Amerindians raised enormous logistical and cost-accounting problems in the fur trade. The food exchange redirected a trader's energy from the outer, commercially valuable, portion of a wild animal to the nutritive muscular and fatty layers between fur and bone. In moving from one trade commodity to another, new meaning was invested in the exchanges with Amerindians. To them, an animal's flesh figured in reciprocity, gift exchanges, and social customs. Its exchange therefore suggested the beginnings of numerous costly social obligations. Because the exchange of food led to the strengthening of social ties, hunters often brought flesh in lieu of skins – frustrating traders, who sometimes turned away such provisions in times of plenty.[35] Amerindians who traded skins, meanwhile, usually included meat as part of the trade or gave it as a gift before handing over skins.

More significantly, Amerindian traders made distinctions between these different trade commodities. The fur hunt was sometimes restricted within family territories, while the meat hunt, important for survival, was not. Outsiders in a certain region were therefore able to hunt big-game animals for food while being prohibited from hunting small game such as beaver and muskrat. Amerindians also observed special rituals involving animal skins. Ojibwa and numerous other groups burned skins after the deaths of relatives and sometimes in mourning stopped trading furs for a year. Traders often rushed to the camp of a grieving family to save furs owed to them. They also knew that in times of mourning these people might withdraw completely from the profitable exchange of the fur trade. Yet such mourning rituals did not interrupt the food exchange with Europeans. Notations about wild meat are omnipresent in the records of the fur trade. Wild meat formed a key component of ceremonies, diplomatic meetings, and friendly social intercourse between Amerindians and newcomers throughout the fur trade period.[36]

Traders also adopted Native traditions in the exchange of food. Anxious to establish social links with bands, they reciprocated with consumable trading commodities such as liquor, tobacco, and food from their own supplies.

Like Amerindians, they showed keen interest in the habits and locations of the wild animals on which they depended for survival. Philip Turner and many others in a northwest posting mapped where wild animals were located. Ross Cox was likely not the only trader for whom rattlesnakes, "the howling of wolves and the growling of bears" frequently occurred in nightmares.[37] A few traders even wrote openly about their interest and participation in Amerindian religious practices. George Nelson, for instance, turned to Wisconsin Chipewyan conjurers for advice, and his post of men even enacted a conjuring ceremony in which they sang, smoked, and danced around the post's hearth so that "something shall be cooked in that place."[38]

The trade in wild animal flesh, then, significantly changed the character of the fur trade itself. Posts rarely became, as their planners and subsequent historians imagined possible, outposts of empire or European "civilization" inland. The charcoal remains of the trading posts on the banks of the Saskatchewan, Bow, and Athabasca Rivers are clear evidence of the shanty villages that these posts became. There camps of "home guard" Natives lived alongside Europeans and supplied food. Natives in need were provided with food from a community supply of goods. Those who arrived and shared their food surpluses were given gifts or traded goods.

The North West Company's Fort George was such a village. It contained an "Indian Hall" to accommodate the regular visits of chiefs and to host their ceremonies. Stores and houses, trading rooms and shanties, filled the compound. Although only a handful of Montrealers were actually posted there, the fort's population was estimated to be as high as eighty men "and near as many women and children." Hardly a bastion of European commerce, Fort George, like its counterparts, was a mixed-blood community where only blurry social lines were drawn. All the while, the energies of all were directed at survival.[39]

John Franklin, who used the HBC post system to reach the Arctic on his overland exploration, saw firsthand the way that food requirements dominated the life and character of such posts. He counted at one seventy Canadian and Métis traders and sixty women and children (and undoubtedly dogs) eating seven hundred pounds of buffalo meat daily. The collective food requirements of such posts, where so many people could unexpectedly gather in times of want, pressed traders to measure meat carefully by the pound. George Hudson noted the "trifle of provisions" that arrived in five canoes in 1784: ninety-seven pounds of bear meat, twenty-eight pounds of fat, one hundred pounds of pemmican, and one hundred pounds of dried meat. These quantities might seem large to modern readers accustomed to a relatively stable food supply. Traders, however, were always anticipating a lean winter ahead, when little food would reach a post and when a daily meat ration among many people could range between six and twelve pounds per day per person.[40]

The problem of provisioning settlements became all the more serious in the case of brigades that linked the western post system. By the early nineteenth century, canoe trunk lines linked Hudson Bay and Montreal to the Rocky Mountains and beyond. The distances to be covered by canoeists before freeze-up necessitated a desperate race over western Canada's vast geography. Brigaders therefore had little time to hunt. The limited cargo space on northern canoes also reduced the quantity of dried goods that could be taken inland. Whether from York Factory on Hudson Bay or Fort William on the lakehead, then, brigades were actually supported by small quantities of European food, while each man burned from four thousand to five thousand calories daily.[41] Voyageurs could usually get beyond the rapids and portages of the shield and into the northern posts near Lake Winnipeg. There, however, local hunting bands usually met brigades at set locations along rivers and lakes to trade food. There, also, large supplies of pemmican, fat, and dried meat were taken aboard. This was the area where, with little exaggeration, Alexander Henry the Younger complained of "the vast quantity of provisions we require yearly to carry on the trade in the Northwest."[42] At posts where Natives returned in summer and fall, food requirements soared depending on the time of year and the number of individuals occupying what became temporary communes.

Traders likely adopted Native customs around food exchange because they had little choice in the matter. The records of Anthony Henday, probably the first HBC man to visit the prairies in present-day Alberta in 1754, suggest how such Europeans were quick to conform to the customs of the country. Leaving York Factory to go inland and invite hunters to trade with the English, Henday travelled with the Cree and Blood into the interior, their pace established by food requirements. They left York Factory on June 26. Three weeks later, they encountered Cree, who informed Henday that he had reached "the dry or inland country." Relations between Henday's party and the strangers were promptly established with the exchange of tobacco from the English side and dried and pounded moose from the Amerindian side. By the end of July, Henday's party was moving rapidly, ten or twenty miles a day, and his guides were moving just as quickly to find food. By July 28, the hot prairie weather upon them, Henday wrote that there "was nothing to eat, nor nothing to be got." Two days later, he reported that they had "seed not one Beast." His party located Saskatoon berries along creek- and riverbeds, "a fine bed of raspberries, of which I did eat till I was like to burst, and about two miles further we came where were the finest berries I ever did see or taste, they are the size of a black currant."[43]

The Amerindians with whom Henday travelled not only devoted their time and energy to the chase but also shaped social relations around the collection and distribution of wild meat. The people whom he encountered used animal skins for their clothing, bone for tools, and sinew for ropes.

Animals provided the necessities of life. More fundamentally, they figured in Amerindian spirituality and became symbolically fixed to clans and tribes. There was great variety in Amerindian animal cosmology. In the northern forest and subarctic regions, where the success of big-game hunting was uncertain, Amerindians adhered to complex magic traditions and hunting rituals. They carefully considered their behaviour in relation to spiritual "game bosses" who controlled hunting success, and they ritualized the treatment of carcasses. These customs and the cosmology from which they were derived seem to have been altered by groups such as the Cree, who began migrating to the plains in the late eighteenth century to rely on the more abundant buffalo.[44] These plains people, however, continued to practise a variety of hunting rituals. They performed dances and other ceremonies involving animal symbolism; the buffalo dance was observed faithfully. Hunters left totems of skulls and skins at their teepee entrances. Elsewhere, the conjurer's shaking tent offered a central meeting place between humans and animals. There the spirits of animals counselled men: the squirrel, bear, or buffalo, each with its own personality, offered hunters advice.[45]

Animal flesh also worked to join peoples, as Henday discovered on July 30, when his party finally located and killed two moose. He recorded that the Amerindian hunters had "a noble feast, attended with drumming, conjuring, smoking, talking, dancing and singing." In this moment of conviviality, the trader's assessment of the plains changed dramatically. The day of the moose feast, Henday described the "level land, willows and cherry trees and fields of tares as full and large as ever I seed any in England."[46] His assessments became more positive between that day and August 17, when his party killed more than eighteen moose and innumerable elk. According to the tradition of the region, the Cree and Assiniboine used guns to hunt the big game located in stands of forest; however, they switched to the much more quiet bow and arrow on the plains when they hunted buffalo. This remained a favourite weapon of stealth for a century since gunfire scared off herds.

The new surplus of meat allowed the hunters to take only the animals of choice: they selectively killed cows, not bulls, since cow meat was the fattest. Henday shot a bull that was "nothing but bones, so took out his tongue and left him to the wolves." He fetched only the heart and "brisket" of a shot moose. And with such plenty around them, Henday witnessed the concord established by food reciprocation. He was invited to numerous feasts held in nearby hunting camps (no fewer than seven on one day!), where he noted "provisions good and plenty" and "fine sweet eating" of buffalo hump and moose nose. The English visitor's attempts to move onward slowed and finally stopped altogether: "travelled none," he stated on two consecutive days, "all hands employed eating and smoking, and I am not behind hand, thank God a good stomach." His evaluation of the surroundings became more generous as they provided more meat. He described the interior in terms of an English countryside with "tall cherry trees, filbeards and nuts large and fine," "the country and weather so fine and pleasant beyond descriptions, I cannot think myself at present in North America." And, finally, he made what became a characteristic response of newcomers to the western environment: he named it according to the meat available. He christened the "buffalow plain," the "wild horse plain," the "plentiful plain," and the "Sporting plain" in the land of natural bounty.[47]

Henday's journal underscores crucial differences between traditional Native hunting practices and those of later sportsmen. His companions travelled quickly in times of scarcity and stopped when they located game. They slaughtered as many animals as they could in periods of opportunity. When few animals were killed, hunters consumed or preserved much of the flesh. When many animals were killed, hunters immediately consumed great quantities of meat. The generosity of Amerindians who shared their own small supplies humbled many traders. They were overwhelmed by the feasting traditions involved in successful hunts; journals often refer to Amerindian feasts where gluttony was common and guests were expected to eat all set before them.

Not surprisingly, these feasting traditions and the hunting practices supporting them seemed wasteful to Europeans. Amerindians, however, believed that in season and in the right place animals gave themselves up to the hunters. They believed that animals were really spirits that "donned fleshly robes from time to time for human benefits"[48] and that their actions as hunters were judged within this spiritual dimension, the "manitou" world of animals. This animistic belief led some Amerindians, particularly on the plains, to believe that animals were superabundant. Plains people believed that the buffalo herds, which seemed to be beyond number, came from the ground each season. From the same perspective, the hunter respected every opportunity to hunt an animal that made itself available. He also remained thankful to the animal and respected numerous traditions when he butchered, consumed, and sometimes disposed of the animal's remains.

These beliefs contrasted with those of most eighteenth-century Europeans, who described the natural world in mechanical terms and saw the animal kingdom living on parts of the Earth in finite numbers. Classical and Judeo-Christian beliefs tended to place animals below humans in the divine order. Cartesian thought itself encouraged a view of animals as sensory machines guided by instinct and little else. Newcomers to North America, then, were quick to criticize Amerindian animism and hunting traditions that seemed to result in excessive waste.[49] James Isham, who spent his career on Hudson Bay at York Factory, wrote that local Cree hunters were "ofte'n starv'd and in Want of food." Yet they did not cure the meat from the animals that they killed. They sometimes took only tongues or heads and "let the body or carcass go a Drift with the tide." He added that it was no wonder that "godalmighty shou'd fix his Judgemen't upon these Vile Reaches, and occasion their being starvd and in want of food, when they make such havock of what the Lord sent them plenty of."[50]

If they lived in perpetual uncertainty, traders also lived in what Richard White has well described as a middle ground between European and Amerindian cultures. Relations with Amerindians arising from the provisions trade should not, however, be confused as idyllic, peaceful, or harmonious. Fur traders and Native provisioners often regarded each other with suspicion. Their relations frequently broke down into dissension and misunderstanding. Both groups usually sought to procure the most for the least, whether hunters for their precious commodities or fur traders for their European goods. Europeans reluctantly gave credit for an upcoming hunting season, while hunters often cut off the trade in provisions if their terms were not met. William Walker was dismayed in what became the worst provisioning year of 1780-81 when he learned that "there is no beast resting nigh hand, which I believe we shall be very hard put to it for provisions."[51] He blamed Natives for deliberately burning the plains near his post. He might have been confused about grassland management: burning forage grasses to keep them greener and thus attract wandering herds. But traders were probably not incorrect that some hunters manipulated game populations to enhance their bargaining positions. Duncan McGillivray reported his concerns one September at Fort George that "tho' we kill abundance of animals to maintain the people, yet the Buffaloes are not so numerous as usual in these parts, [we] are therefore of opinion that some Tribe of Indians hover about us and frighten away the animals to some other place less frequented by men."[52] Robert Longmoore saw hunters burning the grasses around Hudson House in his first season inland. He was consequently driven into a trading relationship with them. When they learned of his dangerously small stock of provisions, they drove up prices; when his liquor supplies ended, so too did their buffalo supplies.[53]

Provisioning problems prompted traders to use physical force. It was over provisions stolen or unfairly traded from Amerindians that fur traders often found justification for violence. It was at Isle-à-la-Crosse that HBC employee Peter Fidler encountered the "particularly violent proceedings" of the first clashes between Montreal men and HBC men. A grim case was recorded by W. Ferdinand Wentzel at Grand River when his NWC post began a vicious competition in 1800 with Alexander Mackenzie's XY Company nearby. In October, the NWC house set aside half a keg of gunpowder and began "firing at every thing we could" to scare away the game nearby. The better-supplied Northwesters then began buying up all provisions from Amerindians to starve out their competitors. By November 18, the French master of the house was asking for mercy, but Wentzel wanted to secure better terms and recorded that "it is now no time for him to repent." By 5 December, Amerindians followed NWC directions and burned the trade goods that they had procured from the competitors. By December 10, an ominous silence fell over the XY Company house. Starving inside, the men barely had the energy to check their nets for fish. The post's factor again asked for provisions to conduct himself and his men to Slave Lake. "He told us that he was near loosing [sic] one of his men through weakness to day visiting the nets, and that he had to eat the cuttings of green skins he had to make windows of in the fall." In a triumphal note, Wentzel agreed to buy up all the XY Company goods on hand at a huge loss to his competitors in exchange "for 24 skins of goods, 72 lbs. of pounded meat, and grease and barley corn."[54]

Europeans, so dependent on Amerindians and competing with each other, tried to strike a compromise with the land by establishing seasonal posts on the much wealthier plains. There they could offset the "debt of nature" that they were accruing in the fur trade farther north. When dispatched with brigades, the pounded, dried, and pemmican flesh of buffalo on the plains could reach amazingly distant regions of western Canada. A formal distribution system was beginning to take shape by the 1790s. Cumberland House and other posts along the Saskatchewan River began to serve as depots that promptly dispatched upriver any surpluses. The creation of provisioning posts in the heart of buffalo country and the development of Assiniboine and Cree buffalo hunters as provision hunters by the 1790s brought a large meat supply to the fur trade. As Arthur J. Ray has shown, by the first decade of the nineteenth century these buffalo hunters were stocking the North West Company with more than 140 bags (90 pounds each) of pemmican each year from Red River and 300 to 500 bags from the Saskatchewan region – nearly 48,600 pounds.[55] That precious supply allowed the trade to expand to the subarctic region, where the best furs were traded but where traders were least able to trade provisions.

The specialization of the plains hunt, soon taken up by Métis hunters, was initially difficult to encourage. Traders long resented the power of plains hunters, who, from the beginnings of contact, enjoyed considerable bartering power and independence from traders. Plains people were only persuaded to provide food for traders if they were offered specific, low-priced trade luxuries. Thus, while northern hunters preferred the Europeans' firearms and powder, their plains counterparts continued to use bows and arrows and achieved even greater independence from traders. When later, in the mid-nineteenth century, the American skin trade moved northward, such bartering power increased further: hunters could then choose between American traders along the Missouri or British traders along the Saskatchewan. But more fundamental still, these hunters traded from a position of relative food surplus, required fewer obligations from traders, and, when they chose to trade, demanded goods such as liquor and tobacco at low prices. Almost predictably, provisioners such as the Gros Ventres (the "Big Bellies") remained the most independent from Europeans, who, in turn, characterized them as the most surly, unpredictable, and "savage."[56]

Barely able to attract plains hunters to secure their food, traders therefore had to build numerous posts deep in the interior, close to the hunt itself. When trade expanded from areas of the Saskatchewan River, companies built "wintering" posts closer to game areas in the forest and on the plains. In this way, provisioning posts attracted sufficient supplies of food from plains hunters. Archibald McLeod's journal at Fort Alexandria in 1800 provides a vivid record of the way in which the fur trade adapted the metropolitan need for fur to the uncertainty of provisions inland. Fort Alexandria sat on the upper waters of the Assiniboia River, about nine miles from an HBC post on the Elbow River. There and on the Qu'Appelle and Red Rivers, nearby Assiniboine hunters traded almost exclusively meat. The Northwester Daniel Harmon recorded that the Cree stayed in the woody parts of the countryside around Alexandria hunting moose, elk, and beaver, while the Assiniboine hunted primarily buffalo.[57] McLeod's trade was devoted to procuring the meat of the animals killed by these hunters, with only marginal returns in skins. McLeod relayed these products to posts along the North West Company's northern system. He consequently knew "our hunters" by their names and maintained interest among them through credits and gifts of rum. He promised that, for every ten animals killed, hunters would receive two gallons of mixed rum.[58]

Through such trade, Europeans acquired buffalo, elk, moose, red deer, and other meat and dried, packed, and prepared it for transport. They also transformed some of it immediately into pemmican for transport in the spring. Each step of this process involved Amerindians: males hunted while elderly females cured meat according to traditional smoking methods. This durable protein – if rains did not ruin it – went west in carts and then into canoes that eventually served the Athabasca brigades moving frantically from Fort William to the northern fur trading posts.

McLeod's 1800 journal describes this life in a plains post. By February 25, after a slow winter of trading mostly small quantities of red deer flesh, Cree and Assiniboine hunters finally began arriving with sleds of buffalo meat; thirty-two bags of pemmican were made by that day (each bag weighing eighty-five to ninety pounds). By early March, McLeod reported that there were eighty-five buffalo cows in the "meat house" and that the men were busy filling kegs with grease and hanging salted meat and tongues in the spring sunlight outside. On 4 March, the trader proudly recorded his post's sixty-second bag of pemmican. Men were already moving the heavy sleds to the lower fort along the Elbow River to get them as far east as possible to supply the brigades. When the fiscal year ended on 7 May, McLeod's post had packaged its 125th bag of pemmican (10,625 pounds) and some 73 kegs of grease (5,110 pounds). Typical of most journal writers, McLeod did not explicitly record the Europeans' reliance on Amerindian labour. But he did note that women from the post's community were drying meat that was starting to mould in the victual shed.

These plains posts dealt in quantities of flesh that might now amaze western Canadians. Qu'Appelle Lake Post, farther to the east, became a large-production butchery. The men there traded buffalo meat from Assiniboine, Stone, Saulteaux, and Métis hunters near modern-day Moose Jaw, Saskatchewan; then they dried it and tied it into bales. A cart was sent every month back to Fort Pelly, formerly Carleton House, on the Assiniboine River.[59] Fort Pelly was served by numerous other posts established in "buffalo country" in the hope that one or more would be fortunately situated near a herd and the Amerindians hunting it. "Guard posts" were built near the Red Deer River Post at Touchwood Hills, and farthest west was a strictly wintering or provisioning post, Where the Bones Lie. One or all of these posts traded meat from Native hunters, and, like the Touchwood Hills post in 1863, they were occasionally able to dispatch carts full of meat. On one occasion, carts loaded with 2,276 pounds of fresh meat were sent back to Fort Pelly, probably for processing and prompt relaying to the brigades.[60]

At Cumberland House, strategically situated near numerous waterways, provisions from the plains were stocked and redistributed to trading regions short of food. An impressive relay system soon established itself, and by the 1830s Métis hunters from Red River began to specialize in providing buffalo products to the Hudson's Bay Company.

The environmental stress accompanying such hunting pressure has been studied not only on the plains but also in the woodlands and subarctic regions. On the plains, Alexander Henry the Younger recorded that in 1807-8 his small post of forty-one people consumed in one winter 63,000 pounds of bison meat taken from 112 cows and 35 bulls. Meat also came from three red deer, five large black bears, four beavers, three swans, thirty-six ducks, and some eleven hundred fish of different species. With expansion of the trade and increasing competition between companies before 1821, the harvest of wild animals possibly became a significant drain on the environment. Arthur J. Ray points out that in 1795 there were twenty-one trading houses operating just along the Assiniboine River, and, if consumption at each was only half that at Henry's post, this area of the trade required about 1.3 million pounds of bison meat annually.[61] Both Ray and Charles A. Bishop have suggested that in northerly areas big game was being overhunted in the period of fur trade competition, when the low prices of trade goods and the increasing need for provisions among Europeans prompted Amerindians to overhunt local large animals. Once using such animals for food and clothing, these people now hunted small fur-bearing animals to buy goods from Europeans.[62]

Visitors who saw the quantities of meat periodically on hand or being prepared for retransport frequently mistook what they saw as evidence of wildlife superabundance. A Montrealer who visited HBC posts in 1838 and wrote about his experiences in *Tait's Edinburgh Magazine* described a plenitude at the posts that he visited. He saw the carcasses of a buffalo and three deer suspended on chains being barbecued.[63] Longtime employees in the fur trade, however, rarely described an Edenic plenitude. Misconceptions about the quantity and availability of wildlife in the west, if they were entertained at all, were erased from traders' minds in the first few years of their service.

The vicissitudes of wild meat supply in fact left the fur trader a cynical observer of nature. He rarely believed that wildlife was superabundant and that nature was inherently bountiful. Traders discerned a natural law of plenty and poverty that determined their fate. Even that law, however, was inscrutable, as Norman McLeod wrote in 1800. After watching a December day change rapidly, beginning as "one of the finest mornings I ever saw" and becoming grey with what seemed like hurricane-force winds, he remarked that "such is [the] instability of earthly enjoyments!"[64] Traders were reminded of human limitations when they were detained at portages ("by incidents and foul weather which is not in the power of us individuals to avoid," as one trader lamented)[65] or when they faced hunger when wildlife inexplicably disappeared. Certainly, they felt a stinging rebuke from a power beyond them when they faced starvation. Many more faithfully observed divine service when their provisions ran low. William Walker, as acting chief trader, read lessons and prayers just before he had to switch to short rations at Hudson House early in the winter of 1781.[66] James Sutherland was initially posted at Lake Burlingoro, near Portage de Delisle in Saskatchewan, where HBC men decided to build the post when their provisions ran out. He wrote one Sunday in 1793 that he performed "Divine Service with a Sermon which treated on Patience and Suffering and Contentment with that lot where providence has appointed us, a discourse well suited to our present circumstances."[67]

Undermining traders' confidence further was that even Native survival strategies, on which Europeans ultimately depended, frequently failed too. Sutherland saw two starving families arrive at his post in January that year. "They are glad to eat the rottenest of our fish, what I shall do I scarcely know, I cannot see them starve and I have not victuals to give them, and now I have 20 Indians in my Room I cannot stir, and the House is so cold."

His poor supply was revealed on February 1 when he admitted that "I scarcely know whether the chield of three years old, or the woman of four score is the greatest chariety."[68]

Traders, then, easily discerned human impermanence in nature. They frequently recognized a violent and unpredictable harshness in their environment that worked to obliterate the presence of Natives and new-comers alike. John Macdonnell saw nature in this light on his first journey to the northwest. When his brigade passed older French forts established by La Verendrye and his sons near Lake Winnipeg, he remarked that there "is now not a vestige remaining except the clearing ... This place is overgrown with brush so as [not] to be known except from the traditions of the antients."[69] Sutherland, writing on the lonely shores of Lake Burlingoro, was quite taken aback when he discovered "the antient remains of an Old French House." Amerindian traders had told him that it had once been in the area but that its precise location was "out of their memory." Only a mother of one of the Cree traders at Sutherland's post (whom Sutherland estimated to be "four score years of age") remembered the French trading there when she was a young woman. Sutherland estimated the post's di-mensions as best he could but commented in an account to London that the remaining structure with "the slightest touch moulders to dust." He then carried a log back to his post and "tied it to the Judge of my House as a rare piece of antiquity," he said, "in this Wild Country where history is unpreserved."[70]

Meanwhile, their own precarious food supply inland led fur traders to observe closely the habits and natural histories of animals. Their study can be mistaken for scientific inquiry. It did have correspondences with the European interest in natural history, which, by the nineteenth century, was prompting scores of people to collect and systematically classify natural specimens. But a trader's interest arose mostly from dietary limitations in an inland posting.

Not surprisingly, "obliging and intelligent" employees at HBC posts soon contributed to English naturalist societies both collections and observations of animals, birds, and Native material cultures. As early as 1770, the British Royal Society formed a museum from the material sent to its members from Andrew Graham and other HBC personnel. HBC ships, like one returning to London in 1771, carried skins and birds that traders dispatched for natu-ralists in that society. Traders also dispatched arctic specimens, deer, and birds to curators at the British Museum.[71] Naturalist David Douglas, collect-ing specimens in the Columbia River area in 1824 for the London Horticul-tural Society, relied on the information and assistance of fur traders, particularly Chief Factor John Mcloughlin. In the 1860s, Robert Brown listed the many "intelligent collectors" living on Vancouver Island, the main-land, and seemingly throughout the interior regions of British Columbia.

All of them were employed or retired fur traders. The governor, James Douglas, was a "good horticulturalist" who gave "great assistance to naturalists by his extensive acquaintance all over the country," Brown wrote. He described HBC men on the mainland collecting insects, minerals, and plants. Near Victoria and Clayton, others were ready "to supply seeds and trees" and anxious to correspond with British naturalists. A resident of the HBC post Fort Yale was studying *coniferae* and other varieties of trees. Chief Justice Matthew Baillie Begbie, famous as the "Hanging Judge," was a "likely individual for a naturalist to apply to for information on the zoology of the southern portion of the country."[72]

The trader's naturalist interests often led to exchanges with numerous collectors at home. In the 1860s, Bernard R. Ross, the chief trader in the impoverished Mackenzie District, published descriptions of Native uses for botanical and mineral products and an exhaustive checklist of mammals, birds, and eggs observed in his district. Naturalists were numerous enough among district HBC staff that Roderick Ross MacFarlane, himself an old trader in the area, recalled that no fewer than sixteen of his coworkers, including Ross, William Hardisty, and J.S. Camsell, helped him with his bird and egg studies in the 1860s.[73]

The Edinburgh naturalist and writer Andrew Murray recognized the potential for coordinating such interest in the late 1850s. Acting as a secretary on an HBC-sponsored seed-collecting party in the Oregon territory, Murray related to the Royal Physical Society of Edinburgh in 1859 that "the enormous extent of their territory forced strongly upon my attention. Thousands and thousands of miles still inhabited only by the 'wild' and all this territory dotted over by the trading or hunting stations of the Company." On returning home, Murray began working with the society and the company's governor, George Simpson (himself a naturalist with a collection in his Montreal home), on what seemed to be a great idea. Simpson endorsed Murray's plan, seemingly self-evident in importance, to distribute five hundred copies of a natural history survey to the fur trading posts scattered throughout the company's vast trading territories: "here was a great opportunity for enlarging our knowledge of the natural history of a considerable portion of the globe." Four pages in length, the survey contained no fewer than 235 questions pertaining to plants, gums, poisons, wildlife, fossils, and Native cultures around the posts. His questionnaire was little different from the one distributed by the Smithsonian Institution's Joseph Henry in 1869. Included was a circular on the proper treatment and packaging of specimens.[74]

The "first fruits" of the project arrived within a year in wooden crates. Four "magnificent" reindeer heads arrived at the society in impressive shape considering their voyage of thousands of miles by sea. Specimens of alpine hare, Quebec marmot, muskrats, and beaver followed. York Factory employees contributed owls and American falcons. Specimens and notes sent by HBC staff shaped Murray's papers to the society later that year.

But traders also worked on an informal basis with other naturalists. John Richardson, who accompanied John Franklin on the 1825 overland expedition, sent letters, such as one that arrived at the Mackenzie River district, asking traders there to collect sheep, goats, and "any small quadrupeds, such as mice, rats, [and] any large birds of the grouse kind."[75]

But there was something far less formal, more utilitarian, about the fur trader's study of the natural world. Fur traders apprenticed as naturalists while they lived as the land's newest dependants. They never saw a paradise in the west. Fundamentally, they did not achieve any real independence in terms of food sources. Quite the opposite, they constantly depended on the provisions trade undertaken by specialist Natives. Although some of the social organization that grew out of the trade has been named "fur trade paternalism,"[76] the term does not fully capture the interdependency between traders and Natives who provided food.

By the mid-nineteenth century, the fur trade appeared archaic to outsiders in terms of business organization and indulgence of Amerindians. In this period, newcomers in the west shared few experiences of the fur trade. They were now guided by the century's almost irrefutable belief in progress and confidence in human ability to improve nature. Not surprisingly, fur trade traditions rooted in social interdependency clashed with the era's ethic of individualism. In 1888, the old fur trader Roderick MacFarlane, posted in northeastern British Columbia at Stuart's Lake, saw the result. That year he wrote to the premier of the province, Alexander Davie, to warn him of the decline in game around Fort St. James. He noted the rapid disappearance of lynx and rabbit, and he predicted imminent starvation among nearby Native people. Fort St. James was notoriously difficult to provision, and traders and Natives had long exchanged any surpluses to continue the trade and, indeed, survive.

MacFarlane's letter was referred to the Department of Indian Affairs, established soon after the region was transferred to Canadian care, where the request was handled by the cost-conscious commissioner of the Northwest Territories, Edgar Dewdney. MacFarlane wanted permission from the government to extend relief to destitute Amerindians since "such was the custom in the North West Territories and some other portions of the country."[77] But Dewdney dismissed the request. He claimed, erroneously, that the Stuart Lake area was one of the "easiest countries for Indians to live in," and he cited the abundant ducks and geese that he believed were available nearby. The Amerindians in question, he said, had been improvident in looking after their future needs, and he cautioned the premier against "acting on reports of the HBCo's officers residing far in the interior, who have always been accustomed heretofore in cases of distress to assist the Indians themselves."[78]

Traders such as MacFarlane were seeing significant changes in the ways that newcomers and Amerindians interacted. New ethics were challenging a societal organization based on the exchange of wild meat. Newcomers arrived not only with new values but also with new expectations about nature itself. As will be seen, colonial farmers were confident in their ability to improve nature and harness its wealth. The era beginning with the transfer of Rupert's Land to the newly confederated provinces of Canada in 1870, addressed in the next chapter, marked a significant departure in the way that many westerners began to view wild animals. Traders such as MacFarlane would witness the transformation of fur trade society. Amerindians and their hunting cultures were being displaced by a European order. And wild animals would occupy a new place and serve a new purpose in what farming promoters soon termed the "last best west."

2
The Territorial Period, Game Crisis, and the Western Domestication Movement

In 1870, the confederated Canadian provinces took control of Rupert's Land and the former trading regions of the Hudson's Bay Company. Although key social and economic changes long predated the "transfer," this administrative turnover marked the history of wildlife in western Canadian society. Immediately after the transfer, the federal government through its Department of the Interior and the few settlers induced to move west began to promote an agrarian society. Newcomers usually brought with them a philosophical and social prejudice against western traditions of subsistence hunting. Their ethic of individualism, moreover, challenged customs involved in the food exchange. At the least, newcomers viewed wildlife as irrelevant to relations between First Nations who were soon signing treaties and Euro-Canadians who were seeking independence as yeoman farmers.[1]

Promoters and government agents helped to develop the agrarian image of the west throughout the 1870s and 1880s. Many boosters dreamed of spurring enough immigration that a garden would thrive where once only fur-bearing animals had ranged. Their brochures, posters, and immigration propaganda made only passing references to western wildlife. Wild animals were often pictured as a quickly disappearing element of a rude region undergoing great improvement. Ironically, it was in the period immediately after the transfer that farm promoters characterized the region as historically abundant in wildlife. They described the land as once supporting unimaginable numbers of wild animals, land that now would yield to farmers immeasurable wealth.

But these newcomers neither transformed the region nor linked it harmoniously to a transcontinental civil state. The western lands did not yield to improvement easily. Newcomers were few in number, and immigration stalled. Most people with ties to the fur trade era looked suspiciously at the great plan of Confederation. Moreover, western improvements portrayed in the first immigration ads contrasted with the reality of western life. Rather than embracing the new order, westerners in the 1870s and early 1880s faced subsistence crises. As a result, they attempted to link their society more firmly to the past, particularly to the fur trade era and wildlife resources that had long supported the social relations of the west. One of the immediate priorities of the period was indeed to domesticate wildlife. Domestication and hybridization schemes gained impressive support, not coincidentally, by the time of the Northwest Rebellion in 1885. To contemporaries, it seemed to be certain folly to sweep aside the wilderness and supplant wildlife with domestic animals unsuited to the climate and geography of the region. Rather, westerners believed that wild creatures should be interbred and tamed.

Another feature of the transfer period is worthy of closer examination. If in the fur trade wildlife joined peoples together in subsistence activities, in the period after 1870 wildlife was appropriated for the first time for political campaigns, boosterism, and a new community identity. In a period when the west underwent a change in image from a fur trade hunting ground to a settler garden, wildlife gained new imaginative value. Although the complete transformation of animals into symbols was a twentieth-century phenomenon, the period after the transfer already suggested ways in which wildlife, especially the quickly vanishing buffalo, could find resonance deep in the human imagination and reappear in times of crisis at the heart of a nascent regional identity.[2]

An intensive campaign by Upper Canadians gathered enough support to have the fur trade regions turned over to their care in 1869. In newspapers such as the Toronto *Globe* and in writings by a minority of westerners, the "expansionist" movement had begun to gain momentum in the late 1850s and 1860s.[3] The critical question was whether the west should be left as a fur trade region – that is, a "barren wasteland" suitable only for the breeding of wild animals – or become an extension of Canadian agricultural lands. By the 1860s, Upper Canadians had persuasively rejected long-standing geographical assumptions about the region and, as Doug Owram has pointed out, successfully pressed the British government to end the Hudson's Bay Company's ancient monopoly and transfer control of the region to Canadian care.[4]

Expansionists raised up new images of the region and designated new uses for its animals. Thomas Rawlings – who wrote the circular "What Shall We Do with the Hudson's Bay Territory?" – asserted that, whatever the qualities of the rest of the wilderness in the interior, the prairies "teem with verdant grasses," and he encouraged their rapid cultivation. The image of a region "teeming" not with fauna but with flora, not with wild animals but with wheat grasses, became (not accidentally) persuasive. Advocates of agricultural improvement contended with entrenched ideas of wilderness where wild animals literally and figuratively threw up impediments to the land's improvement. Expansionists even imaginatively removed wildlife from the fur trade regions in their bid to make them appear more suited to gardening and farming. For instance, Reverend Griffith Owen Corbett, a farming promoter and resident of the struggling Red River community, published various accounts of the region in the London *Times* and *Star* throughout the 1860s. Corbett asserted that the prairie sprawling beyond the Red River settlement was "like a nobleman's estate in England, Scotland, or Ireland." He told readers of the *Times* that "there are the woods, the groves, the lakes, and the rivers."[5] This "paradise of fertility" was patently Edenic in the way that its *ferae naturae* was either tamed or disappearing in regions awaiting settlement.[6]

Canadians were confident in the region's potential for improvement because of ideas associated with mid-Victorian liberalism. Certain that an individual could improve a region's soil, Upper Canadians and other colonizers believed that, through enterprise and initiative, humans could make the earth productive. The expansionist's confidence was not tempered by the fur trader's understanding of western geography and long-standing experience with limited food supplies. Liberalism allowed newcomers to believe that as individuals they could change the wild animal domain into the "garden" that God had intended it to be. Even John Stuart Mill had looked to the expanses of Canadian frontier lands as ideal settings for his yeoman individualism, a key feature of the century's liberal philosophy. Liberalism would in turn become a guiding political movement in Canada's newest farming communities.[7]

Agricultural promoters assumed that companies searching only for the skins of animals had neglected Rupert's Land, its people, and its real resources. Few questioned the mandates of subduing wilderness regions and civilizing the Native peoples living in them, for such land, as one settlement brochure later claimed, is of "no use to any country unless it is made productive."[8] The region's animal and human populations were equally associated with the original, fallen, natural state that required an almost evangelical conversion. George Brown, a leading force in the acquisition of Rupert's Land, imagined resources of "vast importance" in these interior lands and urged his fellow Canadians to take up this higher task: the region, he bluntly stated, "should be brought into the limits of civilization."[9] A fellow expansionist, Alexander Morris, told audiences in Montreal in 1859 that the "assaults of civilization have commenced simultaneously from the East and the West." He said that agriculture was starting in both the eastern colonies and Fort Vancouver and that now farmers were turning ploughs toward the interior lands, allowing the "rapid planting of Anglo-Saxon civilization on their virgin soil."[10]

Behind much of the agricultural image of the region were ideas and ethics that conflicted with traditions of the fur trade. Following a number of philosophical propositions, the farmer tended to scorn the chase after wild animals, whether for their skin or for their flesh. Farming communities preferred private rather than common property, and by the nineteenth century the accumulation of property suggested a higher form of society. The Scottish Enlightenment writers had described the soil's improvement as God's command to humans. Agriculture, attaching humans to the soil, indeed formed the basis of a sedentary society believed to be of higher sophistication than the loose associations of people who continued to rove in hunting and gathering bands. Humans improving the earth were also accountable to their neighbours. As a sedentary people began to observe each other's rights of possession, stable property relations and a nascent system of laws began to guide agricultural societies. These assumptions were broadly accepted throughout western Europe. By the mid-nineteenth century, liberalism appealed to farming promoters because it emphasized an individual's merit. The land, then, should provide for the individual whose hands had improved it.

Newcomers tended, then, to condemn hunting and gathering traditions based on the reciprocation of meat and gift exchanges. The individualism of the nineteenth century discredited the "custom" of the northwest. Indeed, administrators in Indian Affairs, within the new Department of the Interior, were quick to reject fur trade customs of food reciprocation, as might be expected from a government department unable to bear the cost of administering Rupert's Land in 1870. Indian Affairs agents, in particular, had little money to perpetuate food exchange customs of the fur trade era. Lawrence Vankoughnet, for instance, toured western reserves in 1884 during a time of critical food scarcity and criticized food exchanges still taking place, by then almost always to help destitute Amerindians. "I consider the custom a most irrational one that has prevailed in this respect," he wrote to his superior. Rations, he wrote, should be "deserving" gifts, and it was unreasonable for Amerindians to believe that he should "give a feast for every man, woman and child" at the government's expense. The department's rationing policy would soon be organized according to merit, and Amerindians dependent on government rations would have to earn them through work, usually by participating in reserve farming programs.[11]

The conviction that civilized farming societies rose in degrees of improvement above primitive hunting societies united farming promoters against numerous Native requests for assistance in the immediate post-transfer period. The provisions hunt itself was fully discredited in liberal thought. Already by 1860, the expansionist paper the *Nor'-Wester* succinctly summarized how farming communities viewed hunting and gathering avocations. At that time sending three buffalo-hunting expeditions from its parishes each year, Red River had become an occupational "homeland," as Gerhard J. Ens has characterized it, centring on the hunt for buffalo. Hunters profited by then from both the provisions needs of the fur trade and the new markets for robes in St. Paul.[12] The editor of the *Nor'-Wester*, John Schultz, thought it a fitting occasion to comment on the "bearings and influences of buffalo-hunting" since it was the "ordinary pursuit of a large proportion of the Red River people."[13] The hundreds of men who set out for provisions, he observed, killed far more than they actually needed and sold a portion of what they did not use for clothing, groceries, and other necessities. He thought that "careless or slothful" habits led to hunting: "Hunting is not the *cause* of unsettled, indolent habits, as a *result* or consequence of them – that is, that the plain-hunters do not become careless or slothful by following this occupation, but follow it because they are so." The editorial then pointed out that the hunter was a mixture of Native and French blood, thus having certain character traits that predisposed him to undertake this lifestyle of hunting and gathering.

Most of the editor's criticism fell on social and economic problems imagined in the hunt and the trait of "extravagance" that hunting seemed to encourage. "The quantity of meat provisions consumed by the hunters is something enormous." Although only six or seven hundred in number – counting men, women, and children – the hunting community "misused" buffalo meat that could feed six or seven thousand people in Britain, France, or Germany. One buffalo hunter's annual wasted meat, the editor asserted, "would supply a small family of Europeans for the same period." Extravagance then led Métis hunters to their own financial undoing. Frequent periods of lethargy turned into inevitable times of want, when meat supplies were used up and families faced starvation. The result was that hunters went into debt to survive.

The editor stated that "The hunting life denotes a rude or primitive state of society. History teaches that a people who live by hunting are only in the first stage of civilisation." Since the professional hunters remained "passionately fond of their occupation," there was little sign that they would raise themselves up with their own exertions. Instead, they "look forward to the summer's duties with the greatest longing: the pleasures of the chase form the all-absorbing topic at the fireside and by the way." While the editor could approve of "the eagerness and the relish with which the gentleman-traveller betakes himself to buffalo-hunting," he condemned the provisions hunt on social and economic grounds. He promised, however, that the Métis would not stop hunting and undertake higher stages of social improvement until governments restricted their wandering lifestyle "or the ruinous annual slaughter [that] will exterminate the buffalo."

Immediately following the transfer of Rupert's Land, numerous commentators believed that the hunt "brutalized" and "made savage" its participants and that the extermination of wildlife held out the possibility that

Amerindians and Métis would, without alternative food sources, undertake more assiduously pastoral or farming lifestyles.[14] The importance of wildlife in the subsistence strategies of Native people could indeed make settler communities apathetic about conservation measures. As late as 1906, when the new Alberta legislature began amending the older game ordinances of the Northwest Territories, wildlife was associated with an unsavoury wild past and rougher forms of societal development. One legislator held that hunting should be unrestricted, thereby hurrying the extinction of wild-life, "on the ground that its presence was inconsistent with the advance of civilisation."[15]

Agricultural promoters, then, could see signs of progress in the thinning wild animal populations in the former fur trade regions. The final dis-appearance of the buffalo could be viewed optimistically since Aboriginal people who depended on the hunt would be forced into more sophisti-cated, regular, subsistence occupations. Now "abandoning the precarious mode of living by the chase," Amerindians were looking to "the more reli-able returns from the cultivation of the soil and raising domestic herds," as John Macoun stated in his immigration publication in 1883. Ironically, he wrote these words not long before the Northwest Rebellion, inflamed partly by widespread starvation and disease among First Nations people and the incapacity of the land to provide agricultural bounty. Like many others, Macoun believed that plains people had grown lazy in the era of large buf-falo herds, when "food was abundant; buffalo robes and skins [provided] for clothing, [and] tents and lodges were plentiful."[16]

Since progress was transforming the Canadian west, government admin-istrators could avoid preventing what was viewed as a natural, inevitable, or even providential course of events when the buffalo rapidly disappeared from Canadian ranges in the 1870s and in 1881 roamed south across the American border never to return. A visitor to the west in 1874 was surprised by the few buffalo left and suggested in a report to the Department of the Interior that, if the American export of skins and pemmican be stopped, "a rapid increase in their numbers might be anticipated" in Canadian terri-tory. The report even suggested that the measure would allow Native people to continue to use buffalo for food and clothing.[17] But it is telling that the minister paraphrasing the report did not mention this possible course of action. To him, it was far better to introduce into "the magnificent grazing country from which the Buffaloes have recently been driven ... some hardy race of domestic cattle."[18]

One reason why federal bureaucrats were hesitant to do much about the buffalo – beyond their threadbare resources in the first place – was a general view that an ideal settler society would rapidly push aside the wild elements of the region. The *Medicine Hat News*, appearing in that town soon after construction of the railway, often exaggerated the degree of improvement on the prairies. It described the rapid building of towns such as Maple Creek, Regina, and Medicine Hat as a marvellous harbinger of progress. The newspaper looked forward to an almost complete geographical improvement and stated blatantly that the town "cares little for the traditions of the red man. The thoughts of the population are given over to the attainment of wealth." Confident in their future status as the "Denver of Assiniboia," the townspeople were angry at eastern Canadians who lamented the cost of building the CPR and who thought that "this land should have been left to the buffalo and the hunter."[19]

But even before construction of the railway, most newcomers were optimistic that not only the buffalo but also all wildlife in the west were becoming "rapidly extinct" to make room for settlement. Lord Dufferin, speaking to audiences in Winnipeg in 1877, was in awe of this "peculiar theatre of rapid change and progress" when he travelled over the prairies. He said that the land "but yesterday was absolutely bare, desolate and untenanted, the home of the wolf, the badger and the eagle." Now he "passed village after village, homestead after homestead ... corn-fields already ripe for harvest and pastures populous with herds of cattle stretched away to the horizon."[20]

Contemporaries usually understood that the disappearance of wild animals from their native ranges implied that newcomers could then claim the natural wealth. The sheer number of buffalo before the transfer suggested a richness of the soil that could be tapped by settlers. Soils that once supported such a large ruminant population were now free to support cattle and crops alike. The colonists at Selkirk had already drawn such conclusions in 1818, believing that "in a country possessed of so many natural advantages our members would soon multiply, and we might cherish the hope of becoming in the hands of divine Providence, the humble instruments of introducing the benefits of civilization." They believed that the Red River Valley "was a Paradise ... The Climate is healthy, soil good and fruitful and abounds with buffaloe or wild cows, deer and Horses."[21] With the territorial period beginning in 1870, western promoters continued to cite past superabundance or rapidly disappearing wildlife populations. And they began to return to a favourite theme of agricultural vitalism: natural, if not superabundant, wealth that once allowed wildlife to flourish in such numbers could now be tapped in farming. John Macoun, whose government naturalist work often supported western promotion, helped to prove the west's agricultural potential by its present, or more often its past, wildlife abundance. He devoted a lengthy chapter on the wild animals of the northwest in his handbook for prospective settlers in 1884. He also suggested vitalism in wildlife populations at the 1888 Senate inquiries into the natural resources of the "Mackenzie District," a study of the still largely unknown regions north of the North Saskatchewan River. Macoun suggested that, where wildlife was abundant, domestic animals could flourish. He stated that an examination of the grasses in any region

> settles at once the question with me of its climatic capabilities; and the country produces naturally always the animals suited for that locality. The deer, such as our jumping deer as it is called, ceases to exist as we go north, and immediately another deer takes its place, with a foot better suited for the arctic regions – I am speaking of the cariboo. Then we find the wapiti always existing along the base of the Rocky Mountains, and eastward to the prairie and copse wood country. The moose is more a copse wood animal, and is more fitted to go through it than through thick woods; so that any animal you will find in the country indicates the character of the country.[22]

The certainty that cattle would replace buffalo and deer seems to have led senators to publish a map in 1889 showing the distribution of wildlife populations in western Canada. The map showed the southern limits of the musk-oxen, reindeer, black bear, and Virginia (jumping) deer, the range of the moose, and the former range of the buffalo. An accompanying map showed "the barren grounds, arable and pasture lands, northern limits of trees and of the possible cultivation of potatoes, barley and wheat." Both maps gave generous northerly arable limits to Canada's new Northwest Territories. By 1889, newspaper readers in Toronto received similar reports. They also welcomed the news of a lost herd of buffalo (the wood buffalo) discovered in the Mackenzie District, a discovery that likely raised the possibility of a more northerly agricultural frontier. Newspapers such as the *Lethbridge News* in 1888 were also reprinting "telegraphic dispatches from Ottawa" reporting "the existence of two bands of buffalo numbering around two hundred and fifty in the northern portion of the territories." The close association between wild animals and terrestrial wealth finally appeared in a Manitoba government brochure from the 1880s. The pamphlet lauded soils in the province and their "capacity to support life," and it spoke of the province's "variety and abundance of wild animals."[23]

Numerous outsiders and politicians in Ottawa could therefore look back with optimism at the dark events of the late 1870s, when the Canadian buffalo herds had begun disappearing from their ranges. By then, the skin trade and provisions hunt had pushed the animal onto a path leading to rapid extinction that soon affected Amerindian hunters. After 1881, starvation took a grievous toll on numerous plains First Nations. Disease moved easily into makeshift reserves, while hunters directed their efforts at the remaining wildlife. In the southern prairies, this included herds of antelope; prairie chickens, eggs, and even gophers became staple substitutes. Serious shortfalls in available wildlife were sporadically met in government rationing programs administered in fits of "economy." Salt pork and other poor meat undoubtedly made another adverse impact on the health of plains people, to the point where one chief told a government doctor that he wanted "medicine that walks ... Give fresh meat to my people and they will get better."[24]

The "Indian question" being raised in Ottawa invited a harsh solution by liberal-era government bureaucrats. In what was a popular view, the problem was not so much the land as its natural wealth. In former times, it had borne massive wildlife populations that in turn had encouraged indolent character traits and arrested social development among plains people. Senators who discussed the issue of "destitution among the Indians" in 1888 believed just that. With the help of a seriously distorted view of superabundant buffalo and game populations once roaming the prairies, they took up the questions of a St. Boniface member, who asked the government which measures should be taken to ameliorate the condition of the people in the Northwest Territories. In response, a senator stated that

> When the white man first appeared he found them [Amerindians] scattered over those broad prairies – prairies covered with the buffalo, their rivers teeming with fish – their forests abounding with moose and other large animals constituting abundance of food for them, and we may add, that the position of the red man before the advent of the white, was a happy one. The Indian had no ambition beyond obtaining his daily food ... Of course the territory must be used for the white races of the earth, coming like a torrent to supplant the poor red man, and to disturb all his hunting grounds – disturb his paradise upon earth.[25]

John Schultz, at these debates, had to remind senators that, "strange to say," Amerindians faced frequent periods of food shortages before Europeans arrived, even when buffalo roamed the plains. But the senators reached consensus that the land was inherently bountiful and that the government's assistance to Native people, whether in payments or in provisions, might only make worse the indulgent effects of such natural wealth. Before Europeans arrived, First Nations were believed to have become "the most criminally improvident." The government's task, then, was not to continue to pauperize Amerindians through handouts but "to teach them industrious habits, and to educate them to the extent of providing for themselves."[26]

Although the "food question" raised concerns, senators remained confident that the land could yield wealth to the working settler. Their confidence shaped Senate inquiries such as the 1887 committee "Appointed for the Purpose of Collecting Information Regarding the Existing Natural Food Products of the North-West Territories, and the Best Means of Conserving or Increasing Them," headed by John Schultz. The Riel Rebellion of 1885 was sparked to some degree by the destitution of western plains people and the economic crisis of the Métis. It was an irony not only that scarcity of meat had disrupted relations between people but also that the soldiers sent west were themselves meat eaters. Meat, especially beef, climbed to yet higher prices in 1885. With order re-established, the committee looked into the problem of food supply, the ongoing problems posed by the loss of the buffalo, and possible caloric replacements in natural food, whether from wild meat or from plants. Informants were asked about the prices and types of food available to Amerindians at the time of the transfer. They were asked "what were the rations allowed by the Hudson Bay Company and other traders to their employees?"[27]

Summarizing his committee's findings, Schultz stated that in former times western natural food products were "very equally distributed." Now that near extinction of the buffalo had "altered" this distribution, he told the Senate that there were three major food sources left in the west to be encouraged: in descending order of importance, fish, wild rice, and rabbits. He seems to have overlooked the other source of meat protein – still available big game – for strategic reasons. He wished to encourage fishing among Native people, not big-game hunting. The Sioux Wars to the south, he thought, began on reserves placed within big-game territories of the Black Hills. Hunters who had acquired and perfected the use of Winchester and breech-loading rifles on wildlife had turned them on American settlers. Schultz, then, wanted to see plains people raised up as fishers, not hunters. For that reason, he envisioned a new tradition for the plains provisions trade whereby it "may now to a large extent be reversed in the feeding of the plain[s] Indians with fish caught by the fishing Indians" in the northern, well-watered, forested regions.[28]

The proceedings were linked meanwhile by a common thread of optimism that the hunting conditions that had led to indolence among people in the fur trade no longer existed. In the plains, where farming promoters invested most of their hopes, nature had provided so generously to First Nations people that the same natural wealth was now assured to the land's improvers. Turning his attention to Native people in general, one inquiry informant distinguished between the plains and the "wood" according to different hunting traditions: "In hunting the moose, deer and cariboo, the wood Indians had a more arduous task, having to ride early and often pursue the game all day, while the plains Indians mounted their horses, killed the buffalo, leaving the squaws to dress the game and do every thing else, while they returned to the wigwam, lounging about it, eating and sleeping until more food was wanted."[29] Even with wildlife depletion now widespread and plains people now subsisting on miserly rations of bacon, salt beef, and salt pork, Schultz's committee was able to end its published report on a reassuring note for the individual, the one willing to work hard, that "nowhere has Nature showered blessings with a more bountiful hand than in the Canadian North-West."[30]

In many respects, however, the wealth of Rupert's Land was by no means certain. Even in the period before the transfer, the buffalo herds were in decline. As the *Nor'-Wester* had imagined, the commercialized plains provisions hunt was making a dramatic impact on the sizes of the northern herds by midcentury. In American territory, the skin hunt and the inroads of railways inaugurated a massive slaughter, pushing the buffalo toward extinction. In British Rupert's Land, robe hunting took place alongside provisions hunting, both supporting the economic vitality of the fur trade. Although robe hunters in some respects were more discriminate than skin hunters (restricting their killing to winter months, when robes were fuller), provisioners led a comparatively massive destruction of the animal. Female buffalo – the most prized in the provisions trade – could not maintain sufficient populations in the face of increasing hunting. By the 1820s, plains Amerindians in modern-day Alberta and Saskatchewan were shifting to market hunting to meet rising demand for buffalo robes and flesh in the fur trade, and Métis hunting communities were fully specialized in market hunting soon after. Buffalo herds were then accessible only in western hunting locations, and they were exposed to more sustained slaughter by larger, often competing, groups of hunters. By the time of talks about the transfer of Rupert's Land, buffalo populations were likely thinning. As early as 1867, for instance, Fort Edmonton's chief factor believed that "the Saskatchewan can never be depended upon for large supplies of provisions, as in former years."[31]

By the mid-1870s, the end of buffalo days could be anticipated by most westerners. To old-timers, the loss of such a resource heralded not progress but the complete untethering of links between provisioners and traders. By 1875, one informant for Indian Affairs gave the buffalo at best eight to twelve years before its extermination. The food question thereafter became a pressing social matter in the west, yet the *Nor'-Wester* continued to claim wildlife abundance as a means of boosting the region, claiming that the northern posts were self-sufficient in moose provisions. But a food emergency was obviously occurring by 1877 at Red River and the other traditional hunting communities on the prairies. That year the newspaper *Les "Métis"* reported that the Hudson's Bay Company in Red River had managed to send to Montreal 74,000 buffalo robes.[32] But prices were steadily dropping as markets were becoming saturated with wares, and such low prices were accelerating the hunt for even more products. The paper's readers would have understood the implications of this intensive hunting pressure.

The clearest indication of crisis was an escalation in prices of pemmican, dried meat, and fresh meat. In 1870, when the Saskatchewan herds were still abundant, Red River community members enjoyed access to a large supply of meat at low prices. Although prices rose and fell according to the seasonal availability of buffalo herds, meat was usually priced according to the amount of labour involved. There were intermittent inflationary pressures on these prices, and such pressures affected prices at Cumberland House, one of the depots collecting meat products for redistribution. There was also, in the period 1815-23, an unexplained shortage of meat, fat, and dried meat that inflated prices. The rest of the fur trade period, however, showed remarkable stability in food pricing. The meat trade followed market demand, and, when free trade was introduced in the 1840s and American markets began to divert supplies, fur trade provisions rose in price accordingly. Yet prices at the time of the transfer were low by contemporary standards. In fact, the stability in pricing probably benefited the federal government in making promises to Amerindian bands in the west and in signing some of the first treaties. The Department of the Interior and its Indian Affairs branch, for instance, were able to purchase HBC meats at Red River at low prices by 1871: pork sold at twenty-five cents per pound, beef at seventeen cents per pound, and "dried meat" (likely buffalo) at fifteen cents per pound.[33]

By 1879, the disappearance of the Saskatchewan herds caused prices to escalate. Pemmican, in some instances, rose some 1,150 percent over its price at transfer, fetching one shilling, three pence, per pound. Dried meats similarly rose some 400 percent over their 1870 prices.[34]

This does not mean that prices were absolutely higher even by 1880. In the buffalo days, pemmican prices rose according to the season, the cost of transport, and the size of the sold product. For instance, Samuel Bedson (discussed below) remembered pemmican valued in the "old days" as low as five and six cents a pound and as high as fifteen to twenty cents a pound. What he was likely remembering were price differences in times of good hunting versus poor hunting, not ever-growing inadequacies in supply. By 1879, likely when local game meat was being bought up to meet provisioning demands, the Hudson's Bay Company could still sell "at cost" to Indian Affairs (in orders of ten thousand pounds) pemmican at eleven cents per pound – dispersed to meet Treaty 4 and 6 annuity payments that year. But in most of its dealings even with the federal government, the company was now raising retail prices dramatically. By 1877, pemmican was assessed at fourteen and fifteen cents a pound when it was transferred between employees and company posts. But settlers and missionaries purchased pemmican at a staggering twenty-five cents a pound. Retail prices of dried meat went from ten cents a pound in 1877 to eighteen cents a pound between 1881 and 1883. Fresh venison prices continued to vary, while in 1886 moose meat could sell at a high of nine cents a pound, and two years later deer meat could find a market at two and a half cents per pound.[35]

Escalating meat prices at places such as Cumberland House eventually meant that flour and bacon could be imported more cheaply than hunted meat could be purchased locally. By 1893, this was clearly the case.[36] The high prices of meat products were probably most acute elsewhere until 1888, when the railway began bringing barrelled salt beef and pork to the plains. But before that, meat of all description was becoming scarcer in the market. The Honourable James McKay, himself a buffalo hunter and provisioner, and one of the first entrepreneurs to begin preserving buffalo on his private land, sold to the government some seven thousand pounds of pemmican at twenty cents a pound. As late as 1881, provisioners at Fort Walsh supplied the government with pemmican for the destitute plains people who had not located any buffalo herds. Their pemmican sold between ten cents and twenty-five cents a pound.[37]

Although some of the HBC shipments of meat were old buffalo stock, deer and moose flesh was beginning, by the end of the 1870s, to replace buffalo products in HBC accounts. Not only was deer hunting comparatively labour intensive, but also its flesh was more difficult to preserve – requiring immediate drying in thin strips. Deer or moose meat, then, was more expensive than buffalo meat, and the cost was borne by settlers dependent on it for protein. Deer and moose were nevertheless replacing buffalo in settler areas, as HBC accounts suggest; "deer pemmican" appears for the first time in accounts at Cumberland House in 1880.

In response to these changes, Cumberland House personnel quickly transformed their provisioning system. Lac du Brochet, one of its outposts to the north, now supplied new quantities of meat for redistribution. Bills of lading in 1888 record a shipment to Cumberland House of no less than 5,250 pounds of dried deer meat and 2,450 pounds of pounded deer meat. In addition to sinew, there were 676 pounds of soft fat and 1,342 pounds of hard fat accompanying the shipment. The considerable size of the deer hunt can be estimated from the number of tongues reported in the shipment, the first of the season: no fewer than 1,113 from Lac du Brochet alone. An inventory states that remaining stock included another 7,500 pounds of dried meat and 93 bags of pounded meat. After reaching Cumberland House, most of these meat products were transferred to other districts. Some went to the Saskatchewan River, Norway House, Swan River, and Cumberland's own outposts of Le Pas, Moose Lake, and numerous Christian missions in Manitoba.[38]

The immense pressure on woodland areas to provide meat products continued throughout the period. The fact that Lac du Brochet, by 1888, reported a stock of no less than 7,945 pounds of pounded meat, 7,700 pounds of dried meat, and 1,250 "cured deer tongues" ready for redistribution suggests some of the readjustments that Hudson's Bay Company was making in response to the end of the buffalo era. Cumberland House, meanwhile, continued to stock deer products in the period when prices began falling. An 1893 inventory shows 100 pounds of dried meat (six cents a pound), 1,204 pounds of pounded meat (six cents a pound), and 1,288 pounds of pemmican (twelve cents a pound).[39]

The new profit incentives for trappers, whether Métis or First Nations, to supply meat alternatives explain why northern Manitoba communities were soon facing periodic deer scarcities.[40] Native people at Lake Winnipeg began "strongly complaining" as early as 1877 about the "disastrous destruction of game, specially moose and deer," in the country around them. They demanded a law to restrict the season when outsiders could hunt in their region.[41] Similar grievances were heard at the first treaty missions in Manitoba and the Northwest Territories. In light of new provisioning activities and more intensive pressures directed at local ungulates and bird species, and even fish stocks, W.F. Whitcher was likely not exaggerating when he stated in 1884 that not only farmers and sportsmen but also the plains people were interested in "defending feather and furred, and hoofed game from the same fate that has befallen the buffalo."[42] From 1873, when the interior minister, A. Meredith, sketched out the food question darkening administrative considerations, westerners as a whole faced uncertainty in their food supply. Concerns were voiced in some of the questions given to informants for both the 1887 Natural Food Products committee and the 1888 inventory of the Mackenzie Region. Questions to informants included "Can you give any reason for the occurrence of years of comparative plenty and comparative scarcity?" Another question asked informants whether they could specify the cause and nature of the disease "which periodically killed off rabbits."[43]

Both newcomers and senators, then, might have been optimistic about the west's imminent improvement, but most settlers and those whom the western historian W.L. Morton characterized as members of the "old order"[44] were alarmed by pressing food problems. They also feared the unravelling of ties that once bound peoples together. Not surprisingly, then, in the 1880s western political and social elites began looking back to the fur trading era as a period of comparative social stability. Such conservatism already had political value by the election of 1870, when the *Manitoban* backed former HBC man Donald A. Smith to guide the community into the democratic era. Just before the election, it strategically added *Herald of Rupert's Land* to its masthead in a blatant reference to a bygone era when peoples and animals had been placed together under a single government.

Westerners could now fondly revive memories of the buffalo hunt,[45] remembered as an effort that brought community members into some accord. Alexander Begg in 1884 singled out from seventeen years in the west his memory that "it was the rule of the plain not to hunt the buffalo singly."[46] The Campaigner in 1898 described community virtues in the brigades: the elections of officers, soldiers, chiefs, and councillors and the Catholic Métis organization that enforced strict rules about theft in the camp, stopped hunting on Sundays, and maintained discipline during the hunt itself. In its folk retelling, the hunt appeared as a tightly bound, hierarchical social organization that regulated the activities of its members. Precisely such virtues were later identified in western magazine and newspaper accounts, which drew pictures of the hunt as harmonious, disciplined, and stable under the HBC regime. An 1898 account of "An Old Time Buffalo Hunt" that took place "while yet the flag of the Hudson's Bay Co. floated over the bastions of Fort Garry" noted its rigid discipline: early starters were curbed because self-serving individualism endangered the success and survival of the community.[47] Western writers were quick to assert that "every Northwest Canadian" in 1892 had to watch for erroneous historical representations "of that great company which gave its name to ... Rupert's Land." H.M. Robinson's narrative of the "Great Fur-Land" in 1879 already eulogized "the last vestiges of what were once the most perfectly-organized, effective, and picturesque periodically-recurring hunting-excursions."[48]

Memories of the hunt sharpened as westerners faced chronic agricultural problems. After the transfer, they were more than aware of a persistent dependency on pemmican for protein and therefore anticipated imminent social crisis when it disappeared from the marketplace. It is perhaps not surprising that Manitoba's French Métis, facing the most uncertainty immediately after the transfer, began cultivating cultural links to wild animals and taking up conservation practices. These measures occurred as their political status became imperilled with English migration into Manitoba and when, by 1877, French was challenged as the language of government and Catholicism as a creed of life. The newspaper Les *"Métis"* sounded the call to action by making numerous references to an imperilled natural world. The newspaper discussed the troubled state of the fur trade and the dropping prices of buffalo skins, and it urged the creation of a board of commerce to stop the further loss of fur traders to Fort Benton, this to preserve what was feared to be Winnipeg's crumbling status as the commercial gateway to the northwest.[49]

The same year that political difficulties mounted, 1877, French community members read reports of the disappearance of the western bison herds and the impoverished plains First Nations congregating at Cypress Hills. The newspaper's editor also published the first game preservation laws enacted in the province. That year the Honourable James McKay, a former fur trader, announced to French readers his presidency of the Winnipeg Game Club, which aimed to preserve game in the province and uphold the new ordinances. This was likely the forerunner of the Winnipeg Game Preservation League, created in 1882, with another old-timer, Colin Inkster, as president. Bouts of bad health in 1877 seem to have prompted McKay to sell the wild animals in his "buffalo park" – the first of its kind in the west – at the back of his property.[50]

Readers evidently were also working to connect symbolically their community with threatened wildlife populations. Manitoba Catholics in 1877 sent to Rome a gift of animal skins marking the episcopal jubilee of Pius IX. Among them was a "magnificent" black moose pelt donated by James McKay (who had shot the moose). The Sisters of Charity had prepared the pelt and added a border of papal colours. Another skin was donated by the Fort Garry HBC factor: a rare wolf skin exquisitely ornamented by a St. Boniface congregate. The skins were of "a very pronounced local colour," as the editor of *Les "Métis"* pointed out.[51]

Meanwhile, the social implications of declining wildlife populations were alarming members of the North-West Council, some of whom had long personal histories in the west. W.H. Kennedy, who had arrived at Red River in 1860 during the heady buffalo days, first turned the council's attention to the plight of plains people, understood as being completely dependent on the hunt. Kennedy began corresponding with observers about the declining buffalo as early as 1873. Among informants was a young Charles Bell, who sent a letter outlining what was interpreted as an ominous movement of plains people from traditional hunting grounds and their convergence at Cypress Hills, where the last herds were located. The council's investigation in 1877 of ways to preserve the last animals led to the famous buffalo ordinance that year, what Robert G. McCandless called a "home-grown" conservation measure. David Laird, the lieutenant governor, tabled in 1875 the council's recommendation to the federal government and suggested that "game and wild animals and the care and protection thereof" be under the authority of the council. He stated that "the protection of the buffalo and the regulation of the hunt, as well as the questions of a like nature, would seem to be capable of being more effectually dealt with by local legislation." Matters of game – not only those concerning buffalo – became inseparably linked to local issues of political and economic autonomy. But the council's buffalo ordinance was shaped foremost by the concern to maintain wildlife populations for the sake of social harmony. It attempted to preserve the hunt as a community venture and to reserve it for Native hunters. It reworked departure dates for the twice-yearly mass hunts and prohibited early starters who might disperse the animals. The legislation was blatantly self-interested from council's perspective: its advocates believed that Amerindians and other hunters would have fewer social ties – and pose greater threats – to settler communities if they existed in roaming, starving bands.[52]

The Historical and Scientific Society of Manitoba, starting work in 1879, was motivated by the same conservative spirit. Depicted as promoting Manitoba's interests and attending to the province's "urgent future,"[53] its first activities actually suggest a groundswell of support among old-timers anxious to conserve features of the past for social harmony. Métis politicians such as Premier John Norquay (soon losing power to Grit politicians) attended the first meeting. William Clark, a former HBC chief factor, served as one of the society's presidents. Its mandate sought to collect books and preserve a library of maps, manuscripts, prints, paintings, minerals, and objects that generally illustrated "the civil, religious, literary and natural history of the lands and territories north and west of Lake Superior" – the old HBC trading areas.[54] The aims of the society were strikingly similar to those of the Macleod Historical Society, which formed in 1884. Since "the history of the early inhabitants of the country was rapidly passing away," the Macleod society "was resolved to form a museum where the relics of the aboriginals ... together with those of the *flora* and *fauna* of the district" could be held, the Macleod newspaper reported. Five years later, when the Macleod Game Protective Association formed – a topic discussed in Chapter 5 – the society claimed to have "the nucleus of a good museum."[55]

Like the editor of *Le Manitoba*, alarmed that colonization was "pushing before it the aborigines and their game and fur trade," members of Winnipeg's historical society perceived the possible social chaos attending the buffalo's demise. Charles Bell, president of the Board of Trade, became president of the society in 1888. He drew from his own reports to the North-West Council on the matter and on the disastrous implications for Native society, particularly the dispersal of plains First Nations and Métis bands from traditional territories. Now, over a decade after the last free herds of buffalo had left the Canadian west, Bell advocated the study of the "habits and resorts of the wild animals of the Northwest" now that "the advance of civilization is surely driving away animals abundant but a few years ago." The society published naturalist observations made by fur traders such as Roderick MacFarlane and heard numerous papers on the old buffalo hunt and the history and prehistory of the region. It also attempted to collect fur trade documents as a means of identifying the locations of posts that had disappeared. Public talks featured old-timers who spoke about old ways. One was hosted by John Schultz, who spoke about the "Old Wing Trail" now that settlers had "obliterated its once deeply marked triple track." He said that is was "like the old buffalo paths of Southwestern Manitoba," which "in some places [can] be distinguished," but "the fence of the old and the new settler bars the way."[56]

Concerns for social stability did not, however, immediately rally westerners behind conservation efforts. The era of conservation was still decades away. Progressive-era confidence and American initiative were necessary to begin the conservation movement in Canada, discussed in more detail in Chapter 5. In the context of the 1870s, however, an early intervention occurred in

Samuel Bedson, buffalo domesticator, 1885
National Archives of Canada, C 28219

western communities. It centred mostly on the possibility of either domesticating or hybridizing the last buffalo within settlement communities. This technique had already been attempted in the United States. Plans to domesticate or "colonize" wild animals for human benefit had also appeared early in the fur trade. In 1844, HBC employees at Fort Edmonton tried crossing buffalo with domestic cattle when they collected some thirty buffalo calves and ranged them with the fort's cattle herd.[57] In the immediate aftermath of the transfer, however, westerners turned to domestication schemes for their perceived social and economic benefits. Rather than preserving the old order, then, these westerners were attempting to link elements of the fur trade society with the new farming society.

Domestication schemes in Manitoba began after Donald A. Smith, in 1878, allegedly loaned the warden of Stony Mountain Penitentiary, Samuel Bedson, the sum of one thousand dollars to buy some of the last of the buffalo near Winnipeg. They were largely the collection of the ailing James McKay, who had gone into partnership with another fur trader and gathered the animals from returning buffalo hunters in 1873. Captured as calves during the hunt near Fort Ellice, they had been allowed to wander around Winnipeg town limits for a number of years and had later taken up residence in McKay's buffalo park. After Bedson purchased them, they were transferred to Stony Mountain, near Canada's fifth and smallest federal penitentiary.[58]

Little is known about Smith's interest in these buffalo except that this conservation initiative coincided with his growing concern about the rapid disappearance of Métis culture in the settled portions of Manitoba. There was likely some financial reward in the scheme for Smith; after Bedson's herd had grown to over one hundred animals, eventually to be sold to the famous C.J. "Buffalo" Jones of Kansas for a reputed sum of fifty thousand dollars, Smith retained twenty-seven animals, giving five to the Winnipeg Zoo and the rest to Rocky Mountains Park (now Banff). In 1889, one source stated that three of the crossbred buffalo produced at Stony Mountain remained on Smith's farm, where they were to be further crossed with Durham cattle.[59]

More information is available about Bedson. Born in Bentley, England, Bedson was thirty-four years of age in 1873 when Stony Mountain Penitentiary was established. Originally, he had been appointed warden to oversee "Stone Fort," where offenders had been held during the Riel resistance. When troops had gone home, Bedson had been left behind to supervise the small prison that for years had no walls around its grounds. After the penitentiary was established in 1873 as the prairie region's federal house of correction, it incarcerated convicts and the insane from all over the west. Eventually, Stony Mountain held some of the most celebrated participants of the 1885 Northwest Rebellion.[60]

It was around this place of incarceration that Bedson placed some of the last buffalo in the Canadian west. Both inside and outside the penitentiary, Bedson attempted to reform representatives of the former era to make them fit for settlement. He established a special school for Amerindians where he taught skills such as shoemaking, to the benefit of two Sioux horse thieves in 1876. The prison's reform agenda, meanwhile, was pursued through corporal punishment, detention, and solitary confinement; convicts were to learn proper social behaviour toward their betters, recognize social hierarchies, and respect private property.[61]

An adherent of British conservatism and a supporter of the Church of England, Bedson avidly participated in All Saints Anglican Church. He acted as rector's warden and eventually donated to the church the bell that rang on Sunday mornings. He set up curling rinks in the winter and a golf course in the summer and even a racetrack and a hunting club. He invited friends for wolf and fox hunts in aristocratic style. Bedson was remembered to have worn a red coat and breeches on the bald prairie, riding with hounds and members of the hunting club in Winnipeg. He was also known to have used convicts from the prison as butlers at his family dinners.[62]

In 1873, the new North West Mounted Police (NWMP) detachment at Fort Garry put Bedson in charge of raising the detachment's cattle, an enormous responsibility given the widespread scarcity of beef supplies. He himself soon witnessed the food crises mounting in the west. During the 1870s, his administrative letters complained of reduced rations at the prison, exasperating both his inmates and him. Over the winter of 1873, he managed to extend considerable provisions to the nearby St. Peter's Indian Band when the disappearance of the buffalo was keenly felt in Manitoba. It was in this context that Bedson patented land in the still remote area of Stony Mountain, where he maintained the NWMP cattle and the buffalo purchased with Smith's funds.[63]

While Bedson's ways conserved British class values and emulated upper-rank recreational activities, they were also classically conservative in another sense. They attempted to link the past with the present, as noted by an American reporter who visited the prison in 1883. Travelling from St. Paul to see Bedson's herd of the "last" buffalo in North America, the reporter was surprised to see far more: other wildlife penned outside the warden's house, adjacent to the penitentiary, which had no walls around its grounds. Inside Bedson's home, wilderness relics were arranged in plenitude. Done up "Indian style," one room contained a skin teepee, fossils, old flintlock rifles reminiscent of HBC days, tomahawks, Amerindian hide robes, and items that supposedly had belonged to Sitting Bull.[64]

In the zoo and buffalo ground outside the house, wild animals abounded, but all had been tamed for the settler era. By 1881, Bedson had purchased moose from an Amerindian at Brokenhead. He trained them and sent two to a Montreal exhibition where they were identified as the only moose in Canada capable of drawing a sled. The same animals returned to Montreal to represent Manitoba in 1889.[65] By 1884, Bedson had a number of wild geese on hand. The following year, a *Winnipeg Free Press* writer was charmed by Bedson's hens, able to "do unusual stunts."[66] Descriptions of Bedson's animals, wild spirits now subdued, probably appealed to newspaper readers during the following months. Riel's Métis followers were rebelling at Batoche. Visitors to Bedson's zoo, indeed, could be reassured by viewing a large collection of tame bears, wolves, moose, deer, and badgers.

Rather than merely preserving wild animals, then, Bedson sought a place for these representatives of the former era within new settlement communities. Although his domestication schemes were sometimes comic in pioneer reminiscences, he apparently took seriously the idea of either domesticating wild animals to serve agricultural purposes or, in the case of the buffalo, hybridizing them with Durham cattle to meet food scarcities in the west. In this respect, he deserves more credit than has been given to him as one of the first buffalo domesticators. To date, the far more showy American, Buffalo Jones, has been viewed as the first to domesticate the buffalo, but he seems to have procured a large number of his famous buffalo from Bedson.[67] Bedson's experiment at Stony Mountain, indeed, grew into a substantial project when the thirteen original animals purchased in 1878 reached between sixty and one hundred head in 1888, probably due to an aggressive recruitment campaign by Bedson.[68]

Agricultural promoters such as Charles Mair, meanwhile, tended to view with more interest the purebred animals at Stony Mountain. These commentators identified the problem of rearing buffalo near communities. To them, the buffalo served as a symbol of the past, doomed to extinction by progress. Bedson's were the "last of the buffalo," as British CPR traveller Edward Roper called them when he made a side trip to see them.[69] Purebreds also captured the attention of a St. Paul writer in the *Nor'West Farmer*. He said that the buffalo's tendency to wander meant that "the only way to get them back is to lasso the vagrants and try to get them to a station where they can be put in a freight car and taken home. One or two have been shot by settlers when their frolics grew unbearable, but as Major Bedson pays readily for damages of that sort, they usually escape capital punishment." The story suggested that such animals were "awkward pets to have around a civilized settlement."[70]

But purebred buffalo constituted only a portion of Bedson's herd. Evidently, the prison warden and many western Canadian observers looked with more interest at tamed or hybridized animals. Bedson himself believed that hybridization remained one of the only solutions to the problem of food supply. This belief was well communicated in the *Canadian Journal of Fabrics,* a Montreal magazine that described Bedson's venture. The article was reprinted by the same publisher in an 1889 travel book, *The Canadian Handbook*, which gave travelers in the west details of the experiment. Bedson, the story said, had clearly shown the feasibility of domesticating and crossing buffalo with Durham cattle and now urged the federal government to "continue the restocking of some of the northwestern plains with these animals." Bedson pointed out that the animals "required no stabling, but run at large both summer and winter, in fact, stabling them would be injurious." Here, indeed, was the logic of conservation in his mind, the ability of westerners to connect pre- and post-transfer eras through domestication schemes; as he had with other wildlife, Bedson found a presence and an economic value for these animals in western pioneer society.[71]

The hybridization scheme attracted keen interest. Ernest Thompson Seton used Bedson's herd for his own detailed studies. The animals were used for his natural histories published through the Historical and Scientific Society of Manitoba. The great naturalist and writer had dismissed the pure stock at Stony Mountain (he said that they no longer freely existed in the province anyway) and turned his attention to the animals bred with the shorthorn Durham cattle. Seton believed that the cross improved on traits of the natural buffalo. He reminded readers that Bedson had made "a great improvement on both of its progenitors, as it is more docile and a better milker than the Buffalo, but retains its hardihood, whilst the robe is finer, darker and more even, and the general shape of the animal is improved by the reduction of the hump."[72]

It is telling that a crossbred buffalo robe was on display in the fur store of George H. Rogers in Winnipeg. This "half-bred" skin from Stony Mountain became "an object of interest to passers-by," who lauded it for its texture and potential value: "excepting in the matter of color," a newspaper report stated, it was "a superior article" to the thoroughbred buffalo skin.[73] Although a buffalo breeding company in Winnipeg was established in 1886 and given coverage in the *Nor'West Farmer* and the *Manitoban Miller*,[74] more local attention seems to have fallen on the possibilities of hybridization. The *St. Paul Farmer*, for instance, became interested in Bedson's herd and ran a story that discussed the hybrids thriving at Stony Mountain by 1888. That coverage was illustrated by pictures of numerous "breeds" – whether the mythical Pennsylvanian species, the wood and plains subspecies, or Bedson's crossbreed. Both the *Nor'West Farmer* and the *Winnipeg Free Press* ran full front-page illustrations of "the varieties of the cross bred buffaloes," which included the Stony Mountain half-breed and Jones's own contribution, the "catalo," his buffalo crossbred with Texas longhorns.[75]

Western papers, even in the unlikely place of ranching-country Alberta, followed with interest the "half-breed" experiment. In issues covering reports of starvation in bands north of Edmonton and the problems following the previous cattle-killing winter, the *Lethbridge News* published numerous accounts of Bedson's "ranche," his selling prices for flesh and robes, and his success in crossbreeding. Reports pointed out that Buffalo Jones had already visited Bedson's herd and found the sixty half-breeds on hand by 1888 "the best in the world for ranche purposes."[76] Southern Alberta newspapers, then, applauded the creation of the Northwest Buffalo Breeding Company, which proposed to raise funds to buy Bedson's animals, maintain a purebred stock, and expand the hybrid population at a profit. Each crossbreed would be a "wage-earner," company promoters stated, each being cheap to feed and easy to maintain on the prairie, and sell – trophy head, hide, and meat – for about $235. A story in the Lethbridge *Herald* on "The Departing Buffalo" (1888) pointed out the beauty of Bedson's "practical solution" to the threatened extermination of the animal and the opportunities now offered when it was interbred with domestic stock: "The Buffaloes are as hardy as in their wild state," the newspaper stated. It quoted Ernest Thompson Seton, who had seen the half-breeds in January 1887. Unlike cattle, the animal was able to dig through snow to fatten on grass: "During a blizzard they would lie down in a group and let the snow drift over them. The snow and their wooly coats keep them perfectly comfortable."[77]

Frank Oliver's *Bulletin* even lauded the project. Ironically, the paper advocating farmers' rights and later leading the critique of Alberta's expansive ranching areas promoted Bedson's solution. The newspaper wanted the new Indian schools to raise buffalo in order to release them in western areas unsuitable for agriculture. "The buffalo had lived on them in summer and winter in millions, but when the buffalo were destroyed, there being nothing to take their place, the areas mentioned [lacking hay and not inducing settlement] would be useless whereas if the buffalo were preserved and domesticated these areas could be turned to valuable account."[78] The *Bulletin* followed up its coverage by pointing out that the government, "at great expense," had established an experimental farm in the northwest and was about to establish another one in Manitoba "for the purpose of introducing varieties of foreign agricultural products to the farmers of the Northwest. On these farms the domestication and breeding of buffalo should be instituted and receive principal attention." The newspaper, true to liberal principles, further recommended that "these farms should breed the pure animal and leave to private enterprise mainly the work of crossing with common cattle and developing, if possible, a mixed breed that would be superior to both originals."[79]

Whoever would be leading the effort, commentators advocated an immediate and concerted program to propagate a domesticated, interbred buffalo in the west. The *Winnipeg Commercial* proposed that the government place such a herd at Banff.[80] At the food source inquiry, Charles Bell recommended that "under an intelligent superintendent" buffalo be reintroduced to the west "as it is so well suited to the North West, capable of domestication, and breeds well in confinement and affords better meat." Bedson, a key witness at the inquiry, pointed out that his was "the largest herd now to be found on the continent." He claimed that in eight years it had grown from eight animals to sixty-seven or sixty-eight. He spoke about the potential of crossbreeding and recommended that the government take up the work.[81]

But interest began to wane in Bedson's buffalo when western development gained pace. Wild animal domestication disappeared from the imaginations of westerners by the 1890s. John Schultz, through his inquiries in the Mackenzie Region, advocated domesticating the caribou near the Hudson Bay coastline to feed Native people, who were threatened by the 1890s by the scarcity of natural food in this "divested" region. But such northern places and people were distant from the concerns of southerners. Newspapers now confidently predicted that settlers would more than survive on their crops and animal husbandry. Scientific advice abounded on how to tackle problems in cattle, pig, and chicken raising. By 1896, with the beginnings of the Liberal administration and later land booms, the insecurities of old-timers waned as their number declined. Agricultural newspapers (unlike

French Métis newspapers, which continued to celebrate the fur trade past) eulogized the first sodbusters and marked the first successful crops harvested in their communities. In 1889, after a series of negotiations, Bedson sold his herd to Buffalo Jones. Transported by rail to Texas, they disappeared in western Canadian memory as a more confident liberalism began to change environmental opinion. Newspapers described old-timers congregating near the Winnipeg train station to watch the last buffalo being loaded onto freight cars and hauled by rail to the United States. The *Winnipeg Free Press* covered the stockyard chaos attending the shipment and described what was said to be the last stampede in the west when a number of buffalo broke away and thundered down a city street. The paper took the opportunity to record the memories of "a hunter familiar with their habits in the old times."[82]

Interest in domestication rose and fell with Bedson's attempts, suggesting that western Canadians still doubted their ability to master nature. Domestication schemes gained adherents when individuals feared both the social consequences of the end of the provisions trade and the economic disappointments of slow western development. What happened at Stony Mountain had a larger social context in which expansionism had come, at least for a time, upon rocky ground. It certainly contradicted some of the original promises of settlement promoters. John Macoun's *Manitoba and the Great North-West: The Field for Investment, the Home of the Emigrant* was illustrated with pictures showing the original hopes of expansionism. These pictures showed magnificent, ordered farms being established after only "Two Years on the Prairie." The idealized farm was self-sufficient with mixed crops and neatly organized between crop fields and domestic cattle herds.[83] In much of the period, many Manitobans and inhabitants of the Northwest Territories saw little of this successful farm improvement. They were also less optimistic in their ability to sweep aside a natural world with agricultural improvement. Their pessimism about nature's wealth, the real food requirements of the 1870s and 1880s, and concerns about social stability prompted many westerners to re-establish links with the fur trade era by conserving wild animals.

Such conservatism found continued expression in certain communities. Ranchers revived memories of the buffalo to support their interests. They abhorred sodbusters and their busy improvement schemes.[84] They, too, identified their land as original buffalo territory and imaginatively connected their domestic stock with these wild, woolly predecessors. L.V. Kelly clearly articulated this conservatism in his work *The Range Men*. There memory of the buffalo suggested that the free-range rancher was the rightful heir of its natural world. Kelly introduced his rangemen as beneficiaries of the "luxuriant grasses" that the "buffalo had chosen as their breeding grounds." He drew explicit connections between the natural historical past and his romanticized free rangers by reprinting photographs in his book that showed mountain sheep, elk, and buffalo as "Native Livestock." A photograph entitled "The First Herds" displayed bison at Banff – possibly some of Bedson's originals – suggesting that the free-range ranch was the natural continuation of a long-standing land use, one that should not be violated by misguided bids for agrarian improvement. As in southern Manitoba, the buffalo and other wildlife were used to link new western communities to the old order before them.[85]

The farming promoter, too, could draw on the same memories but for different ends. It is difficult to fully understand why a settler near Stettler, Alberta, filled most of his home with items from the HBC period. His collection was so extensive that it surprised even the federal bureaucrats appraising it for possible inclusion in the national parks museum collection. His farmhouse held not only old HBC guns and memorabilia but also a large number of animals, birds, butterflies, eggs, dinosaur bones, fossils, Amerindian curios, and even human skulls. The collector had about 100 specimens of butterflies, 240 birds' eggs, numerous skulls, horns, and dozens of animal trophies, including three massive buffalo heads.[86] The collecting impulse, in this case, is difficult to attribute to particular interests. Farming communities, however, often collected wildlife relics and, in town museums, used them to celebrate progress. In the next chapter, I examine some of the lore surrounding wildlife in settlement communities. By the period of the wheat boom, farmers were confident that progress was sweeping through their region. Writing in this period of confidence, Major Robert Larmour in 1907 reviewed William Francis Butler's *Great Lone Land*. He suggested what would now be a common use for memory of the buffalo and noted Butler's admiration for the western wilderness: "I would say that 'I see' that same wilderness to which he alludes fast becoming a veritable garden. In times not so very long ago that Great Lone Land gave life and sustenance to millions of the wild buffalo, while now, instead, it yields sustenance sufficient for millions of human beings ... the higher order of life."[87]

3
From Meat to Sport Hunting

The first decades of the territorial period were marked by disappointments in western development. Settlements grew slowly. Western promotion stalled as economic recessions hit central Canada in the 1870s and 1880s. European immigrants chose the American frontier over the distant and remote lands west of Winnipeg. Even when they were laid, the CPR tracks carried few settlers. Surveyors' pegs soon rusted. Over many townships, buffalo grasses still swayed.

After 1890 and until the First World War, however, remarkable environmental changes began to transform diets and mentalities. Especially after settlement gained pace, newcomers started to replace wild meat with imported or homegrown alternatives. By the end of the First World War, railway extension, farm and ranch expansion, and technological improvement offered a variety of cheap protein substitutes.

A major change during this period was the move from meat hunting to sport hunting. Sport hunting was already popular in Europe, the United States, and central and eastern Canada. The middle classes followed established etiquette in the sport and promoted conservation measures to protect wild animals as "game." Sport hunting clubs proliferated, and a service industry grew around this leisure pursuit. These hunters also venerated a separate natural realm, understood positively as "wilderness." They also used the term "wild life" to describe their quarry. An ancient pursuit of the upper classes, sport hunting had gained broad popularity among urban and town citizens. These hunters believed that they rejuvenated themselves in nature.

In the Canadian west, sport hunting groups dominated the hunt only after fundamental economic and social changes had taken place. By the end of the Great War, professional and middle classes within towns and cities were able to determine local hunting practices and form the first fish and game associations. These groups aggressively promoted a sport ethic among marginal and poorer groups within communities. But their teaching was successful only after economies themselves had improved and overall demand for wild meat had declined. Farmers could still claim rights to fish and game resources for their subsistence. But by the interwar years, sportsmen claimed fish and game resources as their own.

In the period before the Great War, issues surrounding the hunting and use of wild animals revealed a widening distance between west and east, farmer and town dweller, immigrant and charter communities. But probably most significant was a divide now appearing between Amerindians and newcomers. Before 1919, settlement communities started to gain some independence from wild meat and separated themselves further from First Nations people, whose cultures remained closely tied to a provisions hunt. A traditional economy, in which wild meat had formed an important currency, was becoming obsolete. In this chapter, I explore in more detail the transformation of the western hunt before the end of the Great War.

The Mountaineer, in a letter to the *Macleod Gazette* in 1887, summarized what many believed. "We have already exterminated the noble bison, the elk, deer and sheep will soon follow. Many of us well remember when our prairies teemed with buffalo, and the river bottoms ... abounded with elk and deer." Settlers such as the Mountaineer saw their region undergoing momentous change and wildlife disappearing around them. The sportsmen

Buffalo bones in Saskatchewan, ca. 1910. Pioneers photographed bone piles like these near railheads on the prairies. Collected for export to American fertilizer companies, these bones marked the end of an era.
National Archives of Canada, PA 66544

forming the Macleod Game Protective Association as early as 1889 believed that "these great plains, which a few years ago were a hunter's paradise, are now barren of all large game."[1]

Yet newcomers were not objective enumerators of wild animal populations around them. Settlers almost invariably believed that their "last best west" possessed a past or passing abundance of wild animals. Many believed that history was replacing prehistory and that, consequently, domesticated animals were displacing wild animals. Settlers also swapped stories of the unimaginable abundance of wildlife to suggest the wealth of a land that was now bounded by survey chains. In his classic study of the North American buffalo, Frank Gilbert Roe recorded some of these "traditions" concerning the buffalo in settlement communities. Newcomers exaggerated the animal's range, species taxonomy, and behaviour in what amounted to popularized hearsay. Whether they witnessed it or not, settlers recounted prairies "black" with buffalo. Most townships circulated an account of the "last" buffalo seen before it disappeared to leave its land to settlers.[2] Every community also had a venerated old-timer who claimed to remember clearly the buffalo herds that had covered the land. Newspapers reprinted old-timers' testimonies and termed the buffalo the "monarch of the prairie";[3] settlers party to a cooperative regicide now claimed the realm. Newspapers, indeed, reprinted scores of settler and Native legends concerning the behaviour of herds, their disappearance, the mysterious sighting of the "last" buffalo on someone's land nearby, or, more often, the ways in which the buffalo had been hunted and killed.[4]

Many settlers viewed this wildlife extermination as a sign of the progressive development of the land. Some newcomers photographed themselves next to the giant buffalo bone heaps that formed near railway crossings for export to US bone carbon fertilizer companies. The Hugh Lumsden photographs of skeletons of some 25,000 buffalo piled at Saskatoon in 1890 caught for posterity a moment of change that, to say the least, settlers found breathtaking. The bones, forming a pile regarded as one of the largest in Canada, had been collected for the most part by Amerindian and Métis hunters for five to seven dollars a ton. The Lumsden photographs gained their impressive scale, though, after a young settler, symbolic of changing proprietorship, stood beside the mountains of bones.[5]

Newspapers and pioneer conversation ceaselessly returned to the case of the buffalo in the early settlement period. The *Medicine Hat Times* reported the discovery of a trail made by a buffalo herd near the town in 1886 and the secondhand report that an "Indian came across them and slaughtered four – two bulls and two cows. There was eighteen in the herd." It urged that "provisions should be made for the protection of the remaining few of that once numerous race of animals."[6] Reports came in of CPR travellers who were easily duped into believing that herds of cattle near Maple Creek were buffalo – to the point where one of them "got his rifle ready and was about to begin firing on them" from the train window.[7] The chronology of the buffalo's disappearance blurred in the popular consciousness. Indeed, pioneers and visitors believed that the extirpation of wildlife would naturally follow the transfer of lands to a sovereign and civil state. Achilles Daunt, in a narrative entitled *In the Land of Moose, Buffalo, and Bear*, published the same year as the Riel Rebellion, believed that settlement was becoming so substantial that, even in the boreal forests near Lake Athabasca, wildlife was being hunted to extinction. In this distant region of present-day northern Alberta, the author suggested, the last of the woodlands species of buffalo was being hurried to its demise by Amerindian (likely Cree and Chipewyan) and Métis meat hunters. The author drew on the theme popularly sustained by the Riel Rebellion that "In a few years the romance of the prairies will be a tradition of the past. Nay the pig has already replaced the buffalo, and the policeman has supplanted the Indian."[8] Buffalo Jones, the famous American showman and buffalo domesticator, visited the same region in 1899 and offered his opinions on a subsistence hunt no longer viable even in northern Alberta. The Cree, Chipewyan, and Slavey people there would have to "make fences, cut hay, capture the moose, reindeer, musk-ox, buffalo and other animals" if they expected to survive.[9]

The popular belief in progress undoubtedly influenced these local traditions. The settler's tendency to see change hurrying the disappearance of wildlife was everywhere a theme. It can be seen in Charles Mair's poetry. Former expansionist and itinerant western resident, Mair had been a key participant in mobilizing pressure on the British government to transfer the HBC lands to the Canadian government. Although he is also credited with sparking some of the first Canadian interest in preserving the last of the buffalo, this point needs some clarification. The poet was chiefly interested in the implications of progress propelling western society forward. To him, the disappearance of wild animals provided a valuable benchmark of change. It was his poem "The Last Bison," published in the *Dominion Illustrated News* in 1888, that demonstrated how the agricultural promoter could view the declining Canadian buffalo herds. Mair retold the tragic but, in his view, inevitable extirpation of buffalo herds in the larger march of progress. His poem connected the animal's tragic decline with what he saw as the closely related decline of the Amerindian populations of the Saskatchewan River valleys "Whose faded nation had for ages held, in fealty to Nature, these domains." Mair saw progress as inevitable and the buffalo as

> All vanished! perished in the swelling sea
> and stayless tide of an encroaching power
> whose civil fiat, man-devouring still,
> will leave, at last, no wilding on the earth.

Mair also saw significance in the sheer abundance of buffalo herds, "which overflowed the plains," and left little doubt that natural abundance welcomed western newcomers and the soil's improvers, whose "civil fiat" was predetermined and inevitable.[10]

Typical of agricultural promoters, Mair also confused the first wild foragers with the first inhabitants. From a pioneer's viewpoint, both representatives of the older fur trade period were meeting a similar fate in the march of progress. Sodbusters, making their first few cents by picking buffalo bones off their land, were particularly alert to signs of wildlife extinction. Charles Short, one of the original settlers near Highwood River (in present-day Alberta) in 1884, remembered looking through the woods behind the rotting Spitzee Post. "All through those woods there, there were scores and scores of buffalo heads, at least Indian heads you see. And were always under the impression, told they used to get their liquor there from these fellows, you see. And then go off into the woods and die. There were two or three who were probably shot, but it looked to me as if they just got drunk and died." Along the Highwood and Little Bow Rivers, the first settlers in the 1880s came across countless wolf skulls and bleached buffalo bones. These bleak relics referred to the past and a debauched and violent era.[11]

Not surprisingly, the disappearance of the buffalo was of interest to Frederick Middleton's army personnel dispatched to quell the Northwest Rebellion in 1885. These shoe salesmen and office clerks who mustered to the call must have taken some comfort in believing that progress was on their side. Many quickly learned how to shoot rifles by aiming at buffalo skulls when they arrived in the west. As one diarist noted, "the last of the buffalo in the country was killed, we are told, last summer."[12] Another soldier described an entire company who fired their rifles (unsuccessfully, it turned out) at a lone antelope near their camp in present-day Saskatchewan,[13] the very hotbed of rebellion against the "civil fiat." William Francis Butler, whose reconnaissance during the Riel Rebellion took him to distant reaches of the prairies, devoted a book to the theme of environmental progress. Native people, forests, and wild animals were quickly fading from this "great lone land." Left behind were deserted camps devastated by smallpox and the acres of buffalo bones bleaching on the plains. Everything seemed to be hushed before the first sweep of providential change. Like Mair, Butler found it a depressing but amazing sight to behold. When he later visited Calgary in 1883 as a representative of an English colonization company, he saw the western section of the CPR completed and reported in the *Calgary Herald* "the great change he found throughout the Territories since his former visit"; places "which were then a dreary waste have since sprung up and become flourishing towns."[14]

Popular spectacles seemed to justify some of that optimism. Settlers shot or chased away animals as soon as lots were surveyed. Run from farm and town peripheries, shot off the land, or simply poisoned as nuisances, hoofed animals fared badly in the first settlement lands of western Canada. Bear hunts became civic events. The *Macleod Gazette* celebrated the shooting of an enormous cinnamon grizzly "making himself conspicuous" on frequent visits to a hotel's trash can in town and recounted the way that individuals hunted it down, in this case, for its pelt.[15] The *Calgary Herald* noted numerous bear sightings in 1883, still early in the town's slow development: "reports have been brought in each week of their having been seen in the vicinity," the editor reported. The newspaper urged city hunters to take up the challenge since few had yet risen to the call: "we think the fact of an Indian having killed four on Monday in the vicinity of Morley should stir them up to fresh activity."[16] CPR train crews were meanwhile running bears before their engines, chasing them into ditches, and firing at them with Winchesters.[17]

Bears and other carnivores dangerous to humans, sheep, cattle, and chickens were of more than practical concern to a settler facing thorny undergrowth and massive tree stumps on his land. In the Lower Mainland of British Columbia, a bear crossing town limits undermined efforts to boost a community's reputation. The editor of the New Westminster paper, the *Mainland Guardian*, reported a "scene on the street at Vancouver" in 1888 in which a large crowd had gathered outside the Dougall House and Cosmopolitan Saloon to watch a trainer wrestle a bear. The animal had got loose and nearly attacked a child nearby, and the editor chided organizers for allowing the spectacle to take place in the first place: "It was a brutal exhibition which would not be tolerated in a civilized community: but there were magistrates, police, and other city officials amongst the gaping crowd, and all enjoying the vulgar comedy that was so much like a tragedy." Had the bear killed and eaten the child, the editor wondered, "would not that be a good advertisement in all the cities of Europe? An encouragement to fathers and mothers to bring their children to the 'queen' city of the west?"[18]

Elsewhere, newcomers freely shot just about everything that moved in a combined effort to hunt food and clean up a rough settlement's reputation. With "almost every" train on the new line between Banff and Calgary passing large herds of antelope, passengers and crews were spending "whole stores of ammunition" in the often vain attempt to shoot animals from railcar platforms. The *Calgary Herald* reported that one visitor to the town had succeeded in shooting one antelope, breaking its leg with a first shot and amazingly, considering the difficult marksmanship in such conditions, finishing it off with a second shot. "The train was stopped, and the carcass picked up and taken on board, and was found to be very palatable."[19]

Wolves so detrimental to herds on Alberta's struggling free-range ranches began appearing as trophies in shop windows in High River. Stuffed coyotes decorated the interiors of barbershops. In Calgary, a businessman's group calling itself the Pack of Western Wolves had as its special trophy a wolf head that in 1893 was used for studio photography. The visiting lieutenant governor of the Northwest Territories, Charlie Mackintosh, had his picture taken with it.[20] The wolf seemed to perfectly embody the troubles that newcomers encountered while improving wilderness areas. A Lethbridge paper, for instance, reported the wolf problem facing Magrath community members in 1913. They had supposedly never faced wolves and coyotes "as ferocious as they are this year." Here the wild animal became both a metaphor of the wilderness and an embodiment of everything holding back western ranchers from success – an acute issue since ranchers now faced competition with farmers for land. The newspaper reprinted the "almost incredulous facts" being learned by ranchers about the animal. Although several wolves had been killed on the ranches, one animal was described in detail. "He is a leader of a band of coyotes, numbering about thirty and he is said to be as fleet of foot as a deer, and his cunning and ferociousness is incomparable." The paper stated that "this gaunt, silent pursuer and his howling kinsmen" would hunt down and hamstring range cattle and then devour them. "It is a peculiarity of the wolf-leader that he rarely enters into the slaughter himself, but is satisfied in wounding the beast, leaving it to his followers."[21]

Settlers, then, were able to understand more concretely conceptions of wilderness when they read newspaper accounts of snarling wolves, coyotes, bears, and the like. Taxidermists, too, modelled vindictive and mean spirits in the snouts of specimens that appeared in hotel lobbies and city hall entrances. Newcomers, not surprisingly, associated their hostile environment and western climate with animals that challenged their right to be there. A missionary in northern Manitoba, for instance, saw "something sublime and exciting" in a winter blizzard "when like some great wild beast it has broken loose from its bounds." As late as 1928, when the museum in Calgary opened, wild animals were still being linked with obdurate wilderness conditions. Citizens seemed to sigh with relief that so many wild animals were displayed in their museum. Established in the Travellers' Building, the museum was opened by the mayor, Fred E. Osborne, whose speech praised the work of volunteers who, gathering many of the wild animals no longer near the city, had proven that Calgarians were "making advances mentally, culturally, and I hope, spiritually." He thanked the numerous citizens who had contributed pieces, including a massive wood buffalo, weighing 2,240 pounds, shot in 1909. "Calgary has taken the opportunity of preserving for futurity those specimens that would be extinct in another thirty years," he stated. Undoubtedly, his audience cheered after the speech.[22]

But there were persistent weaknesses in the triumphalism of settlement rhetoric. The notion that wilderness was disappearing before settlement did not decrease dependencies on wild meat. Furthermore, wild animals still present in farming areas were being hunted down by visiting sportsmen. The west offered them wilderness conditions and good sport. Indeed, before the Laurier-era land booms, the CPR track completed in 1886 was used more by visiting sportsmen shooting wild animals than by hordes of settlers. A good portion of the company's revenues was derived from romantic sightseers and sportsmen who saw the west as an Edenic wilderness.

Sport hunters who visited the west were part of a surging popularity in outdoor recreation among the urban middle classes in the last decades of the nineteenth century. The same hunters were already using new railway and steamship services to find sport in the Muskoka region of Ontario, the northern shoreline of the St. Lawrence in Quebec, and the hunting grounds of New Brunswick. They were among the first to take advantage of passenger service now available from Montreal to Vancouver. H.W. Seton Karr was aboard the first CPR passenger train from Calgary on the "Royal Route" to Alaskan shooting areas in 1886.[23] Others were lured west by the promises of Newton H. Chittenden, whose promotional brochure described "the sublime grandeur, unsurpassed beauty ... [and] the incomparably rich fields for the hunter and sportsman."[24] These publications hurried Londoners to "this new North-West of ours" before others made the region as commonplace as a London suburb, as one confessed.[25] Others followed the attractions laid out by J.H. Hubbard, president of the Manitoba Gun Club, who lectured at the Colonial and Indian Exhibition in England. Surrounding his audience were stuffed birds and heads of game that Hubbard and others had shot in the Northwest Territories. As he said, "never before have the natural history and sport attractions of the Canadian Northwest and Rocky Mountain regions been brought before the European public so forcibly as during the past two months," when the railway was nearing completion.[26]

Urban conditions in eastern Canada, the United States, and western Europe were driving the middle classes back to nature and onto this rail line. In the 1880s, criticism of poverty and unsanitary living conditions in the growing cities was prompting a widespread "purity" movement in Toronto, Montreal, and numerous American cities. Pushing for urban reforms, scores of city residents were also searching for outdoor recreation beyond city limits. During visits to the west, they hoped to find the "bracing," clear air of nature and respite from coal-polluted urban life.

Back to nature, as a movement, found many expressions. The health benefits believed to be derived from sport hunting gave it unprecedented popularity in the last years of the nineteenth century. The virtues of the sport hunt were promoted by individuals such as British Columbia's chief game guardian. Arthur Bryan Williams had arrived from England in Vancouver in 1888. He had intended to move to California but stayed in British Columbia after becoming struck by the natural beauty of the region and the abundant wildlife available for sport hunting. A longtime hunter with "traces of primitive man" in his blood, as he said in his published autobiography, he offered guide services for a number of years. In the late 1890s, with no previous experience for the job, he was hired to fill the province's new position of game guardian. He clearly floundered in his mandate to single-handedly watch over a province some seven hundred miles long and four hundred miles wide.[27]

Nevertheless, Williams was encouraged by the increasing popularity of sport hunting in the province, especially by 1911, when hundreds of Vancouver and Victoria hunters headed into nearby forests. He believed that hunting produced "a healthy, hardy race" and that a thorough knowledge of the use of firearms might "some day be of great service in the defense of the Empire."[28] Throughout his career, he maintained correspondence with hundreds of like-minded sportsmen who turned to hunting for health reasons. He reminded one of his correspondents, ailing with sickness, that a source of health awaited him in the forests. It was his own experience to be "wet to the skin for weeks at a time and feel no bad effects though I at once get ill on my return to town." He therefore urged the man to go hunting, for there "is nothing like fresh air and a bit of sport for setting a man up."[29]

The provincial game office was beginning to draw an important economic return from big-game populations when foreign sportsmen visited and left money in small towns that provided guides and supplies. Williams hoped that the guardians he was appointing in more populated areas could successfully reserve smaller game such as deer for settlement use and undertake a concerted conservation campaign to have the larger grizzly, elk, caribou, and moose populations preserved for skilled, wealthy, visiting hunters. By the first decade of the twentieth century, he had effectively overseen the promotion and maintenance of a highly popular transportation system that linked the Lillooet, Kootenay, and Lower Fraser districts, accessible by rail, and the magnificent Cassiar region, accessible by steamship.

For Vancouver and Victoria residents, Williams believed that properly regulated hunting could create a healthy urban population. He was not alone in this belief. Numerous middle-class magazines devoted to hunting and fishing underlined the benefits of such sports. In *Rod and Gun in Canada*, western Canadian hunting trips were lauded as a prescription for the ill effects of city life. This escape into a region unmarked by human artifice was believed to make the urbanite all the more productive when he returned home after a hunt. One sportsman writing about big-game hunting in British Columbia in *Man-to-Man Magazine* in 1910 spoke of the benefits of living in Vancouver, so close to hunting regions. On a Saturday morning, "you climb on to a train. A real gun is strapped over your shoulder and you are dressed in boots and khaki. In a few hours you are making your way through a God-made wilderness. In the afternoon you bag a bear or a deer.

On a Sunday you bring down a mountain goat. You are back at your desk Monday morning ready for a hard week's work."[30]

The slow fits of initial immigration undoubtedly underscored some contradictions developing between what westerners promoted about the west – attempting to dispel its associations with a wilderness region – and what transportation and service industries were promising. Tourism promoters were busily presenting the west as a pristine wilderness region. Although promoters of back to nature could easily idealize country life, its adherents in western Canada were not hoping to find farmyards in their rail tours. They were looking for natural conditions that contrasted with the contagion, overcrowding, and physical "softness" of city life. From the outset, visitors aboard railways turned a blind eye to the homesteader's small shack and the towns about which westerners were anxious to boast. Mrs. Phillipps-Wolley, accompanying her husband, Clive, aboard a CPR train in 1887 on a big-game hunt, was one such visitor. As she wrote to a friend in England, "What a land this is for an angler!" Seeing many lakes in western Ontario from the train window, she believed that they were pristine, that "on half of them probably no birch-bark canoe has ever floated – no fly ever been thrown." But most of her awe was reserved for the reaches of the rail line beyond Manitoba, where she could watch nature "in her very wildest moods" from the comfortable Pullman coach: "Inside the Pullman car all is luxury; outside is Nature in her most rugged mood. The cars are on cradle springs, and rock evenly as they rush along the line. Lying in a cozy bed, I drew up the blind of the window which ran beside my pillow, and as I dozed away looked out upon the wild Canadian night."[31] John Sheldon, penning a promotional brochure for the Canadian government in 1887, described to readers the view from the rear platform of the Pullman car. "In no other way is the sublimity of those vast solitudes to be so impressively perceived ... A railway train is a mere worm pursuing its sinuous course ... Successive scenes come quickly into sight, and are ever changing as in a veritable panorama."[32] In fiction, the west held out the dark allure of Harold Bindloss's novel *Prescott of Saskatchewan*, published in both Toronto and London, in which the rail journey is equated with a descent into wilderness. The heroine, Muriel, wearing "travelling tweeds" too hot for the prairie summer, watches with growing apprehension as the wilderness west of Ontario sweeps past the train window. Finally, in Winnipeg, all that connects her to "luxurious civilization" are the electric lights down the street. "She wondered with a stirring curiosity what awaited her in the wilds where man still grappled with nature in primitive fashion."[33]

English sport hunters were so anxious to reach unspoiled wilderness regions that they were susceptible to CPR promotional maps, which soon advertised "unexplored" areas throughout the western provinces. Such were promised in the editions of *The Sportsman's Map of Canada and the Northwest*

Territory, in which a blatantly misleading term, "unexplored," appeared over large areas of Quebec, Ontario, and the northwest.[34] As late as 1905, the world-travelling Frederick Lort-Phillips and his wife, seeing a CPR brochure highlighted by these "unexplored" areas, decided that their next journey would be to western Canada: "there was not only hunting to be considered, but the added delight of being the first Europeans to penetrate those inland waters, and the prospect of some useful mapping to be done."[35] Although the areas had been thoroughly mapped and described in topographical surveys since the 1860s, Lort-Phillips included a hand-sketched map of the Fraser River and the interior lakes that he visited in his memoirs, published in 1931. But he was not alone in searching for pristine wilderness in the west. The hope of finding natural, not settled, areas attracted H. Somers Somerset; "'Unexplored' figured so largely and alluringly in one and prodigious accounts," he said, "that this untravelled region promised a certain amount of novelty and adventure."[36]

To suggest the wild dimensions of the west, the CPR's westbound "annotated timetable" consistently suggested to readers that game abounded beside the track.[37] Still meagre passenger rosters prompted the company to use such promotions to round up easterners and outfit them for shooting trips. In the first years of the CPR, groups of five or more sportsmen journeyed west "at greatly reduced rates," and the Dominion Express Company offered reasonable fees for camp equipment, tents, and other necessary rentals.[38] And in 1887, the new rail line to the Canadian west was featured in the *Sportsman's Guide to the Hunting and Shooting Grounds of the United States and Canada*, a compilation of some three thousand proven shooting areas. The directory listing 208 railway and transportation companies that offered services to North American sportsmen now advertised the western spaces. Largely unclaimed by any form of settlement, this dominion land was "open to all" for hunting. Hotel rates and livery fees were on par with those of other locations, and there were dozens of recommended lakes and areas for sport at Medicine Hat, Qu'Appelle, Regina, Swift Current, Wapella, Wolseley, and dozens of locations in British Columbia. "Good grounds" to hunt antelope, elk, bear, duck, goose, and prairie chicken awaited hunters near Medicine Hat. Qu'Appelle offered good hunts in deer, bear, grouse, wolf, fox, and rabbit. Throughout British Columbia, deer, bear, mountain sheep, "panther" (mountain lion), and elk awaited at Hatzic Lake in Mission and near whistlestops at New Westminster, Port Moody, Revelstoke, the Shuswap, and Victoria.[39]

The train therefore became the means and even the end of back to nature, especially when "palace car" tours allowed hunters to venture into the western game fields soon after completion of the CPR. Thomas Martindale, a wealthy writer and hunter from Philadelphia, decided to travel along the track after becoming convinced that Canada offered the

"The Game and Fur Trophy in the Canadian Court," 1886. Describing the Canadians' impressive Game and Fur Trophy at the Colonial and Indian Exhibition in London, 1886, the *Illustrated London News* praised the abundant wildlife to be found in the "noble forests and rivers of the Dominion." J.H. Hubbard, a sportsman from Winnipeg, helped stock the taxidermy display and gave lectures on how to access the western game regions through the new railway line.
Illustrated London News, 14 August 1886

last wilderness areas for sport hunting. Disappointed with hunting conditions in Maine, where he had found about fifteen hundred sportsmen in the woods during one deer-hunting season, he joined one of the many western shooting tours sponsored by an American excursion company. He and other travellers moved along CPR tracks and lived aboard the private car, Yellowstone, while being "luxuriously housed and fed." In the morning, the author wrote letters about the prairie while staff made beds and prepared breakfast. In the evening, he sat down to dinners of wild roast goose, teal, prairie chicken, fresh peaches, sweet potatoes, and even ice cream. Of the thirteen aboard Martindale's car, two were Englishmen. One had just finished elephant shooting in India and was en route to the Rockies for grizzly bear. Others, including five women, were happy just to shoot prairie chickens, ducks, and other wildfowl near Winnipeg, trying to get in the last shooting of the season.

Near Regina, a party of men and women overtook Martindale's excursion. "They eat and sleep in the car, and have been, so far, very successful in shooting and hunting," Martindale wrote in a letter home. He said that the group expected to leave Regina on a side trip for antelope and bear.

Throughout their western tour, the party shot just about everything possible. At one point, Martindale claimed to have seen more sport hunting at Crane Lake in present-day Saskatchewan than he had seen anywhere. In one day, he shot Canadian geese before breakfast and resumed shooting midmorning at the lake, where he shot ducks, snipe, and geese, the water "literally covered in places" with wildfowl. Returning to the train for supper, he shot prairie chickens along the road, and in the last light of day he continued shooting, close to the car. "What exhilaration was crowded into those twelve hours!" he wrote. That night the group had a sing-song in the car, with one of the women playing the piano.[40]

In the 1890s, the visiting sportsman found a sprawling sporting ground in the prairie and western woodlands. There he could hit a bird "even if he shut his eyes when he fired," as T.R. Patillo described sport hunting near Red Deer. Patillo and his hunting companion, dressed in suits of dry grass colour, sloshed through marshes near Red Deer Lake to slaughter hundreds of wildfowl. He wrote that one morning he and his friend became "drunk with excitement" as "the ground all about was dotted with dead and crippled geese." Having shot for hours at flocks nearby, and his trip nearing its end, Patillo returned to board the train in Calgary with a wagon "literally packed with geese, ducks, and chickens."[41]

For many reasons, early settlers did not interfere with these sportsmen. One reason was a pressing need for their hunted game. Patillo did not report it in his narrative, but he was undoubtedly selling his wagonload of wildfowl to game butchers in Calgary. Whatever agricultural boosters said about town or regional self-sufficiency, settlers typically faced chronic food shortages. With settlement rapidly increasing after 1896, new demands for hunted meat, especially in Vancouver and Winnipeg, again exceeded supply. British Columbia's "beef famine" began in 1893 following the rise of urban centres in the Lower Mainland and Victoria. After the great settlement boom of 1897, the west fell into a sustained period of supply crisis in which local dietary needs were being met by hunters, professional provisioners, individual sport hunters, and game butchers.[42]

Increasing consumption of wild meat in the west is a difficult historical phenomenon to examine, largely because it went unrecorded in most sources. In the Yukon, far into the twentieth century, wild meat continued to take a prominent place in the diets of unapologetic northerners. However, in more southerly pioneer societies, the tendency was to disavow what was an embarrassing dietary shortfall. This was even the case when, in open game seasons, creaking, blood-soaked, meat wagons arrived in town from marshlands and hunters brought sides of moose or deer to sell at railway stations.

Federal and territorial government statistics obscure the pioneer's diet. These records attempted to chart progress, not local dependencies on wild

Duggan and Shaw's butcher shop, Camrose, Alberta, ca. 1910. Pioneers relied
heavily on wildlife for their subsistence. Game laws permitted newcomers not only
extensive hunting freedoms but also allowed for the sale of meat.
Glenbow Archives, NA-3462-24

animals and provisioning networks that included Amerindian hunters.
Dominion trade, export, and food-processing statistics did not include
the large quantities of wild meat being sold in communities or exported
illegally to other parts of Canada. Newspapers, arguably the richest documentary source on this matter, mentioned only in passing this reality of
pioneer experience. For instance, in 1888, the New Westminster *Mainland
Guardian* carried advertisements of the wild meat butcher, W.H. Vianen,
who offered "Fresh and Salt Water Fish" and "Game in Season." In early
October of that year, Vianen displayed a deer weighing two hundred pounds
at the store; he shipped about two thousand salmon to different locations
following the fall runs; and, by early November, he and other game butchers were handling sacks of wildfowl.[43] But these butchers received little attention in the papers. Only a careful reading of a shipping section can identify
boats, such as the *William Irving*, arriving from Hope carrying a deer with
the cattle and hogs coming downriver.[44] Photographic evidence can fill in
some of this documentary vacuum. One photograph preserved in the
Glenbow Museum shows the interior of the Duggan and Shaw butchery in
Camrose, Alberta, in the 1910s. The picture shows a mother buying meat
over the counter, her baby stroller nearby. The community's dependence
on wild animals is clear in the scene: a massive bull moose and numerous
deer hang from the wall behind her, and rabbits cover the counter.[45]

Some dimensions of wild meat consumption become more obvious in
the writing of game ordinances as well as the files of game guardian offices

established in new provinces. In the territorial period, the Department of the Interior had moved rapidly to have game protected by volunteer "guardians." By 1885, thirty-two guardians had been appointed throughout the territories from Moose Jaw to Calgary to enforce game ordinances. The 1884 ordinance had a prime objective to conserve "an important source of economic food supply."[46] That year William F. Whitcher visited the Northwest Territories to provide Rocky Mountains (Banff) National Park with game laws. He deemed "excellent" the game ordinance already in place. But he stressed the need for game guardian appointments since it was rumoured that St. Paul and Chicago pot hunters were planning to visit the region "under the impression that shooting, egging, etc., are free in that remote part of Canada." He stressed the widespread reliance on wild meat by pointing out the desire among settlers to have feathered, furred, and hoofed game protected by law.[47]

The importance of game as a food source appears in the written ordinances of the last decades of the nineteenth century. Most of these ordinances were shaped around community food needs. The 1898 Northwest Territories game ordinance specified a closed season on big-game animals but waived all restrictions for an individual who hunted "for the purpose of food for himself or his family." The ordinance stipulated that travellers, families, or persons "in a state of actual want may kill any bird or animals ... and take any egg or eggs ... for purpose of satisfying his or their immediate wants but not otherwise."[48] The so-called traveller's proviso was respected in the 1890 Manitoba game ordinances and occasionally reappeared in laws after the turn of the century.[49]

Ordinances, meanwhile, encouraged a large trade in wild meat. Game hunters and butchers, although restricted to open seasons, could sell, trade, or barter their meat. The first game guardians appointed in western locales had wide latitude to check any "shop, storehouse, warehouse, restaurant, hotel, or eating-house, or any delivery cart or any waggon," suspected of containing game meat out of season, suggesting the various venues and vehicles that carried such fare. In British Columbia, the meat trade thrived well beyond the 1911 game act. Defining no fewer than forty-four sexual and species classifications of animals and birds, the legislation prohibited hunters from shooting twenty-six types of wild animals and selling their meat. These were almost exclusively the female and young members of species. But the ordinance continued to allow the "buying, selling, or exposing for sale, show or advertisements," within season, caribou, buck deer, hare, bull moose, mountain goat, mountain ram, and plover.[50] The wording of an 1897 ordinance allowing game guardians to enter "any shop where game is usually exposed for sale" also suggests that game butchers were well known in communities and pursued their livelihood on boats, in hotels, and from the back doors of restaurants.[51]

Popular backlash against changes to game ordinances further suggests the importance of wild meat in western diets. A letter writer complained in the *Macleod Gazette* in 1887 about reductions in the duck-shooting season, saying that in September "bacon straight is so unpalatable, and fresh meat so difficult to get and keep, it is a severe trial to the most law abiding citizen to be forbidden to kill ducks that have been ready for table for some weeks."[52] Newspapers often sided with readers to argue against changes in game laws simply because settlers were still dependent on hunting to feed themselves. Their concerns seem to have been well founded when one makes estimates of the beef supply in the west. The 1881 federal census displays the small numbers of animals sold per one thousand people according to province (Table 1).

The larger supply of domestic animals in British Columbia at the time of the survey was unavailable to most colonists because of high prices. Since western residents had little access to domesticated animals, they relied on wild game that they hunted themselves or purchased from provisioners. In fact, the census enumerated occupations of residents and provided a glimpse of occupational "hunters." These individuals, making a living from hunting wild animals and birds, would not all have been provisioners. Although the 1888 census does not define its terms, the 1891 census groups together "hunters, trappers, scouts and guides" as one occupational category. With this qualification in mind, however, the 1888 census reveals a startling number of "hunters" in western electoral districts compared with central and eastern provinces, a number far higher than the national average, as Table 2 indicates.

Interestingly, while occupational hunting proliferated in the west, the number of taxidermy establishments at this time was low. This statistic reveals two different uses of wildlife between western and eastern populations

Table 1

Number of animals sold in 1881 per thousand people

Province	Cattle	Sheep	Swine
Prince Edward Island	139	540	246
Nova Scotia	143	343	127
New Brunswick	110	276	186
Quebec	117	321	245
Ontario	188	389	414
Manitoba	**74**	**21**	**283**
British Columbia	**276**	**216**	**210**
Northwest Territories	**31**	**4**	**12**
Canada	152	346	301

Source: 1881 Census

Table 2

Ratio of occupational hunters to total population, 1881

Province	Ratio of "hunters" to population
Prince Edward Island	1:21,000
Nova Scotia	1:3,900
New Brunswick	1:3,400
Quebec	1:1,200
Ontario	1:2,100
Manitoba	**1:55**
British Columbia	**1:57**
Northwest Territories	**1:43**
Canada	1:770

Source: Derived from 1881 Census occupation tables and total population tables

– one population using wildlife primarily for meat and commerce, the other for sport. The 1891 census shows that there was one taxidermist in Winnipeg, two in New Brunswick, and three in Nova Scotia. In central Canada, where occupational hunting was at its lowest national level, no fewer than twenty-three taxidermists in Ontario and thirty-one in Quebec plied their trade.[53]

The availability of beef in the west likely varied according to a settler's environment and proximity to rail lines. Early commentators noted that beef prices in southern Alberta reflected surpluses being redistributed to Winnipeg and British Columbia by the 1890s. The ranching industry had first imported herds in 1876 and 1877 and had started exporting beef to Winnipeg (1885) and Britain (1887) when rail lines were complete. Before the railway, however, most of the west suffered from a chronic shortage of beef even in areas of established settlement. The Winnipeg newspaper *Les "Métis"* lamented the fact that, even with rising numbers of cattle in the Winnipeg market, and milking cows selling at lower prices in 1877, butchers had not lowered prices of meat. The reasons were many. Transportation, storage, and range problems meant that there was comparatively less fresh beef on the market.[54]

But even after the building of the CPR, western communities did not necessarily gain access to cheaper beef products. Edmonton, still distant from a railhead, experienced meat supply problems well after construction of the rail line. Newspaper editor Frank Oliver sent estimates to the 1887 Senate natural food source inquiry of the dressed weight of wood buffalo, musk-oxen (eaten only when deer was not available), jumping deer, moose, and reindeer. Meanwhile, Richard Hardisty, at Edmonton, confirmed the rumour of exorbitant local beef prices (fourteen cents a pound!). Bacon was selling at fifteen cents a pound and pork at nine cents a pound. But even along the rail line, bacon still sold at twelve cents a pound. Considering that beef was available to eastern buyers at about three cents a pound, western prices were staggeringly high. At St. Albert, one settler noted that game birds sold at ten, fifteen, or twenty-five cents per pound; geese at fifty cents each; partridge or prairie chicken at ten cents each; and fish at twelve cents per pound.[55]

Fort Benton importers, particularly T.C. Powers and Company, were bringing large orders of beef into Canadian territory for as low as three cents a pound, but this barrelled beef sold for higher prices the farther inland it was carried and when it was converted to retail. Periodic climatic and political disturbances also caused meat supply crises. In 1884 and 1885, troops went west to quell the Northwest Rebellion, the CPR's construction continued to bring out hundreds of workers, and settlements were becoming larger in southern Manitoba. All these developments ensured that beef fetched as high as fourteen cents per pound on the market. The first land rush in southern Manitoba and the accelerated growth of Winnipeg introduced new food demands by the 1890s; in British Columbia, the most acute beef supply problems occurred in 1893, after the Hall mines opened in the Kootenay areas and mining and lumber camps opened in distant reaches of the province.[56] Certainly, increasing urbanization affected prices, and the most spectacular urban growth began to occur in the west, in Winnipeg and Vancouver, by the 1901 census; the population in British Columbia jumped from 98,000 in 1891 to 178,000 in 1901 – most of it in urban areas. Calgary, Edmonton, and Saskatoon showed similar population explosions in 1911 and 1921.

Wild animals therefore provided an important protein alternative when domestic products were not available. And the railway likely caused even wild meat prices to escalate. Although a significant infusion of imported products vented pressure from the market, the first settlement booms raised demand for game meat to new levels. The railway seems to have drawn away from local use the wild meat in high demand elsewhere. By the 1890s, meat was so scarce that disease among rabbit populations was big news in communities. The Manitoba legislature initially protected rabbits. By 1887, their cyclical population booms rendered protection unnecessary – and a dollar could purchase twenty-five rabbits on the market. But seven-year rabbit cycles could just as easily impoverish westerners. It is telling that the *Saskatchewan Herald* in 1890 printed recipes for alternative dishes made with gophers "when game becomes scarce."[57]

Meanwhile, the small numbers of beef producers placed high prices on their product. Infrequent exports after 1888 in British Columbia suggest that the ranching industry was barely meeting local demands as urbanization in Vancouver and Victoria gained pace. And the mining and outlying districts simply were out of reach of beef stores. When customers in the booming Cassiar district did procure products in north-central British Columbia, they cost between fifty and sixty cents a pound in 1875.[58] Record prices like these had the effect of drawing what few beef supplies were available away from southern areas, such as those reaching the Klondike gold fields. Patrick Burns began redirecting his growing supplies northward, for obvious reasons, when hotel restaurant owners in the Yukon would buy beef at a dollar a pound at the height of the gold rush at the close of the century.[59]

Settlers, then, frequently went hungry and purchased what they could from game "provisioners," including Amerindian hunters. Or they ate whatever they could get their hands on. One Moose Jaw sodbuster described how his family made it beyond the first few years of land breaking and capital improvement:

> Early in the spring [of 1885] Dad took the shot gun and went out to the river to hunt ducks ... In one place the river bed was narrow. The suckers trying to get upstream were so thick their fins were sticking up out of the water. Dad found a net made out of slender willows hid in the bushes. It was made so fish couldn't get out again. It had been made by Indians. Dad placed it in the water where it was shallow and wide. He built a wall of stone on each side out to the snare so the fish had to go into the net. The next morning it was packed full, three or four barrels full. They were cleaned and salted for summer use. Each neighbour did the same until all were satisfied.[60]

The Highwood River rancher George Lane was famous for his prairie chicken hunts. But black-and-white photos of the lanky rancher, hands filled with birds, reveal a larder-filling strategy. Ranchers tended to choose their land according to pressing dietary needs, as Elizabeth, George's wife, later recalled about her own father's arrival at Highwood River. He chose land "where there was deep black soil, no forest and no boulders to move, where the rushing mountain river abounded with trout and where wild geese, wild duck and prairie chickens were plentiful."[61]

Since wild meat of any description was still being used to meet local subsistence needs, it is not surprising that a rapid depletion of fish and game followed the first settlement booms at the turn of the century. Hit hardest were fish stocks in lakes and streams adjacent to towns and growing cities. The federal Department of Marine and Fisheries, maintaining control of prairie fisheries until 1930 and overseeing many of the inland streams and lakes in British Columbia, became concerned about the problem after settlement increased. A departmental guardian posted at Peavine, Alberta, remarked in 1909 on the difficulties of upholding the ordinances in regions desperately in need of fish. "I've come to the conclusion," he wrote, "that under present custom, that ... [the fisheries] will soon be a thing of the past here." The many lakes nearby were being fished without licences. "Last year

One day's catch from Lake Minnewanka, Rocky Mountains National Park, ca. 1890. Railway employees relax after catching enormous lake trout at what is now Banff National Park, Alberta. The period of railway construction, mining booms, and – by the turn of the century – rapid farm expansion on the nearby prairie made a marked impact on fish populations throughout the west.
Glenbow Archives, NA-237-38

during spawning times people from around here clubbed, shot and speared any fish they came up with, even went so far as to dynamite the lake this winter."[62] Lake Winnipeg fishermen were certain that whitefish populations were being so quickly depleted that they compared the scenario "to the story of the buffalo."[63]

Raids on lakes near settlements completely discouraged the thinly dispersed representatives of the fisheries department. For the most part political patronage appointments, these guardians did not really attempt to restrict newcomers from overfishing. Few would have had the moral courage to do so since they would have been taking food off tables. Meanwhile, with as many needs elsewhere, pioneers were coordinating a labour force of First Nations and Métis people to collect and export local fish stocks. Pigeon Lake residents in Alberta were sending their soon dwindling whitefish stocks to high-priced markets in Calgary and the Kootenay-region mines of British Columbia by 1902.[64] In 1904, a Winnipeg company took the initiative of shipping prairie whitefish to Edmonton and, from there, sending them on to eastern destinations via the railway. At the same time, these lakes and streams began meeting enormous local food requirements. Some two hundred settlers of German, Russian, and Ukrainian background were visiting

Buffalo Lake in these years, each party taking an estimated four hundred pounds of pike with each visit.[65]

Fishing made a dramatic impact on northerly stocks with the first settlement booms in the south. By 1899, it was estimated that Lac St. Anne and Lac la Biche were already "exhausted" from overfishing. With commercial fishermen wanting to redirect northern lake fisheries to town and city markets in the south, the Department of Marine and Fisheries finally stepped in the same year. Its local representatives believed that, "on the whole, lakes north of the Saskatchewan River must be regarded more as a source of food to resident half-breeds and Indians than fitting objects of mercantile exploitation."[66]

It is doubtful that the department could really provide effective enforcement. The prairies fisheries regulations were only copies of the Manitoba laws until the 1910-11 Alberta and Saskatchewan fisheries commission came up with regulations more suited to local needs. Initial choices for guardian roles were also wanting. Most guardians were appointed in the same manner as employees for the postal service, rewarded for political support. With conservation matters becoming truly critical in the first decade of the century, the federal administration learned of the decrepit condition of its western workforce. Some guardians were actually too gouty and lame to patrol. One in northern Alberta was blind. Even if a guardian was conscientiously upholding ordinances, he was usually overstretched in huge patrol districts. It became a truism in town newspapers that unpaid guardians were useless in their enforcement capacity and that paid ones only looked the other way while neighbours overfished. Many did little more than report the evidence that they uncovered, such as at the Highwood River in 1910, when settlers, ranchers, and other people were found "lime bottling," dynamiting, and even shooting fish in the river.[67] Few unpaid guardians would interfere with this scramble for protein. And they likely believed with their neighbours that foreign game thieves were visiting their locales to haul away what they themselves were not using. As early as 1889, the *Regina Leader* heard "the latest rumour from Winnipeg," that Toronto pot hunters were proposing to take a refrigerated car into the Northwest Territories "and filling her up with game for the eastern markets."[68] Substantiating such reports is difficult, since the story of outsiders stealing local fish and game recurred in many western towns and became a driving force behind local conservation efforts.

The railway, beyond raising prices of local game meat, was being used to illegally export wild meat out of the west. Sportsmen in Vancouver complained that in open season "every train has a large cargo of moose and deer, all of which are heavy animals, consigned to addresses in the Canadian cities, where the meat fetches a very high price."[69] In southern Alberta, both the head and meat trade were supplementing pioneer economies, and aboard "nearly every eastern-bound train [were] heaps of gory trophies in the shape of deer, bighorn and grizzley heads."[70] Early rail passengers would not have missed the sight of residents selling game meat at stations and piling moose beside each other in freight cars. In 1889, settlers near Red Deer informed the territorial government that locals were not killing animals for their own domestic use "but for the purpose of exporting to Calgary and other points for sale, prairie chickens and partridges and other game birds, which breed and are found in the district ... [This] selfish and barbarious practice is fast depleting the District of its game."[71] At the turn of the century, restaurant owners in Vancouver were serving local wild partridge and pheasant out of season – and disguising them with fancy French names such as Roast Gillinotte. That was when new sporting groups began urging trolley car conductors in Richmond (then a favourite wildfowl sporting field) to check under passengers' coats for out-of-season game birds for sale to restaurants in Vancouver.[72]

Contraband game exports constituted only one of many problems facing new governments. In the first years of Saskatchewan's provincial history, the chief game guardian (appointed in the agricultural department) became concerned about market sales of game birds and a perceptible decline in sharp-tailed grouse and prairie chicken in many regions of the settled country. He thought that a prohibition on the sale of grouse would be prudent since "some parties make a practice of shooting these birds for sale to hotels and restaurants, and even peddle them about the streets."[73] That winter he learned that in distant Ottawa an Ontario game warden had seized a trunk filled with prairie chickens checked as train baggage from Regina. Market shooting became the most dramatic during duck-hunting season. Settlers were given generous bags until the First World War. Their duck hunts often became bloody, destructive events. In Moose Jaw, an enterprising butcher contracted hunters, supplied them with ammunition and food, and enjoyed the returns of their hunt, some fifteen hundred birds in the 1911 season alone.[74]

Although prairie Amerindian bands faced bleak hunting prospects, woodland and mountain bands who enjoyed treaty privileges found profit in selling meat and by doing so revived the provisions networks of the fur trade era. In northern Manitoba, they sold directly to the buyers coming north, such as those (discovered by game guardians) who purchased untold numbers of moose from Cree, smoked the meat in woodland camps, and then exported everything, skins and all, to southern markets probably centred in Winnipeg.[75] Not only urbanites but also farmers were buying this meat. As late as 1915, during peak wartime meat pricing, settlers claimed that it was too inconvenient and expensive to buy a hunting permit and ammunition. They purchased wild meat from Amerindian hunters instead. That year in Beausejour, Manitoba, deer meat was about nine cents a pound, probably a good price by any contemporary standard;[76] indeed, one lawyer (likely a weekend sportsman) addressing the "problem" of such pantry hunting stated that a deer fetched the equivalent of nine dollars on the market. Game licences then issued by the Saskatchewan government cost four dollars, which meant that the licensed hunter "is paying more than the meat is worth."[77] By 1920, one hunter noted that it was still cheaper to buy wild meat from Amerindian hunters than it was to hunt it himself. And wild meat would still have been cheaper than beef. One settler in Regina who had sold no fewer than twenty-three moose in 1919 reported to the chief game guardian that men at many railway sidings were selling moose cows and calves to train crews, who delivered them in Manitoba at the attractively low price of ten cents a pound.[78] Wild meat markets existed long after the war years. In 1921, Gordon Hewitt believed that Canadian wildlife, properly conserved, was a valuable alternative to beef, stating that "one of the most serious problems of the present day is the gradually increasing cost of food, particularly meat." He proposed the harvesting of deer at about twelve cents a pound.[79]

There was little "sport" in this type of hunting, as sportsmen always lamented. Western hunters were too busy meeting dietary needs. They did not fret about trophies or follow any of the sport hunting etiquette listed in membership pledges of town and city game clubs. In Saskatchewan, the game guardian office began compiling statistics that showed the scale of meat hunting. Of the licences issued in 1909, 848 went to farmers, 40 to labourers, 37 to Amerindians, 253 to others of "various occupations," and 40 to individuals having no specific occupation. Following the legislation to shoot cow moose, statistics reveal less sport hunting than larder hunting. The department's affidavit system reported the following bags: of the 1,535 big-game animals killed that year, 874 were moose (351 female), 445 were elk (136 female), 213 were jumping deer (79 female), and three were male caribou.[80]

The issue of selling and buying game meat was thorny, however. Besides the weighty legal tradition in Europe that had reserved game for the privileged few, problems arose when settlers and urbanites began buying wild meat in larger quantities. Game laws in western Canada were written on the assumption that individuals who required meat could hunt animals themselves and that this meat was a resource not limited to particular groups in society. This reflected a legal debunking of what had been a continual attempt to reserve game for royal and aristocratic privilege, which New World abundance, poor supervision, and relatively expansive personal freedom simply would not allow. Game was also too important a food source and too easy to hunt for regulations to do anything but protect it for the common good. The first game ordinances in British Columbia preserved game as such. The 1859 ordinance was written because "birds and beasts of Game

constitute an important source of food, and the pursuit thereof affords occupation and the means of subsistence to many persons in this Colony."
The law made it illegal to sell or buy game such as duck, teal, goose, wood-
cock, and snipe at certain times of the year. Deer hunting was closed from
January to July.[81] These stipulations attempted to maintain meat supply for
society as a whole, allowing animals to reproduce and become available for
the chase when they were most fattened. Game ordinances usually stipulated no fees for licences except for wild meat vendors; furthermore, they
did not exclude groups from the chase, nor did they recognize territorial
limits for that chase.

It would therefore be misleading to believe that there was no game conservation in the nineteenth century. Rather, the spirit of western game ordinances after Confederation was to protect wild meat for the common good.
By 1877, for this reason, ordinances in British Columbia forbade the "careless distribution of poison" by individuals who attempted to kill nuisance
deer, coyotes, and other animals. Deer became a serious problem in new
farming communities when they ate and ruined root crops. But poison killed
animals indiscriminately and thereby wasted a community food resource.[82]
The province's 1892 ordinances also prohibited the export of deer hides for
the same reason. Meanwhile, Manitoba laws conserved game as a community food resource. Legislation was therefore initially generous to newcomers
and Amerindian hunters alike, although the province's attempts to legislate
matters between the Crown and Amerindian peoples went beyond provincial jurisdiction. Ordinances gave Manitobans extensive freedom to pursue
all species of the deer family for much of the year and abundant wildfowl at
other times. Earlier game ordinances in Manitoba granted an open season
of 180 days and no limits on the number of moose, elk, deer, and other
varieties of the "deer family." There was no restriction on duck shooting.
Prairie chicken and grouse hunters still enjoyed a season of 165 days. The
same ordinances granted exceptions in the case of individuals in need.[83] In
the Northwest Territories, wide-ranging hunting freedoms indicate the important place that wild meat occupied in settler diets. The 1895 Northwest
Territories ordinance established a 120-day season for the deer family, bighorn sheep, and mountain goat, with a restriction of six animals of each
species per year. But all such restrictions were waived if an individual was
hunting because of need. The hunter also enjoyed complete freedom to
hunt most bird species year-round, except for nesting grouse and prairie
chicken. They were hunted in a ninety-day season. But in spite of this restriction, dietary needs were easily met in the hunt – the 1895 ordinance
restricted hunters to 20 grouse a day, for a possible bag of 1,800 grouse each
season! By 1903, hunters were seasonally curbed to 200 grouse and prairie
chickens.[84]

Individuals who sold meat were also given the generous freedom that hunters enjoyed. Most were middlemen game butchers and brokers. Established butchers offered wild meat, as we have seen, in addition to supplies of beef, poultry, and pork. Specialized game dealers thrived in towns; J. Kearns, in Fort Qu'Appelle, for instance, sold "fish and game" to townspeople. Kearns, who acted as both auctioneer and commission merchant, probably purchased meat from Native people and occupational hunters.[85] It was not in the community's interest to discourage market hunters and game butchers whose activities placed meat products within reach of settlers. The territorial ordinance of 1898 therefore allowed all meat to be sold or traded either directly by the hunter or indirectly through a middleman. The same ordinance only prohibited the sale of mountain goat and bighorn sheep and restricted the sale of prairie chickens to those who hunted the birds themselves. Meanwhile, ordinances were severe on those who exported wild animals, either in part or in whole, and forbade the export of grouse, partridge, pheasant, prairie chicken, elk, moose, and caribou. This measure ensured either that flesh from animals hunted for skins would not be wasted or that flesh itself would not be exported and thus lost to local needs. Game legislation in British Columbia explicitly forbade wasting deer flesh and prohibited fur trade companies from handling deer skins in 1898.

By the 1890s, new hunting restrictions began to appear in ordinances. Since gun clubs had begun to urge the government to curtail pot shooting and Native hunting freedoms, these more restrictive ordinances might appear to have been written by elites to reserve animals for their own sporting pleasure. But this was clearly not the case. Settlers, like those in the Green Lake and Prince Albert areas, were asking for protection for fish and game because they were still a major source of sustenance.[86] Settlers also demanded tighter laws in light of the increasing commercial fishing operations now redistributing local resources to markets in new areas. Town sportsmen had effected some changes in the 1883 Northwest Territories ordinances, when settlements of territorial Alberta were given much shorter big-game hunting seasons despite the need for food among settlers, but immediately after these measures were adopted the territory erupted in protest.[87] The perception that town sportsmen wished to preserve game for a few weeks of sport or to impress visitors to settlement communities infuriated farmers, who considered the shooting of their own meat "the custom of every free-born son of the soil," as one Alberta farmer put it.[88]

It was in such a context of polarized opinion that prairie sporting clubs began to question Native hunting freedoms enshrined by treaty. In 1893, members of the newly formed Calgary Rod and Gun Club sent a petition to the minister of the interior and the superintendent general of Indian Affairs noting that, "although there are at present large numbers of diverse kind of game in the North West Territories, already a serious falling off can be noticed, particularly in the case of prairie chicken and wild fowl." The letter, signed by the club's president, Edward Hodder, claimed that the game ordinances "are practically nullified and defeated owing to the fact that these laws are held not binding on the Indians, who not only take innumerable eggs of the wild fowl and chicken, but slaughter thousands of the young birds before they are able to fly." About sixty members of the club signed the petition asking the government to place Native people "on the same footing" as settlers and, if that was not possible, to have them "confined to their several reservations during the breeding season for chicken and wild fowl, say from June 1st to September 1." Similar petitions were signed by clubs across the west. The Maple Creek Gun Club, which formed at the same time as the Calgary organization, had nineteen members. The Edmonton Rod and Gun Club boasted a roster of prominent, politically powerful sportsmen, including W.A. Hardisty, Superintendent A.H. Griesbach of the NWMP, C.F. Strange, and no less than eight other members of the NWMP. Meanwhile, the Alberta Gun Club formed in Lethbridge and protested Native hunting freedoms, as did the Macleod Gun Club, the Red Deer Rod and Gun Club, and the Moose Jaw Rifle Association and Gun Club.[89]

Despite the prominent names appearing on these petitions, they hardly formed a consensus for the legislature. Although Alberta's first game laws were written in 1907, soon after the creation of the province, they were debated at length when sportsmen and farmers continued to press for game to be protected for sport or food. As one MLA stated, objecting to any form of restriction on big-game hunting, legislatures, "instead of looking after the preservation of ducks," should "look after the preservation of men, women and children, by allowing them to shoot game when they required it for their own use."[90]

The ordinances at the time of the first land booms probably did not reserve sport hunting for a few as much as protect food for many more people. The more detailed and severe ordinances were passed as settlement began to gain pace. They aimed to protect game resources for new, larger populations on the prairies. In Manitoba, which experienced the first rush of settlers in the 1880s, seasons for moose, deer, elk, and caribou declined from 180 days in 1880, to 150 days in 1882, to only 60 days in 1890. Settlers in the Northwest Territories, who in 1895 enjoyed 120 days of hunting for any species in the deer family, bighorn sheep, and antelope – beyond their dietary needs – faced in 1899 a 45-day season for the same animals. The open season for deer species in settlement regions was reduced even further, to merely 15 days a year.

By 1903, ordinances forbade hunters from shooting any female animals in the territories, a strategy to conserve populations. These restrictions occurred in the midst of the settlement boom, when towns rose in population.

In British Columbia, the critical need for wild meat caught the government and its threadbare conservation agencies completely off guard. The dramatic rise in the populations of New Westminster and Victoria, and consequently the rise in beef prices, prompted an enormous hunt to supply communities with food. By 1905, when the province established the position of chief game guardian and appointed A. Bryan Williams to it, he reported "the enormous increase in the numbers of sportsmen from the towns, particularly at the coast." He guessed that there had been a 25 percent increase in the number of guns in these urban settings. Many a hunter went after grouse species; indeed, railway lines on Vancouver Island began such intensive pot hunting that the blue grouse was almost immediately shot out along their allowances. Williams noted that most town hunters were after small game, fish, birds, deer, and goats in a day or two of sport. "A very small fraction of the population of this Province has either the time, money, or inclination" to hunt the larger moose, wapiti, bighorn sheep, and grizzly bear, he reported. In this, he revealed his two-pronged conservation plan: to set aside big game for high-paying tourists, and to conserve smaller game near towns for urbanites.[91]

These urban sportsmen were, in most respects, pot hunting. Licensing was long resisted in the legislature. But increasingly concerned about the urban hunt, most groups urged the creation of licences beyond the province's existing big-game and visitor licences. By 1909, when the BC legislature set aside the enormous sum of ten thousand dollars for game protection (mostly to appoint more salaried game wardens), Williams noted that the "number of men from the towns who go out to shoot birds is increasing greatly every year" – as was market hunting.[92] W.H. Heald, the game guardian assigned along one of Vancouver Island's railway allowances, estimated that "at least 1500 to 2000 guns left Victoria by the E.&N. Railway on the first three days, personally, I think there were more, and they literally cleaned up everything that they were allowed to shoot from Victoria to Cowichan on both sides of the E.&N. right of way for a half mile at least on each side." Most hard hit was the blue grouse. Heald urged the province's chief guardian to enact a closure on willow grouse and shorter seasons on quail and pheasant. He added in his report that Sunday-night trains during the four-month deer season carried back to Victoria between seventeen and nineteen deer each trip, "and I regret to say, does too are allowed to be killed."[93]

Williams's own statistics for the urban centres in 1911 were startling. "Every week sees scores of hunters returning by train, car, launches, and every means of conveyance, and if the number of head of game could be totalled up, it would be a surprise to most people." His lowest estimate was that in 1911 alone one thousand deer and fifteen hundred pheasants were hauled back to Vancouver in the first few days of the hunting season. The next year, Williams reported that city hunters – men and women alike – appeared in numbers "never seen before ... with every conceivable sort of weapon." He noted that, with "this army of hunters scouring the country, many of them not knowing one species of bird from another and shooting at everything they see, it is really a wonder that there is a head of game left."[94] The hunting licence, finally introduced in 1913, attracted thousands of applicants to the New Westminster game office, which ran out of forms.

Meanwhile, increasing numbers of farmers on the prairies were pot hunting. In Saskatchewan, game populations were not meeting settlers' needs, prompting sportsmen to complain about Native people and meat hunters north of Prince Albert. There elk were believed to be "exterminated" as early as 1918 by provisions hunters. But even in 1906, within a year of the province's creation, 132 volunteer game guardians (most interested in winning half of the fines they exacted from wrongdoers) were being mobilized by the agriculture department's chief game guardian. In the first year of their service, they observed that most violations of ordinances were being committed in areas with large populations of new settlers who had not been informed of game laws.[95] But the problem lay not so much in widespread legal ignorance as in pressing local needs. The chief game guardian in 1918, Fred Bradshaw, underlined the problem growing in northern areas, where Native people hunting in the closed season were apparently depleting such populations. He was concerned that they and trappers were "killing more than they can eat" and that homesteaders, contrary to the ordinances, "kill all the year round."[96] That year Bradshaw received a letter from a Silkie, Saskatchewan, resident who travelled for three or four days into the bush by horse and wagon on hunting excursions. He reported widespread shooting of cow moose, whether for meat or left to rot in the forest, and people using cars at night to drive into hunting locations. A resident of Craik, Saskatchewan, whose excursions took him north, was alarmed by the number of Native and commercial meat hunters working the forests. "That these Indians may in a sense use this meat for food, I do not doubt," he said; however, with Bradshaw's department considering closing elk hunting for three years to conserve populations, the hunter suggested that "you may as well throw the season wide open and let the white get his share of the game with the Indian." The hunter believed that severe penalties should fall on Amerindians killing animals in closed season so that "the indolent inhabitants of that District, will find that it is better to go out and engage in honest labor and earn an honest dollar than it is to depend on slaughtering game and selling it although prohibited by law."[97]

The Saskatchewan game branch was also contending with boosters who exaggerated game resources. In 1919, the Regina *Leader* reported that northern game populations, on which prospective settlers would depend, were abundant. The newspaper quoted one of the department's own guardians and listed three thousand elk, "millions" of caribou, sixty thousand moose, "numberless" musk-oxen, and "all kinds of animals." The department promptly reprimanded the guardian and pointed out that such publicity would make it far more difficult to have further hunting restrictions introduced, particularly a projected three-year moratorium on elk hunting believed to be necessary to conserve the species.[98]

Although settlers faced tightening restrictions on game food, they often evaded the ordinances. Most rural inhabitants ridiculed guardians. Originally, the agricultural department hoped that licence holders, given the power to uphold the ordinances, would effectively discourage neighbours from breaking the law. Since this was not the case, W.R. Motherwell, who soon headed the department, oversaw the hiring of paid game guardians between 1907 and 1912. The program appointed guardians in places such as Kanora and Wadena, where one farmer believed that there was "more illegal shooting done" than in any other provincial constituency.[99] But even paid guardians had little authority in these areas. It was widely known that settlers at Kutawa hated the game act, and they could not be convinced that "such action is necessary sooner or later in order to preserve our wildfowl," as one department employee stated.[100] Guardians, meanwhile, could not deny settlers food. As one letter to Motherwell pointed out in 1908, they were not willing to "squeal on their neighbours." A former game guardian and member of the NWMP, the letter writer even stated that "local men can scarcely be expected to execute the law to the letter and place a certain coolness between themselves and their neighbors."[101] Regina hunters were complaining to Motherwell that his guardians, upholding ordinances during the short hunting seasons, were "conspicuously absent" during the closed season, especially in moose territory.[102]

When they wore their hats as provincial appointees, guardians were usually excluded from settler communities. The report of one Saskatchewan guardian in 1920 was likely typical. During the hunting season, he patrolled his assigned range between the Saskatchewan and Torch Rivers, travelling by dogsled and meeting many hunters. Most of them were farmers or businessmen who lived south of the Saskatchewan River and the nearby Canadian National Railway. He found, however, that townspeople were warning each other where he was patrolling and planning their hunting excursions accordingly. Everyone, including the many Amerindians whom the guardian encountered, had stories of hunting abuses committed by others, "but they were unwilling to furnish the names of the parties or to be brought in themselves."[103]

Settlement areas continued to rely heavily on wild meat to supply larders. But some western populations were becoming less dependent on wildlife by the end of the century, and changes in diet became most pronounced by the end of the First World War. In 1901, the editor of the *Lethbridge News* noted that "the west is becoming more thickly settled" and that stricter game laws were therefore required. He complained about "several" incidents since the opening of duck-hunting season in which hunters had bartered their game. "This should not be permitted," he wrote. He then noted the new demand among sportsmen for no hunting on Sundays: "Wild game requires a day off once a week, and it is only fair they should have it."[104] Townspeople now criticized the "traveller's clause," still granted in ordinances, which was extended even to freighters. In 1903, Harrison Young, a federal fisheries official, wrote to the Edmonton Rod and Gun Club to say that "This country is now so settled up there is no longer any necessity for according any travelling men a special privilege."[105]

The war years seem to have been key in transforming game use. Ammunition rose suddenly in price at that time to completely undermine the economics of larder hunting. In Lethbridge, a local paper even suggested that the high cost of ammunition by 1917 might save threatened duck populations.[106] By 1918, a police report from the Northwest Territories stated that Amerindians near Fort Resolution "are wasting no deer so far ... Many of them are killing no more as the price of cartridges is so exorbitant and they have already all they can make into dry meat."[107] Wartime demands for meat, meanwhile, were skyrocketing, so provincial governments directed more energy to enforcing ordinances and forming public will against the game market, which, if satiated, would have emptied forests and streams of wildlife. Finally, when the war ended, the impressive cold storage and transportation systems developed in part by the Department of Marine and Fisheries during the war years seem to have brought a surplus of beef, chicken, and pork products to western Canadians. By 1917, Winnipeg boasted 2.5 million square feet of cold storage, Vancouver 1.5 million square feet, and Edmonton 800,000 square feet.[108]

Immediately after the armistice, gunsmiths and cartridge manufacturers no longer enjoying wartime demands attempted to promote sport hunting. The Montreal-based Dominion Cartridge Company in 1920, for instance, published its own pamphlet, *The Call of Canada*, in which it claimed that the nation was "the Sportsman's Paradise." Certainly, after the war, sporting ethics were being promoted as never before. The Commission of Conservation, meeting in Ottawa after the war, heard a speech by John Burnham, the president of the American Game Protective Association, that suggests how the war had changed opinion toward subsistence hunting. In his speech, entitled "The War and Game," Burnham praised both American and Canadian legislatures for safeguarding wildlife during the war years "in the face of the clamour for cheap food in the form of marketed game." Burnham argued that war events had proved the utility of sport hunting as a means of training rigorous, disciplined, and skilled soldiers. He therefore suggested that sport hunting was not merely a form of recreation but also a "righteous" undertaking – pointing out that, "of the first contingent which Canada sent to the war, 75 per cent were sportsmen." Their "splendid valour and efficiency" had proved the utility of having North Americans reserve animals for sport hunting. He also discussed the issue of market hunting, which, next "to the advance of civilization," was the chief factor in reducing game. His speech urged enforcement agents to apply regulations that would close down such markets.[109]

Key changes in ordinances, meanwhile, suggest that a shift in the use of wildlife had been effected in wartime. Cold storage of wild meat became closely restricted, and the trade and sale of meats between hunters and nonhunters was prohibited. British Columbia's 1920 amendment to ordinances stopped such sales and required cold storage operators to obtain a licence to preserve game for individuals only during open season. By 1924, merchants and licensed storekeepers, long given latitude to sell wild meat, were restricted to the number of animals that they could individually hunt themselves (in 1924, one moose, one elk, two mountain goats, two caribou, three deer, and two bighorn sheep). Alberta's ordinances shut down game dealers in 1922, restricting them to the sale of certain game birds. Saskatchewan's meat trade was restricted by 1916 to licensed dealers, and the game meat market closed completely in 1917. Manitoba's ordinances also severely restricted meat dealers. By 1913, ordinances forbade the selling of game and many game bird species.[110]

Drawn up in the context of meat shortages during the First World War, these conservation measures inaugurated a period when animals were reserved for recreation, not food. They also coincided with the triumph of wildlife conservation as a national priority, a topic examined in Chapter 5. But this legislative watershed also occurred in a period of changing western subsistence patterns, when many westerners no longer needed wild meat for their survival. Such changes were perceptible in the rising animosity between western urban communities and traditional suppliers of wild meat – Amerindians. In Saskatchewan, the government appropriated more funds for game guardians in 1919 and directed its attention to the "problem" of treaty freedoms. The chief game guardian believed that sport hunters should "give special attention to the Indians in the big game country during the forthcoming summer and fall," as Fred Bradshaw informed sportsman J. Johnston Willett.[111] The provincial game guardian had already encouraged Willett to form a protective game association. Willett stated that he would encourage fellow hunters to exercise the powers given to them in Section 20 of the Saskatchewan Game Act. That section allowed them to stop individuals from violating closed seasons. He promised to do his best as a "humble instrument in such a first cause" and urged Bradshaw to hire three or four resident guardians in key game areas to watch "Charley Greyeyes and

Johnny Rainintheface." Willett then reported that Amerindians were visiting moose-hunting grounds in summer and described their drying racks and piles of moose hair.[112]

Amerindian hunters continued to meet demands for venison, ducks, and eggs in southern regions of Saskatchewan, but with declining dependence on such sources of protein their activities – and those of "pot hunting" farmers and game provisioners – were increasingly condemned. Bradshaw himself was unapologetic about his view that game should be used for sport, not meat. Just after the war, he wrote to one hunter that "Our wild life was never intended to take the place of the butcher shop, and the taking of the meat should be looked upon as merely incidental to a successful hunting trip." What counted for the real sportsman was "the opportunity afforded to get away for a few days vacation in the woods with sociable companions and a chance to match his wits against the monarchs of the forests."[113]

Undoubtedly, Bradshaw was not being completely candid in these comments. Threadbare government resources, particularly in Saskatchewan's Department of Agriculture, would never have been expended merely to protect sport hunting. Game was also becoming important in boosterism. The department's conservation programs, though, were changing opinions about meat hunting as a subsistence strategy. Bradshaw's department sought to uphold "sportsmanship" as a civic duty. The game guardian on one occasion pointed out to a group of sportsmen that "a true sportsman is usually a good citizen. He looks upon the game laws as his code of ethics and tries to live up to them."[114]

The Department of Agriculture in Saskatchewan was also changing its stance on cow moose hunting. The issue gained notoriety in 1917 when ordinances allowed cow moose to be shot, a move to help settlers in their larder hunting. The chief game guardian immediately received letters from wardens in New Brunswick, Quebec, and Nova Scotia unanimously urging prohibitions against such hunting. J.A. Knight, from Nova Scotia, informed Bradshaw that, since cow moose had been protected in 1909, there had been a large increase in the moose population in the province. The issue was now at the heart of conservation efforts, and sportsmen believed that "it does not seem right to shoot the female of any species of big game." One letter writer to the Saskatchewan game branch admitted that he had shot a cow moose only to realize that her two calves would perish without her support. "I have not yet got over the guilty feelings that came over me. When I killed that moose I practically killed five animals." Another sportsman pointed out the problem of hunting for a head, and any cows or does shot were often left in the forests to rot. If in the past cow moose hunting was part of a larger scramble for food, cows now ensured a moose population for sport hunting. W.R. Motherwell himself was moved by the "inhumane and unsportsmanlike practice of shooting female deer of any kind.[115]

With legislative changes by 1920, railway companies stopped shipping female moose (and conductors insisted that the sex of the animal had to accompany wild meat shipments).

As provinces began reserving male animals for sport hunting, the Department of Indian Affairs concurrently began entrenching Native hunting freedoms. It had by no means entrenched them previously. Rather, it had taken the position that provincial and territorial ordinances protected game as a food source for Amerindians as well as newcomers and that the equal treatment of treaty signators under ordinances therefore benefited everyone. This development suggests that western society was gaining independence from both wild meat as a source of protein and the hunters who provided much of it.

Initially, traditional hunting freedoms were guaranteed in most of the numbered treaties. The tradition had been established with the Upper Canadian Robinson-Huron treaties made in 1850 that had allowed "chiefs and their tribes the full and free privilege to hunt over the territory now ceded by them," except for areas from "time to time" homesteaded. Most of the numbered treaties in the western territories continued to respect the right of Amerindians to hunt for their subsistence. In this respect, the federal government regarded territorial and provincial ordinances as important to the Amerindian's as well as the settler's interests, and it asked provinces to act "leniently" toward bands and bands to be "prudent" in their hunting.[116]

In this earlier period, indeed, the Department of Indian Affairs unilaterally limited Amerindian hunting freedoms. Some key legal opinions seemed to support this policy direction. The Manitoba, Kewatin, and Northwest Territories portions of the west coming under Treaties 1 and 2 (1871) contained no special Native hunting privileges. The other treaties contained a stipulation that Amerindians "shall have [the] right to pursue their avocations of hunting and fishing throughout the tract surrendered." They did allow, though, that regulations could "from time to time" be made by the federal government, and they restricted hunting on settlement, mining, and lumbering lands. The key wording of the Indian Act, Section 66, provided that the Indian superintendent general could declare territorial and provincial laws applicable to Indians, "as the case may be, or to Indians in such parts thereof as to him seems expedient."[117]

Before the turn of the century, the department rarely sought changes to provincial and territorial legislation in regard to traditional hunting freedoms. In 1877, British Columbia's Indian reserve commissioner believed that it was important to object to a recent Victoria police court ruling that fined two Amerindian hunters for exposing, against game ordinances, deer skins for sale. He believed that the hunters, given the liberty in 1850 and 1851 treaties to hunt over "unoccupied lands as formerly," had probably been hunting for food and obtained the skins that way – and no "petty court" should rule on an integral means for Indians to obtain their necessary food.[118] But in other respects, the commissioner's office exercised Section 66 either explicitly or implicitly, allowing provinces and territorial governments to establish game ordinances that made inroads upon traditional hunting freedoms. There were two reasons for doing so.

First, this federal bureaucracy was on shaky constitutional ground if it made these hunters exempt from local game ordinances. An important provision of the British North America Act was, after all, found in Subsection 16 of Section 92, which explicitly gave provincial governments full control over game legislation. Justice department opinions therefore favoured the provinces in their authority over game, refrained from disallowing provincial ordinances, and upheld provincial charges made against Amerindian hunters charged with abusing the ordinances.

Second, beyond this legal consideration was the department's fiduciary responsibility and threadbare financial resources. The spirit of game ordinances preserved animal populations for food. Amerindian hunters were thought to benefit as much as newcomers from controls on hunting freedoms. Perhaps the department's Hayter Reed, Indian commissioner for the Northwest Territories, best enunciated this "spirit of the law" policy. In the context of severe food crises in the west, he acknowledged in 1889 that, although Amerindians did not come under the jurisdiction of game laws, "they should as far as possible, be made to conform to the spirit of them." For that reason, Reed ordered Indian agents to refrain from issuing ammunition during the closed season "and to take every available means for marking your strong disapproval of gathering the eggs of birds or catching fish during the spawning time."[119]

Reed himself was reacting to reports from agents who had observed declining grouse populations on or near reservation grounds, suggesting to him that some controls were necessary. In 1893, he successfully prompted the superintendent general to extend game laws to a large number of bands in the Northwest Territories, including the Hobbema, Sarcee, Blackfoot, Piegan, Blood, Battleford, Duck Lake, and Moose Mountain bands. Thereafter, specific bands were occasionally brought under provincial and territorial ordinances when the superintendent saw fit. Reed also travelled about the northwest to explain why he was withholding twine and ammunition from hunters at reserves during closed seasons. He believed that it would require some time "in order that the minds of the Indians may be prepared for the change, and thus avoid the possibility of trouble arising."[120]

Reed's policy applied despite the protests of band leaders such as Astakeesie of the Waywayseecappo's band, who sent a letter to the department through an Indian agent in 1893. The department told the chief that "the protection of game was more in the interest of the Indians than whites and under the Treaty the Government reserved the right to make regulations to govern

Indians at this avocation."[121] There would be no exceptions, as Canadian poet and Indian Affairs official Duncan Campbell Scott reiterated. "It would be much better to aid the Indians if necessary and protect the game than to comply with their wish to be allowed to hunt at all seasons."[122]

Prior to 1907, in fact, the federal bureaucracy rarely questioned the ordinances established by provincial and territorial governments. For instance, it responded to the queries of the Indian agent at Morley, Alberta, that the Stoneys there were under the control of the latest Alberta ordinances. By virtue of Chapter 29 of the Indian Act, the Stoneys had come under the control of the game ordinance of the Northwest Territories of 1895. The department pointed out that "the protection of the game is a matter of the utmost importance to the Indians," and if hunters broke game laws the Indian agent should inform them that "they need not expect the Department to interfere on their behalf."[123]

By the end of the First World War, however, the department began to change its policies and entered more consistently into the controversial issue of treaty hunting freedoms. The increasing presence of sport hunting associations made it plain that ordinances were no longer protecting animals for food as much as for sport. With human populations rising and wildlife resources insufficient to meet the needs of all, provincial governments were now reserving animals for sport. Sport hunting lobbies were now also influential in having legislation amended, almost yearly. The trend was clear in Manitoba by the late 1890s. Amerindians were being charged more frequently with breaking game ordinances. The trend alarmed Indian Affairs agents, who anticipated that, if treaty hunters were hindered, they would become wards of the government. Worried about this outcome, the department urged provincial game guardians to extend leniency to Amerindian hunters. But the province was becoming less tolerant of traditional hunting techniques and the entire issue of treaty privileges. Provincial authorities often agreed that Native hunters should be given freedom to hunt for their food needs – as were all settlers – but they disapproved of hunts in which many animals were killed. The utilitarian ends of these hunts horrified observers. A game guardian stated that one of the Fisher River bands – likely selling some of the meat to settlers – had been "slaughtering moose wholesale and they were supposed to have taken about fifty" that season alone. The band later admitted that a "considerable" number of moose had been killed. Indian Affairs asked the agent to reach a compromise and allow each family to take one or two deer or moose for their own use outside the Indian reserve.[124]

By 1917, authorities in Manitoba informed Native hunters that game laws would apply to them; lawbreakers would have their game guns and traps confiscated if they were caught. An Indian agent from the Fisher River Agency near Lake Winnipeg pointed out that "in consequence the Indians are afraid to hunt and a serious problem faces the government unless the Indians are removed to some locality where they can farm." The agent, though, was leery of the province's claim that the protection of game benefited everyone: "when the Provincial Authorities issue licenses by the thousand to men of means who are well able to buy beef, giving them power to kill the game they profess to protect, their argument appears most ridiculous."[125]

In Alberta, Aboriginal cultures closely connected to subsistence hunting were coming into conflict with sport hunting groups. Bands living along the foothills were hunting antelope, despite its small amount of flesh, and bighorn sheep and mountain goat. R.E. Sibbald, the Indian agent at Morley, left a detailed record in 1903 of the hunting traditions of the Stoneys. During the closed season, the agent tried to keep the hunters on the reserve by having them sell firewood, but he noted that despite his success hunters probably killed the same number of animals in the open season. They generally left the reserve near the end of September. Hunters ventured north, sometimes to the North Saskatchewan River, to lay away dried meat to supplement the government rations on the reserve. One band member reported killing thirty-six bighorn sheep, twelve in one day. Each hunter, Sibbald estimated, killed about ten sheep, goats, or deer. Since there were ninety hunters, he believed that about nine hundred animals had been killed in one season. "I am sure I have not overestimated much, as [I] have seen a family of six eat a whole deer in two days, they are terrible meat eaters if they can get it, and they all look good and fat when they come back." Sibbald urged the Native hunters to refrain from hunting in this way not only because it would lead to the extermination of the animals but also because "as long as they can hunt you cannot civilize them. I have lived alongside of them for twenty six years, and with the exception of a few of the younger ones they are no more civilised now than they were when I first knew them, and I blame hunting as the cause."[126]

By the time of the Great War, such matters greatly exercised Benjamin Lawton, Alberta's chief game guardian. He believed that the Stoneys, who had much of their lifestyle and some of their revenue tied up in hunting, should be placed under the provisions of the Alberta Game Act.[127] But Indian Affairs was now reacting to this development at the provincial level. By 1915, the BC Supreme Court had overturned the conviction of a Sanaach Indian discovered with venison out of season by a game guardian.[128] In 1917, George H. Bradbury anticipated the heavy government expense if Native hunters were denied their freedom, and he began to press his department to entrench treaty privileges: "if the Indians are not allowed to hunt for a living they will certainly become a charge upon the Government of Canada. There is no alternative. If you take away their means of living, then you will have to provide food and clothing for them, and there is nothing [that] will pauperize the Indian quicker than doing this."[129]

The Stoneys themselves reacted against game convictions in a 1907 letter signed by band leaders.

> They tell us that we must not hunt the goat and sheep in the mountains; that we must not kill prairie chickens for all this year; and part of next year, that we must not kill more than one moose, one caribou, one deer and that we must pay $2.50 before we can hunt.
>
> Now, when we made a treaty with your chiefs, we understood that there would always be wild animals in the forest and the mountains. But the white men come every year, more and more, and our hunting grounds are covered with the houses and fences of white men. We are poor people. We do not know how to get money, as white men do. We have much to learn. We are not so strong as the white men, and we need your help. Look upon us as poor people. Our agent tells us the laws that you make, and they are good. We try to keep the laws. Whatever the Government tells us to do, we try to do it, and it seems good to us.
>
> ... After treaty payment in the fall every year, when our hay and the feed for our horses and cattle are all gathered, we like to hunt the deer, the sheep and the goat that we may eat sweet meat. It is like a play time and holiday for us. At that time the meat of the wild animals is sweet to eat. We do not wish to hunt in summer for the meat is not good.
>
> ... Let us still hunt the game in the fall as our fathers did. We work hard and make all the money we can, and we buy what the white men eat, but sweeter to us than all, is the flesh of the wild animals ... Give us freedom to go into the mountains and the forests to look for meat of the wild animals, and the birds, when our children ask for it. We cannot hear them cry for food and we are too poor to buy them meat. This is what all our people wish us to say to you.[130]

A critical case occurred in Alberta in 1910. Benjamin Lawton, through the Crown prosecutor, had charged several Stoneys for hunting without licences and selling game heads illegally. When the conviction was appealed to the Alberta Supreme Court, the matter centred on the applicability of the Alberta Game Act to the individuals in question. The Stoneys maintained that they were entitled to hunt without restriction in unsettled portions of the province. Justice Charles A. Hunt threw out the conviction, stating that Treaty 7 made no mention of the possibility that Native hunters would be restricted. Significantly, Hunt read the treaty to argue that the provincial game act did not apply to treaty Indians.[131] Moreover, he believed that the Stoneys were at most subject to the ordinances of 1893, when selling game heads was not illegal.

The matter was certainly not resolved, but a watershed had been reached in western Canadian society. Natives and newcomers were no longer trading wild animal meat or joining in the same subsistence hunt. Sport hunting groups were anxious to conserve animals for numerous purposes, but dietary need was no longer one of them. The new ethics of conservation were clearly at work in this reorientation to wild animals. Sport hunting groups now fully condemned market hunting in any form. Amerindians who hunted out of season, pot hunters who brought a utilitarian end to the hunt, and illegal meat vendors alike were marginalized. In the case of Amerindians who continued to slaughter animals and exercise treaty freedoms, outsiders viewed their reliance on wild meat as evidence of a stubborn resistance to improvement. Euro-Canadians believed that the traditional hunt gave Amerindians independence from the "civilizing" program of the reserve system. Hunting for food also allowed Amerindians to neglect crops and only halfheartedly take up ranching. At the many national wildlife conferences in the 1920s, when Indian Affairs representatives became the target of abuse from new conservationists and provincial game guardians, the continued use among Amerindians of wild meat was bitterly criticized. The Amerindian's larder hunt was described as anachronistic in the larger progress of western Canadian society. Long believed to be pushing to extinction big-game species "in the wake of the buffalo," as the *Macleod Gazette* had once suggested,[132] the food hunt seemed to threaten the abundance that boosters were anxious to advertise in western areas.

More fundamentally, the widespread protest against Amerindian hunting practices reflected a growing distance between western Canadian communities and Native societies. With the wild meat resource no longer being shared between groups, intolerance of the traditional "avocation" widened. In the 1920s, when wild meat trading was explicitly prohibited in ordinances, an imaginative re-creation of "traditional" hunting practices came about in conservationist publications. By then, many game guardians were urging the federal government to buy out traditional hunting freedoms (some suggested a sum of one thousand dollars per Amerindian), and the proposal to create a large hunting reserve in the north for southern bands was discussed (the bands would then be obliged to stop hunting locally). Alberta's sport hunting groups, some of the most politically powerful groups in western Canada, advanced this proposal. They believed that they could make the deal appealing by promising to prohibit white trappers from invading the same northern hunting areas. The end of wild meat currencies between First Nations and western Canadians, then, brought about some of the movement toward segregation that continues in the present.

In this era, too, the Amerindian's techniques of slaughter led to pessimistic explanations among conservationists. At game conferences, Amerindians were characterized as having once been "natural conservationists," but their interaction with Europeans had "corrupted" them. C. Gordon Hewitt pointed this out in 1921 in his work *The Conservation of the Wild Life of*

Canada, stating that "the Indian, when unspoilt by white men, is traditionally a conserver of wild life, that is he uses it but does not exterminate it."[133]
A leading government official in Manitoba, J.H. Evans, believed that Amerindians, when dependent on animals for food and clothing, had left enough
game to meet future needs but that they no longer did. He believed that the
"responsibility for that rests with the white man. I do know that the Indians to-day are not giving as much attention to that old tradition of leaving
sufficient [animals] to reproduce as they did long ago."[134] The misunderstanding that Amerindians had once been progressive conservationists was
reiterated in Mabel B. Williams's *Guardians of the Wild* in 1936. In a work
highlighting the conservation initiatives of the national parks movement,
Williams tried to explain that Amerindians traditionally believed that it
"displeased the Great Manitou to destroy the lives of animals wantonly."
The "primitive man took no more than he needed, and as he bent above
the fallen carcass he would breathe an ancestral prayer." When the Europeans arrived, they seemed to be great spirits who taught Native people to
hunt meat and fur in exchange for European goods. "The Indian, impressed
by the white man's success, and conscious of a growing feeling of inferiority
before his superior skill and knowledge, forsook the old tribal wisdom which
had taught him to spare the females and young, and take only as much
game as he needed for his own personal use."[135] Conservationists, then,
drew a romantic image of Native subsistence traditions in order to promote
their own approach to resource harvesting, the model of maximum sustained yield.

Wild meat consumption, of course, did not end with the First World War.
Farming communities continued to rely more heavily than urban communities on wild meat, and they continue to do so. Provisioning networks,
too, could rapidly be reinvigorated in times of severe economic distress.
Not surprisingly, the last great wild meat hunt took place during the De-
pression. While unemployed urbanites flocked north to try trapping – creating havoc in existing trapping economies – farmers searched for needed
wild meat. In 1930, one Manitoba farmer with a family of eight asked the
premier, John Bracken, for permission to shoot a moose since he had to sell
his cattle that year to pay for his crop losses.[136] Many residents of Manitoba
on relief petitioned the government for free big-game permits in 1931. That
year big-game hunting licences increased to 3,325; five years earlier, only
1,700 had been issued. Meanwhile, a Saskatchewan game guardian soon
reported that Greig Lake Amerindians were beginning a provisions hunt
that he described as "an amazing spectacle."[137] He came across a camp with
separate drying and smoking tents. Inspecting one, he found eight freshly
dressed hides, half carcasses of moose and deer, a green deer hide, a head,
and portions of meat. He saw duck feathers, a dead mud hen and pelican,
and several fish. Later, in the Cold and Primrose Lakes area, he discovered

Amerindian hunters during the summer "common ... with traders only too glad to deal thuswise." He discovered several men, reputedly white, at or near Cold Lake "who derive quite an income from the same traffic." Everywhere, it seemed, people were again looking to wild animals for subsistence. "Most of these people," a man at Nipawin, Saskatchewan, said, "because of hard times now think that they can go ahead and slaughter all the wild game they need to keep themselfs [sic] alive." He stated that he had heard "several men complaining about having to live on moose all summer."[138]

What game guardians were witnessing was a briefly reinvigorated provisions trade in which Amerindian hunters supplied settlers and townspeople again and traditional exchange relations found meaning. However, these groups were further separated as the century progressed. In the context of failed settlement, and the dustbowl conditions of the Regina region, wild meat briefly circulated as currency between First Nations and settlers. But after the First World War, wild animals were no longer really protected as a food source in western Canada. They found a new use as symbols among western Canadians, who used these symbols to attract newcomers and investment dollars to the region.

4
Boosters, Wildlife, and Western Myths of Superabundance

The improving economy of the Laurier era after 1897 brought hundreds of thousands of newcomers to the Canadian west. A generous dominion lands policy, improved agricultural techniques, and cheaper transportation rates heightened interest in Canada's unclaimed farming regions. At a time of climbing world prices of grain, the settlement boom began. Almost a million hopeful farmers arrived between 1896 and the First World War. For western residents, the hectic pace of regional development presented enormous social and economic challenges. Leaders of new communities wishing to sustain growth had to attract badly needed investment dollars. It became imperative to encourage the building of rail branch lines nearby, to begin capital projects, and to establish a tax base to maintain schools or roads within townships.[1] Territorial and provincial governments had always promoted the region. After the First World War, however, members of communities began to boost their locales to recruit new citizens who could help to make payments on growing debts. In this period, western boosters made numerous claims about their region. One theme of their advertisements and pictorial representations of western Canada was that it was the last wildlife stronghold on the continent. Wildlife was key in advertising regional wealth.[2]

Not coincidentally, communities created these representations of wildlife at a key moment in the history of environmental attitudes, a time when many Americans and eastern Canadians were initiating conservation and preservation policies. In the United States, the near extermination of animals such as the North American bison and the growing fear that "civilization" was crowding out wilderness areas had already prompted George Bird Grinnel, William T. Hornaday, C.J. "Buffalo" Jones, and others to begin campaigns to limit hunting activities, prohibit feather industries, preserve game in parks and "breeding areas," and domesticate animals as a means of preventing the complete disappearance of wildlife. News of their activities circulated in Canada's west. But the conservation message was transformed in its western Canadian representation. Motivated by a spirit of boosterism and the realities of a hinterland economy, many westerners drew on the rising conservation movement to promote their region. They created images of inherent natural wealth in their settlements and an almost inexhaustible supply of resources available to settlers and newcomers. Western promoters tirelessly sustained the image of a western wildlife Eden – now represented in local taxidermy displays, natural history museums, and print advertisements. Locating some of these new images of wildlife and analyzing their meanings for western Canadian residents are the subjects of this chapter.[3] Boosterism contributed to a western conception of environmental superabundance that influenced conservation policies. Early conservation gained support because wild animals, along with other western resources, were inseparably linked to concepts of wealth in the region's settlement history. A study of booster symbolism, then, sheds some light on the pioneer's most fundamental environmental understandings.

No theme became as integral to western promotion as natural abundance. Brochures and posters offered newcomers a plenitude of resources. They identified nature's wealth in western soils, in vast forests found along western reaches of the prairies, in British Columbia's mountain streams. Literature produced after 1890 underscored the westerner's conviction that God had provided bountifully for people in the west, and an almost supernatural beneficence was offered to any settlers or visitors: all could sup, all could be satisfied. This abundance was not characterized as simply *a lot* of resources existing in Manitoba, the Northwest Territories, and British Columbia. The concept was tied more closely to vitalism, recognizable in promotional literature at the beginning of the territorial period: natural wealth lay deep and quiet in western soils, in forests and rivers, and this wealth was superabundant – that is, it could provide constant sustenance to successive cohorts of newcomers.[4]

Residents were quick to realize that indigenous wildlife provided evidence of such wealth. Throughout the period after the transfer of Rupert's Land to the Canadian government, settlement promoters and resource developers frequently used wildlife in advertisements. In them, wild animals symbolized a trove of raw wealth waiting to be mined.[5] But the imaginative link between abundant wildlife and the region's resources was strongest by the end of the century. By the 1890s in British Columbia, wildlife was featured in local natural history museums, brochures, posters, and books. These representations appeared at a time when the economy, based on mining and fishing, was beginning to include forestry. Images of numerous forest-dwelling animals suggested an imaginative corollary in vast timber resources appreciated by outside investors. Often such associations were made when speculative fever ran high in nearby metropolises and where investment capital was controlled. Citizens in Victoria, soon building an impressive

Stereoscopic photo of John Fannin's workshop, ca. 1890
BC Archives, G-03172

natural history museum, became keenly interested in the forests and ore beds discovered in distant reaches of their legislative domain. The city's promotional use of wildlife and its support of the unrivalled natural history museum occurred at a time when Victoria was losing population and business to the soon dominant Vancouver. The business and political elites wishing to anchor their influence in the resource economy constructed the massive legislative buildings in Victoria. As it did in northern mining districts and with the big-game resources found there, the Victoria business community by the 1890s was eyeing the investment potential and the bighorn sheep of the East Kootenays.

The province's official taxidermist, John Fannin, made sure that the wildlife populations of such distant resource hinterlands were well represented in his museum. Fannin was originally a blacksmith naturalist who came to British Columbia with the gold rush. The provincial government hired him to study the agricultural potential of the Fraser River valley and then appointed him provincial taxidermist and museum curator in 1886. Some of the province's most influential citizens backed the creation of the museum when Fannin was hired. They included George A. Alkem, Matthew Baillie Begbie, Dr. William Fraser Tolmie, Mayor Rithet, and others. Alarmed that European and American collectors were exporting artifacts to other museums, the group resolved that their own would "preserve specimens of the natural products and Indian antiquities and manufactures of the Province and to classify and exhibit the same for the information of the public."[6] Their confidence in Fannin's taxidermy skills was well rewarded. Fannin was an able writer and public speaker. His dioramas were breathtaking.[7] By 1898, his museum had been moved from the Supreme Court building into the eastern section of the legislative buildings. Beyond their scientific appeal, the displays undoubtedly promoted the province. In newspapers such as the *Victoria Colonist,* Fannin lauded British Columbia's superabundance of resources by describing unfailing populations of wildlife. In a letter to the paper, Fannin drew attention to the moose available in the booming mining area of Ominica and Peace River, recently discovered and opening up to investment. He claimed that, while wildlife was disappearing before civilization elsewhere, the game haunts – and implicitly the natural resources – of British Columbia were too remote for such extermination to take place. Rather, the province "will hold its share of these noble creatures":

> The extermination of all the game animals from the greater portion of the Continent in the not distant future is, in my opinion, a foregone conclusion ... To those of us, however, who would look upon a country destitute of game as we would upon a waste of desert sand, this is consolation to cherish, and I speak with an experience of nearly thirty years, having during that time travelled over almost the entire length and breadth of the province, British Columbia is a wonderful country full of surprises for the sportsman and tourist, a country wonderful for its vast stretches of virgin forest, which will yield untold wealth to this and future generations ... There is ample food and cover for all our game.[8]

Fannin and others had learned that taxidermy displays were a useful way to represent natural wealth. Western provincial and territorial governments and many city governments followed British Columbia's example and established natural history museums to promote settlement and represent provincial resources. After the territorial partition of 1905, the new governments of Alberta and Saskatchewan hurriedly built natural history museums. The museum in Saskatchewan was initially assembled from the travel-frayed specimens sent to represent the territorial government at European fairs in the late nineteenth century. The famous tornado of 1912 wiped out the entire collection, but the new legislative buildings soon provided shelter for better displays prepared by taxidermist Horace H. Mitchell. The former resident of Toronto worked closely with the province's chief game guardian and, within a few seasons, stuffed some 350 specimens for the museum. He eventually created dioramas of prairie and parkland scenes containing antelope and birds. Through his museum, Mitchell attempted to educate settlers and visitors about the province's natural wealth.[9]

Canadian immigration display, England, 1910. A government promotional display to encourage immigration to Canada in the early 1900s contains fish, grains, fruits, and other agricultural products. Taxidermic samples, like the buffalo and elk heads seen here, were also usually included to convey the Dominion's untapped natural wealth.
National Archives of Canada, PA 76936

This use of animals and birds – fish taxidermy was rarely undertaken since it required the time-consuming "waste-mould" technique – was not limited to provincial or territorial displays. By the end of the nineteenth century, western Canadians had begun crating wildlife specimens for exhibit in central Canada, the United States, and Europe. Calgary resident James Reilly coordinated the Northwest Territories display at the World's Exposition in Chicago in 1893 and copied Manitoba's example by sending every specimen of bird available.[10] These displays replicated those built on a smaller scale at municipal fairs and provincial exhibitions that flaunted wildlife, especially big game. Norman Luxton, Banff's self-styled wilderness man, taxidermist, Indian curio dealer, newspaper editor, and ardent booster, took the lead in stocking many of them, such as one display for the 1908 Dominion Exhibition.[11]

Local residents such as Luxton supported similar promotions undertaken by the Department of the Interior, the federal bureaucracy advertising western lands for settlement. The superintendent of the immigration office, W.D. Scott, realized that wildlife specimens, authentically arranged in overseas displays, could attract immigrants. He began gathering quotes from western taxidermists by 1907 to have stuffed birds and animal heads (including fur bearers, coyote, buffalo, antelope, moose, and caribou) decorate his offices overseas. The department finally began shipping crates of specimens to Europe by 1910 to "show what could be got in Canada."[12] He did not want "rare" varieties, he instructed the two westerners filling one order, Luxton and Winnipeg taxidermist William Calder. Scott wanted species that were abundant and available to all newcomers. He could not resist sending to his London office an impressive stuffed buffalo that had died at the zoo in Rocky Mountains National Park (now Banff). It thrilled Charing Cross pedestrians, who could peer at it behind the office's large picture window. The buffalo was later hauled around Europe to numerous immigration fairs. The CPR was initially sceptical that wildlife would promote immigration (and, incidentally, refused free trans-Atlantic passage to Scott's shaggy buffalo for that reason), but after 1910 the company changed promotional strategies and used wild animals, birds, and fish in almost every European exhibit to advertise western Canada.[13]

Wildlife imagery was not restricted to federal immigration promotions. Numerous individuals were working at local levels to advertise abundance in the west. Some launched the fish and game conservation movement, which gained momentum early in the twentieth century. Although the heyday of protective associations occurred in the interwar period, prewar conservationists understood that wildlife indices could differentiate their communities from others throughout the west. The wealthiest and most respectable citizens led these associations during a period of rising provincial and municipal debt. Many of these citizens were anxious to attract capital to their communities to pay for former booster projects and lure newcomers to fill vacant city lots.[14] Their associations did much more than merely protect leisure pursuits, and their membership lists overlapped with those of numerous other civic and booster clubs. The civic promotion behind conservation can be seen in the work of Richard A. Darker. The wealthy life insurance broker started the Southern Alberta Fish and Game Protective Association in 1907. It brought together the most "respectable" elements of pioneer society. Darker meanwhile served as vice president of the Calgary Auto Club, which promoted the tourist and hunting potential of southern Alberta. The club also advertised new road systems leading to southern Alberta. Darker's efforts were matched by those of A.E. Cross, whose civic, business, and conservation activities overlapped considerably. One of the "Big Four" who launched the Calgary Stampede to boost the reputation of the city, Cross took an active interest in parks protection and angling matters. Some of his letters to the Department of Marine and Fisheries, along with those of Darker, were instrumental in pressuring the department to place the first western fish hatchery in the impractical location of Banff, far from the streams that the hatchery served but close to the thousands of tourists annually visiting the town site – and therefore boosting the reputations of nearby foothills communities.[15]

Darker concurrently offered advice to conservation groups taking root in Edmonton and Vancouver. Associations in British Columbia were attempting to restore depleted wildlife in what is now Stanley Park and to guard game and bird populations in the Lower Mainland and on Vancouver Island. Run by sportspeople, these associations should not be dismissed, however, as lobby groups pursuing their own recreation. In fact, their concern about wildlife usually had a civic purpose. Most western communities supported local "refuges," "preserves," or "breeding areas," though they often disagreed about where they should be situated. The western game preserves not only protected animals and provided game to be hunted outside them but also bolstered provincial and local reputations of natural abundance. First established in the national park at Banff, game preserves were later created in federal western parks and in provincial parks in British Columbia after the turn of the century and in Saskatchewan and Manitoba by the end of the First World War. Before the war, naturalist and famous nature writer Ernest Thompson Seton helped to plan one park near Lethbridge. Townsfolk were pleased to know that train passengers from the east would have a chance to see "the last of the antelope" near their community. Visitors could also see the "last" herds of buffalo and other animals preserved at Elk Island near Edmonton and at Wainwright. In 1914, the City of Calgary, ever intent on attracting newcomers, asked its Member of Parliament, R.B. Bennett, to find funds to have a herd of buffalo established on the Sarcee Indian Reserve near city limits. The plan came to naught, likely because of the prohibitive cost of fencing.[16]

BC Provincial Museum exhibit, ca. 1910. Photographs such as these, used on postcards, promoted the province's abundant natural resources.
BC Archives, B-03776

Wildlife conservation, animal paddocks, and game preserves allowed boosters to proclaim a western abundance that differentiated their region from others in North America. Wild animals affirmed the concept of a new land, the "last best west," that invited newcomers. This wildlife advertised a region only recently opened to settlement. Here sodbusters could stake their claims and become squatters in a land not yet spent of opportunity.[17]

Wild animals represented as superabundant also associated the region with Eden, and – given the connections between the urban reform movement and back to nature – boosters could suggest that the west offered a plenitude that contrasted with the poverty and unsanitary conditions of European and American cities. Natural history museums built from the late 1880s on supported this central proposition of local boosters. Officially serving as naturalist universities,[18] they displayed the popularization of science in society and the economic work that their supporters were undertaking in ornithology and entomology – matters of critical importance to provincial governments. But natural history museums also displayed animals, birds, and fishes as superabundant by overstocking them. The museum in Banff, established on the main street adjacent to the Bow River in 1893, attracted increasing numbers of guests every year. Curator Norman Sanson was dogmatic in collecting and haphazard in displaying specimens. By 1922, the museum contained approximately six hundred birds, stuffed and mounted, to the point where visitors had to stand tiptoe to see specimens displayed on top shelves and kneel to study those on bottom shelves. Albertans, some hoping for remuneration, were sending bird nests, animal carcasses, shells, insects, moths, and dinosaur bones, many of which were accepted and heaped in the museum's back room.[19]

Overstocking Banff's natural history museum was likely a strategic public relations move by James B. Harkin, the commissioner of parks after 1911. Harkin himself directed aspects of the museum's development and designed some of its dioramas. Virtually every aspect of the natural world represented inside his museum was overstocked. Walls were covered with specimens, giant glass jars of Okanagan fruit and containers of fishes and salamanders lined shelves, a moose with stitching coming loose loomed next to elk and bear. These displays helped to lead observers to the imaginative conclusion that natural wealth was available nearby. Adding clarity to the clutter, dioramas told taxidermic stories. Showing animals in natural environments and striking action poses, these dioramas displayed the bounty of the land.[20]

Sometimes spilling over with specimens, western museums carried out a central mandate of boosterism: to prove that the west was particularly blessed by nature. Harkin, of course, was anxious to show his parks as verdant remnants of wilderness. But westerners building their own museums seemed to be intent on constructing the same illusion of abundance. Calgary's natural history museum, funded and stocked by the city's busiest and best citizens, rooted itself in the basement of the Tavernor Block and included a buffalo weighing 2,240 pounds shot by a Calgarian in 1908.[21] Red Deer's municipal library housed a natural history museum by 1905. Winnipeg had many such museums. The Historical and Scientific Society of Manitoba collected natural history pieces, and its members maintained private collections used by Ernest Thompson Seton for his checklists of birds in Manitoba. As in Regina, in Winnipeg the collection was located in the legislative building. Mainland British Columbians supported a remarkable number of natural history societies and museums by the turn of the century. A surprising number of them burned down, but they were soon rebuilt.[22]

Abundance was articulated in the way that these displays were arranged. As Karen Wonders points out in a study of wildlife dioramas, collections often followed criteria of display and technique but were freely reorganized locally by the people building them. Wild animal displays, in particular, lent themselves to didactic and "narrative" purposes, whether to promote conservation or to tell stories of the Darwinian natural world.[23] In western Canada, wildlife displays often served the didactic purpose of revealing the progress taking place in settlement communities. The Medicine Hat exhibition in 1925, for instance, included the "very interesting and instructive" exhibit of the Canada Land and Irrigation Company. It showed buffalo products on loan from the parks department, including coats, auto rugs, a buffalo head, and pemmican.[24] In other representations, wildlife confirmed an abundance persuasively communicated by museum postcards. These photographs strategically brought together a museum's specimens within a single room or hallway entrance. John Fannin himself appeared in one promotional stereoscopic photograph. Other photos were taken of the Victoria collection crowded into what was then the provincial court building.[25] One photo was reproduced in publications such as the Canadian Pacific Railway's *Hunting, Shooting, and Fishing,* in which "unrivalled" hunting opportunities were promised to visitors. The same photographs, meanwhile, were reprinted as postcards and found circulation when they were purchased, stamped, and mailed abroad.

Such images communicated Edenic abundance. Westerners were not interested in re-creating the conditions of a competitive wilderness in their wildlife displays. Their postcard photos showed carnivores and herbivores standing side by side, well communicating the idyllic conditions before the biblical fall from grace. This implicit promotional device also addressed a key contemporary criticism of urbanism in which reformers identified unfair competition in American cities, the problems of big business, and injustice toward the working classes. Crowded into a single photo, the wildlife displays suggested plenitude, freedom from want, and an end to strife. One of many postcard photographs promoting Victoria's museum, then, showed wolves, bears, and coyotes standing on their wooden bases beside mountain goats, deer, moose, and elk – carnivore and herbivore sharing space within the sanctuary of Victoria's judicial building. Since a museum was usually located in the legislative centre of the provincial capital, these displays, arranged alongside the ornate façades and grand portico entrances of legislative or judicial assembly rooms, suggested the peaceful and law-abiding tenor of communities in the west. They certainly proved that these rapidly growing urban areas – population growth in both Vancouver and Winnipeg was out of control by 1911 – were still blessed with close contact with the natural world.

Museum builders also used such displays to differentiate their growing metropolises from others south of the border or across the Atlantic Ocean. Local boards of trade and commerce were particularly adept at using photos of animals to advertise their towns or cities as more naturally wealthy than their competitors in the booster age. The Calgary Board of Commerce, for instance, published a postcard early in the century showing four hunters surrounded by the numerous ducks that they had shot, depicting a message of local abundance. The most intriguing element of the photo is where it was taken: within city limits, not where the ducks had actually been shot. This was a deliberate strategy by city boosters. The same strategy is discernible in a postcard advertising Pipestone, Manitoba, in which citizens show "The Spoils of One Day in Pipestone, Man." The hunters transported the

Banff's Natural History Museum in the 1930s
National Archives of Canada, PA 135005

ducks from their marshland setting and lay them in front of the town's hodgepodge of false-fronted buildings on Main Street.[26]

Such civic abundance was sometimes ritualized in the annual event of the duck hunt, in which, within Winnipeg's city limits, the members of one fish and game conservation association traditionally heaped ducks as high as their clubhouse roof. Photos were usually taken. This event did not celebrate waste, since most of the ducks were promptly redistributed to families for consumption. Such rituals more directly boosted a local reputation or raised funds to support civic projects, both having the purpose of building the community. Anglers from Calgary competed in opening-day contests to see who could land the largest number of fish from the Bow River. With a daily trout limit of twenty-five and no limit on other species, these first-day bags must have been impressive indeed.[27] At these events, a local merchant often offered a prize, and all proceeds from ticket purchases went to Calgary hospitals. By 1910, though, in a letter sent to the *Lethbridge Daily Herald*, one reader took a local hardware store owner to task for offering a prize for the largest number of ducks killed on the first day of the season. The reader pointed out the "far-reaching damage this thoughtlessly worded advertisement may cause ... placing a premium on wanton slaughter."[28]

Advertisers and businessmen were aware, however, that wildlife associated their community with natural abundance when it was hunted and displayed in these ways. No wonder, then, that conservation programs led by game guardians paid by provincial governments attempted to sustain wildlife as much for a province's reputation as for the pleasure of sport hunters. Manitoba's chief game guardian encouraged conservation associations to "make of this province a sportsman's paradise," obviously attempting to sustain an Edenic reputation for the province.[29] Fred Bradshaw, long the wildlife guardian in Saskatchewan, promoted a "more game" movement among provincial fish and game conservationists after the turn of the century in much the same spirit, attempting "to maintain our *desirable reputation* as a province where wild life abounds."[30] Wildlife, then, was rarely only the concern of sport hunters in the beginning decades of the twentieth century. Abundance was an issue to anyone who had an interest in a region's reputation. Natural history museums and boards of commerce used wildlife to issue reassuring statements about conditions in nearby settlements and even urban centres. Wild animals could communicate to the outsider that here, whether in Calgary, Victoria, or Banff, a revitalizing and perpetual contact with the natural world was still unbroken and that citizens lived in original, superabundant plenty.

The proposition that abundant wildlife could advertise natural resources, however, raised problems from the start. As optimistic as these western promotions were, they existed in the shadow of the conservation movement gaining popularity in the United States and subsequently in eastern Canada. There themes of superabundance had been completely discredited long before they appeared in Canada's newest agricultural frontier. High-profile Americans had launched conservation efforts with the final decline of the buffalo, the extinction of numerous bird species, and the disappearance of other game animals throughout the eastern states. Powerful organizations such as the Campfire Club of America and the Audubon Society were taking up the cause of protection. Sport hunting associations themselves were urging governments to stop wasteful hunting and the commercial use of wildlife. In eastern Canada, too, conservation was gaining support. In 1909, the Canadian Commission of Conservation was established following the lead of Theodore Roosevelt, who had inaugurated a short-lived American counterpart. With the North American migratory bird convention and Mexican initiatives following similar priorities, Canada was tied to a continent-wide concern to conserve nature. The Canadian commission itself rallied around the promises of progressivism: that efficient land and resource use, scientific leadership, and federal advice would help provinces to better use forests, fish, and other natural resources. Provincial game resources became one of the commission's priorities by 1917, when it convened a special meeting to discuss conservation strategies. Whether commissioners encouraged the creation of fish and game conservation associations, launched independent resource studies, or promoted "scientific" fur farming, they were

"The Spoils of One Day at Pipestone, Manitoba." Despite a rapid decline in fish and game populations, westerners perpetuated a myth of superabundance, linking what they claimed to be rich hunting opportunities with local natural resources. Boosters deliberately took pictures like this and sent them abroad as postcards to attract investment and settlers.
Provincial Archives of Manitoba, N928

initiating what would become, in the interwar period, the popular era of wildlife conservation in Canada.[31]

There was certainly enough local information about depletion and a widespread pessimistic appraisal of western wildlife that should have countered the creation of a western image of superabundance. The first hordes of American and British hunters were disappointed with the western Canadian territory as early as the 1870s and 1880s. Before the building of northern railways and the launching of steamship services to better game regions in the Cassiar district in north-central British Columbia and elsewhere, these hunters were restricted to areas along the CPR line and American branch lines in southern British Columbia and Manitoba, regions that were soon overhunted. These sportsmen hardly heaped praise on Canadian sport hunting. The British adventurer William A. Baillie-Grohman was probably typical in his pessimism. Like his American sport hunting counterparts, he turned his attention to British Columbia after American fields had been "shot out" by the 1870s. He discovered the Lower Mainland and Fraser River valley tangled with forests and scarce of big game. He soon complained that he had seen in Wyoming and Idaho, "in one single day, more big game, not counting bison, than I have in all the ten or eleven years put together in British Columbia." Baillie-Grohman's dour observations were matched by those of hunters who initially used Canada's new transcontinental railway as nothing more than a fast route to the truly magnificent game fields of

Alaska, largely bypassing Canadian game haunts altogether. These hunters appreciated how quickly even the best hunting regions could be emptied of game. British hunting narratives reiterated the same pessimism by the end of the century, describing areas of southern Alberta that had, within a decade, lost their status as a "sportsman's paradise."[32]

There is some irony, then, that images of superabundant forests and "un-rivalled" hunting and fishing opportunities began to appear in the late 1890s, when in other settings wildlife depletion became a truism of settlement and urban growth. Indeed, just when the era of progressive conservation gained its greatest popularity, westerners were deliberately advertising their region as the continent's remaining Edenic wildlife refuge.

The myth building is best seen in British Columbia. By the 1890s, wildlife formerly used for the meat and pelt trade was beginning to be reserved for sport hunting. The 1893 game amendment ended some of the freedoms of meat provisioners and deer skin exporters. Debates surrounding game legis-lation brought to light a growing cadre of local sport hunters who appar-ently sought to refine hunting in the province and attract foreign, high-paying, big-game hunters. Significantly, these individuals were closely tied to political elites in Victoria, themselves facing some threat from a chang-ing economy and a shift of metropolitan population and wealth from their city to Vancouver.[33]

By the time that the legislature took issue with the game laws, Victoria resident Clive Phillipps-Wolley was already inflating the province's game resources. A British citizen, he had published accounts of his hunting expe-riences in the Crimea. Clive and his wife heard of the opening of the CPR and visited Victoria on an excursion in 1886, a journey that inaugurated a new career for Clive in writing and business. Disgusted with the "choking" fog of London, the couple began to live in Victoria. There Phillipps-Wolley became active in local politics, running unsuccessfully for a federal Con-servative seat in Parliament, and took a lead in civic events, giving public lectures based on his experiences as a world traveller. Letters written home to friends and Clive's law partner were later published in a book called *The Sportsman's Eden*, in which Clive praised British Columbia as the last out-post of wilderness, a region, he asserted, abundant in game and fish.[34]

Phillipps-Wolley became a booster of the city while he concurrently led a circle of sport hunters who attempted to bolster the province's reputation as a big-game location. He was a member of the city's Union Club in 1892 when it lobbied to have some of the province's game laws relaxed to attract wealthy big-game hunters. The club was already the meeting place for for-eign hunters who "gassed" about their sporting exploits; Phillipps-Wolley saw the club's impressive trophy walls and the high social atmosphere around the billiard tables maintaining Victoria's reputation as "the Great Gateway to the sportsmen's Edens of the North and West."[35]

According to Baillie-Grohman, Phillipps-Wolley and others were not above exaggerating game abundance. He cautioned readers of his own narratives about an unnamed Victorian, undoubtedly Phillipps-Wolley, who was publishing hunting descriptions (included in *The Sportsman's Eden*) that exaggerated game opportunities in western Canada to "benefit the land speculators and hotel-keepers" of Victoria. Pressing the legislature to further relax game laws, and writing letters to and leading articles for newspapers, the "individual" in question "gave expression to opinions regarding British Columbia's big game resources which hardly bore out the high opinions which he published." Baillie-Grohman believed that Phillipps-Wolley wrote the articles for "a local circle of Victoria readers" anxious that the "rich men of Europe come out here to hunt our sheep and bear and wapiti, leaving hundreds of pounds in the country for every beast which they took out of it."[36]

Phillipps-Wolley, Victoria's MLAs, and the curator of the natural history museum were all attempting to keep Victoria the "Great Gateway" to the province's commercial and resource development. Meanwhile, the newly appointed game guardian, Arthur Bryan Williams, also promoted British Columbia as a hunter's Eden.[37] Williams, as noted, was a British sportsman en route to the United States in 1886 when "the glories of this wonderland and the magnificent sport" near Vancouver kept him in the province.[38] If his letterbooks are any indication, Williams spent most of his time answering the inquiries of foreign hunters interested in British Columbia as a possible region for sport hunting. He advised them on the best areas to hunt, on the right time to arrive and depart from Victoria, and on steamer and rail service, and he made arrangements with Amerindian guides at places such as Cassiar, the East Kootenays, and Lillooet. Williams tirelessly described the Vancouver area and other regions of the province as "teeming with wildlife."[39]

These boosters immediately formed connections with railway companies, one of the most powerful being the Canadian Pacific Railway. The CPR had always encouraged hunting excursions in the west as a means of profiting from its passenger service. Concurrently, as it promoted the west as a garden for homesteaders, it heavily advertised it as a bountiful game haunt. It supported the promotional tour of J.H. Hubbard, the president of the Manitoba Gun Club, who lectured in 1886 at the Colonial and Indian Exhibition in England on game in western Canada.[40] Hubbard illustrated his lectures with taxidermy pieces that he took with him. They seem to have been particularly impressive. The *Illustrated London News* depicted the massive taxidermy display greeting visitors to the Canadian pavilion that year.[41] By the turn of the century, railway promoters had tapped into the increasing popularity of sport hunting and began using taxidermy pieces extensively. For instance, at the 1908 Automobile, Motor Boat, and Sportsmen's Exhibitions

John Murray Gibbon, the CPR "spin master," at his BC cabin, ca. 1920
Canadian Pacific Railway Archives, 24831

in Montreal and Toronto, pelts, antlers, and snouts adorned western rail cars. Wildlife pieces were subsequently sent to the 1908 Canadian exhibit at the Franco-British Exhibition to cater to the broad international interest in back to nature; the animals were mounted "in an attractive way," as a CPR information memo said.[42] The Canadian exhibit at Edinburgh in 1908 highlighted not only agricultural, timber, and wood pulp products but also specimens of big game. White fox, a buffalo, musk-oxen, moose, and deer were displayed. The most popular item was "a huge bear, said to be the largest ever shot in the colony," a London magazine writer said. "In its paws it holds a bunch of grain, symbolic of Canada's greatest industry."[43] Wildlife imagery also appeared in the 1915 Panama-Pacific International Exposition at San Francisco, where the CPR devised a cinematographic lecture hall surrounded by walls bearing the heads of wildlife.[44]

The CPR promoted Canada as the last wildlife stronghold in large measure because of the brainstorming of former British journalist, scholar, and wilderness novelist John Murray Gibbon, whom the CPR employed as its promotional manager. Throughout the 1920s, Gibbon was involved in numerous promotions that cultivated the image of a western wilderness reserve. He referred visitors to Banff outfitters, served on the board of the National Parks Association, and organized the Trail Riders, a horseback-riding club that explored the Rocky Mountain parks. He referred travelogue writers and filmmakers to key individuals in Banff, such as the Brewster brothers, who could get them great film footage and photos of wildlife. In

Entrance to CPR exhibit, Wimbley, 1925. The CPR aggressively promoted tourism and advertised the potential of Canada's western farmlands by placing images of moose, buffalo, and other wild animals at the forefront of displays and immigration booths. *Canadian Pacific Railway Archives, 10569*

his workplace, Gibbon carefully managed the idea that the west was the last region of abundant game. It seems to have been his innovation to use images of moose and bear in the company's exhibitions and logos sent abroad. His dioramas and miniature railway exhibits in Europe usually contained wildlife specimens.[45] And an abundance of wild animals appeared in virtually all of Gibbon's novels set in the Canadian west, novels likely inspired by his experiences at his Field, British Columbia, cabin. These abundant wild animals found shelter in the west from a rapidly overindustrializing world.[46]

In many respects, this promotional strategy was created to meet growing concerns outside the region about urban development and inequity in industrializing economies. Wildlife depletion, especially in the United States, had naturally given rise to the proposition that the Canadian west was the last northern game refuge. It was already featured in editorials of publications such as *Rod and Gun in Canada*. Since 1905, the magazine had been busy "awakening Canadians to the possibilities of the Dominion as the great sporting and play ground of the world."[47] The editor published letters of rebuke from Americans who claimed that Canadians had not yet realized that their country presented the last of the wilderness regions in North America. "What Our American Cousins Can Teach Us!" exhorted Canadians to realize their "treasure chest of infinite resources in this matter of health-giving recreation."[48] The writer claimed that Canadian authors such as Ralph Connor, Charles G.D. Roberts, and Stewart White had helped to make Americans take notice of the hearty, character-producing wilderness regions of Canada. "Add to these the excellent [hunting and fishing] booklets of the CPR and other railroads, the mass of magazine literature dealing with the attractions of life in the Canadian wilderness and one does not wonder that the eyes of the whole continent are turned upon you."[49]

The work of railway promoters, game guardians, and civic boosters such as Phillipps-Wolley, then, drew on the concern that the United States, once a region swarming with game, had become "irretrievably" ruined by the end of the nineteenth century. They countered this concern by stressing that this was "not the case in the Canadian territory," as a brochure assured its readers, and the editor of *Rod and Gun in Canada* heartily agreed. Thousands of Americans, the magazine claimed, lived in industrialized luxury south of the border and then "hardened" themselves in sporting pursuits in Canadian forests. The "over-civilized" American had to look northward, to North America's wildlife "El Dorado" and the "Gameland our Fathers Lost," to find animals hunted out of the United States.[50]

The same frontier, then, that once separated civilization from wilderness in the American experience had become fixed across the forty-ninth parallel, separating Canada from its neighbour.[51] The CPR's *Sportsman's Map of Canada and the Northwest Territory* drew heavily on this premise by showing railway lines penetrating "abundant" Canadian hunting and fishing areas. These areas – covering the entire Canadian territory but particularly the west – were labelled "Forest Full of Big Game and Small Game," "Small Game Abound," or "Grizzly Bear Very Plentiful." Some game was identified south of the Great Lakes, but the rest of the United States – included in the map – remained conspicuously empty of wildlife.[52] This theme was graphically illustrated in brochures such as the twenty-ninth edition of the CPR's *Fishing, Shooting, Canoe Trips, and Camping*, which went to American and overseas audiences in large quantities by the First World War. Its cover showed a man wearing a Stetson hat and rugged riding attire mounted on horseback in the Canadian Rockies. Reprinted inside was an interior postcard picture of the BC museum in Victoria. It showed elk, deer, mountain lions,

Fishing and Shooting, CPR brochure, ca. 1910. Railway companies like the CPR produced numerous brochures boasting an abundance of wildlife in Canada's west. Many of these suggested that wildlife had taken refuge in Canada after being driven out of the United States, and that unexploited natural resources and homestead lands still awaited in western Canada.
Canadian Pacific Railway Archives, BR 124

raccoons, and other "species of game found in Canada"[53] crowded together. Beneath the photo was a quotation of a *Field and Stream* article: "People have to turn to Canada to find the wild country that we all of us want to enjoy from time to time." The brochure went on to say that "Most of the species now found in Canada were formerly common to the whole Continent. Many of them, however, have been altogether driven out of the United States by the steady march of civilization, and have retreated beyond the international border." Hunting and angling opportunities beckoned to Americans from behind the Canadian border, where animals had taken "up their abode in the great wilderness of the north."[54] The brochure promised a northern refuge where wild animals in the industrial and settled south had sought protection.[55]

The CPR was not alone in these promotions. Western residents were anxious to further distinguish the boundaries of the Canadian Eden to their advantage. By the 1920s, most national exhibitions tended to demarcate an industrializing and mechanizing central Canada from a farming western

Canada. The Toronto Canadian National Exhibition in the period usually included a miniature train that allowed Canadians to get aboard for a western excursion to a mountainous wildlife haven. A 1910 Soo Line brochure adhered to the same promotional strategy by stating that the United States was "gradually becoming a thickly settled country, and even the valleys of the western Rockies are the homes of the orchardist and the rancher." Now wildlife was "'trekking' to the north, where in the vast solitudes of the Canadian Rockies and protected by the stringent game laws of Canada, they will never become extinct." The brochure asserted that Alberta, Saskatchewan, and British Columbia provided the "best big game country in North America, if not in the entire world." Western Canada, then, was a land where "vast solitudes" provided the answer to dreaded scarcity of resources and super population growth. Canadian society enjoyed the immediacy of "still vaster areas of forest and mountain, thickly populated not by man but by all the numerous creatures of the wild."[56]

The idea of a great northern "trek" of animals to western Canada appealed to residents busy promoting their land and welcoming investment. Later civic boosters such as J.F. McFadden never let go of the idea of a great western game haunt. McFadden led the Riding Mountain National Park Committee in Manitoba. Attempting to stir interest in the creation of a federal park in 1928, he pointed out that the province's gains in industrial and mining enterprises meant that "all eyes are focused on Manitoba." The next step was to create a national park that showed Manitoba "also [as] a province of mountain grandeur, of lakes of unsurpassed beauty," where "countless bands of elk and moose and other game still roam at will."[57]

Settlers, town builders, and community leaders, then, closely associated wild animals with the untainted wealth of a natural world. In the period of the first land booms and massive immigration, westerners were representing their region as abundantly stocked with wild animals. In doing so, they differentiated their human homes from others that no longer had such a generous stake in what was understood as a close approximation of Eden. It is no surprise that westerners took interest in a well-stocked natural history museum, the reputation of a local game haunt, or a nearby game preserve. Moose Jaw residents, for instance, avidly supported the opening of a wild animal park established near town limits in 1929. Originally called Chief Sitting Bull Park (though distant from the celebrated Sioux chief's encampment after the military rout of Custer), the park was conceived by town resident Frank McRitchie, who persuaded a local landowner to set aside land along the Moose Jaw River for the preserve. A newspaper advertisement asked readers to financially support the venture. It showed an Amerindian on horseback spearing a buffalo and announced that "The 'Buffalo' Drive Is On." The park would "mean thousands of visitors and wonderful publicity for the City."[58] Funds were raised, and the park was opened. Some five hundred people attended the inauguration ceremony officiated by the province's lieutenant governor. Sioux and Cree chiefs responded to invitations to attend. A competitive anti-American spirit moved over the proceedings. The opening-day brochure pointed out that Sitting Bull's braves had arrived in this area "to seek refuge on the soil of the Great White Queen."⁵⁹ The "vast Animal Park" was now dedicated to Sitting Bull's "name and memory." Only a few animals actually roamed the reserve by opening day: a few bighorn sheep, six buffalo, some elk, and deer. Yet the exercise succinctly expressed what town boosters hoped to say about Moose Jaw and its immediate hinterlands. Wildlife now took refuge north of the border with the United States, a land exhausted of opportunities, and found revitalization in or near Moose Jaw. Young deer and other animals, one 1935 newspaper report pointed out, had arrived in "exceptionally poor condition," and after some time of being protected and fed by park staff they had "developed into beautiful animals."⁶⁰

In this exercise, Moose Jaw residents also seem to have become, as wild game guardians, inheritors of the Earth and all its bounty. At the park's opening, First Nations people lent crucial authenticity to the message of civic progress. A Cree chief "told how his father Chief Star Blanket had shot the last buffalo known to be killed in the district and, as near as the chief could remember, the incident took place in what is now the Wild Animal Park."⁶¹ The same participants were given horses, guns, and blank shells and allowed to run the six buffalo in a historical re-creation of a pound drive. The park subsequently became an important part of Moose Jaw's identity as gateway to the west. By 1933, an inventory counted moose, bear cubs, buffalo bulls, and peacocks, and park attendants now claimed to have "100 mouths to feed." Even as late as 1966, a newspaper report suggested that the park that was "once the hunting and camping spot of Sitting Bull's braves is today a chief recreation spot for thousands of city residents and out-of-town visitors each year."⁶²

Ideas of an abundant northland accompanied many western Canadians – indeed most Canadians – into the age of conservation. By the 1920s, rallying around the idea of a superabundant northland had a lasting impact on regulation writing, conservation initiatives, and popular environmental understandings in the interwar years. The wildlife advisory role of the Canadian Commission of Conservation and the federal-provincial conferences on wildlife throughout the 1920s and 1930s aimed to safeguard what Canadians assumed they had: abundant wildlife. Conservation and preservation were popular in this period because so many Canadians now imagined their territory as a superabundant haven for wild animals. In short, Canadians ardently believed in northern plenty and American poverty. *The Sportsman's Map of Canada and the Northwest Territory* had shown that wildlife abounded above the forty-ninth parallel. That image of plenty was subsequently useful for the American conservationist William T. Hornaday, who published a map depicting America empty and Canada teeming with wildlife as a means of bolstering American support for his projects south of the border. Significantly, that image – and all of its profoundly erroneous suggestions – found circulation in Canada. It was used by Gordon Hewitt, the federal entomologist and the leader of wildlife conservation in Canada, in *The Conservation of Wild Life of Canada*, an interwar book marking the widespread support for wildlife conservation in Canada.[63]

Wildlife used in exhibitions, postcards, and museums became more than a promotional gimmick to encourage western visits and settlement. In the west, promotional activities gave substance to an idea that found currency deep within western Canadian society and perhaps shaped the very direction of subsequent environmental campaigns. Wild animals and natural resources were closely associated, one reason why photographs of duck hunts and crowded taxidermy displays helped to raise speculation in western development. Wildlife imagery asserted the theme of abundance in the Canadian west and provided tangible evidence of the largely incorporeal claims of boosterism. Those boosting new agricultural lands and investment opportunities used wildlife extensively. They arranged stuffed wild animals in legislative buildings. Exhibits featured wildlife as emissaries from a near natural world and suggested that representatives of the wild kingdom found a place in the last best west. Arranged in exhibits, game parks, or poster pictures, wild animals confirmed the special place of this region in the "civilized" world. How such ideas became important in western conservation is the topic of the next chapter.

5
Pioneer Society and Fish and Game Protection

By the First World War, western Canadians had begun to use taxidermy, photography, and illustrations of wildlife to advertise the natural wealth awaiting newcomers to their region. It is not surprising that wildlife – having so many associations with regional wealth – was dearly conserved in booming periods of immigration and social upheaval.

Historians often point to the rise of fish and game protective associations in the late nineteenth century as an indication of changing environmental ethics in North America. Members of these conservation groups, usually sportspeople, had become alarmed after numerous bird and animal species were exterminated and fish stocks, once believed to be superabundant, disappeared in lakes and streams.[1] In western Canada, such associations appeared in the settlement period and gained large memberships in the interwar years. Little is known about such associations, but they gained popularity in the context of social crises. Westerners often became conservationists because they believed that fish and game protection helped to reserve resources for local use, particularly for citizens who had arrived first in the region. Indeed, conservation associations were often led by community leaders who had become uneasy when large numbers of "foreigners" had appeared, registered land nearby, and begun hunting and fishing for their subsistence. These newcomers usually extracted the land's wealth more intensively than individuals who had proven up their homesteads and were now benefiting from social and economic networks within their communities. Beyond the inroads of new environmental sensibilities, the aims and activities of these conservationists suggest the concerns of community groups trying to control the economic and social uncertainties of western development.

Fish and game protectors worked in the context of a land boom, when speculation was growing around values imagined in the soils, forests, and streams of western Canada. These pioneer conservationists were concerned that community members or visitors fishing and hunting without limit would undermine overall confidence in a region after they diminished fish and game species. Protection, then, did not concern merely a few sportspeople within a town or city. A community's most influential representatives often joined conservation efforts because they believed that the work safeguarded the land's value and even the character of society taking root in the west. This chapter evaluates the wealth that conservationists imagined at stake in their work.

Fish and game protective associations were not a new concept when, in the first decades of the twentieth century, they spread to communities throughout the Canadian west. The first associations, established in the United States in the first half of the nineteenth century, are traced to the work of Henry W. Herbert (alias Frank Forester), an English immigrant who began to write in the 1830s about the virtues of fair game and sportsmanship. A proliferation of sporting magazines in the eastern United States appeared at the time when associations formed to promote discriminate shooting and etiquette in the "chase" of animals. While hunters developed a sport around their pastime, they mounted campaigns against the wasteful butchery of wildlife for either commercial use or mass consumption.[2]

These sport hunters had seen game opportunities near their communities rapidly diminish. In the Canadas before Confederation, similar environmental changes prompted individuals to establish protective associations. Fish depletion was so widespread in Upper Canada and Nova Scotia at that time that sportsmen were soon patrolling freshwater streams to protect them from overfishing. Their activities accorded well with the laissez-faire maxims of mid-Victorian liberalism and the realities of colonial financing; a government could only thinly disperse a contingent of guardians who, for the most part, regulated commercial industries. Freshwater fisheries were often left to the communities that grew up around them.

With little real government supervision, these fisheries were some of the quickest natural resources to be depleted, with or without volunteer guardianship. Soon after settlement in the New World, trout streams near settlements were almost immediately barren. If not hungry newcomers netting and dynamiting streams, dirty and unregulated industries, processing plants, and sawmills were quickly depleting fish populations.[3]

In pioneer communities in Newcastle, Upper Canada (where it was common for community members to fish annual spawning runs with pitchforks), the disastrous state of freshwater fisheries prompted some of the first Canadian conservation movements. It was likely the dramatic spectacle of depletion in these northern waters that pushed Samuel Wilmot and William F. Whitcher (both employees of the fisheries office of the Upper Canadian government) to international prominence as two of the first conservation advocates. Whitcher, who later drafted game laws for the Rocky Mountains National Park (now Banff), and gave advice to the Manitoba government on some of its first game ordinances, was himself startled by how quickly the Great Lakes and maritime coastlines could show signs of depletion. He took a prominent role at the London International Fisheries Congress in 1888. There he urged regulation and scientific investigation of the efficacy of fish hatchery programs. Wilmot developed fish breeding as a "science" and later oversaw hatchery programs in Canada. After Confederation, he made sure that ova and fry from Ontario were distributed to far-flung reaches of the dominion. Even British Columbia's depleted streams were sent stock, likely in a failed restoration project.[4]

Some local angling associations were already mustering ranks to better guard against reckless overfishing. Such associations decided allowable limits, season dates, and other matters pertaining to the use of nearby lakes and streams. Government fisheries officers sometimes volunteered in these associations or patrolled streams at the behest of local residents. In Upper Canada, the Wentworth Society for the Protection of Game and Fish was established in a tavern in 1860 after local sportsmen became alarmed since their nearby "noble game and fish" had been "vanishing before the arts of civilization." Members voted John W. Kerr, already a paid fish guardian for the Upper Canadian government, to take a lead in enforcing regulations. The association promptly petitioned the government to establish commercial and angling zones on nearby lakes and to grant special fishing privileges for neighbours living around Burlington Bay and nearby Hamilton. The members went on to urge that commercial ventures be excluded from sport fishing waters altogether.[5]

The Wentworth Society typified nineteenth-century approaches to conservation, which relied almost completely on local individual enterprise. Freshwater sport fisheries were protected by the members of communities, not really by the government, which devoted its few resources to commercial regulation. Local opinion often determined rules and season dates. After all, anglers saw themselves as the only ones qualified to make decisions of this sort: they considered themselves students of nature, observers of a particular species of trout (the regard of Ontarians for the great Nipigon is a good example), believing that they were the only "experts" in the fish's feeding habits, spawning characteristics, and the like.

The crisis in game and fish populations by the end of the century lent significant energy to this local tradition of conservation. By then, mechanized canning technology and motorized fishing crafts had seriously marred what had been considered superabundant fish stocks in the Great Lakes, in the St. Lawrence River, and along the east coast. A broad segment of the American and European publics now saw wildlife populations as overhunted and certain species on the brink of extinction. Given the concurrent rise of an American wilderness ethic, in which Frederick Jackson Turner's ominous statement in 1896 – that the "frontier" had been filled – was to play a part,

The last of the Canadian buffalo, ca. 1910. By the turn of the century, the buffalo became a symbol that garnered support for conservation initiatives. These animals, photographed in their pen at the popular Banff wildlife zoo, were some of the last in the Canadian west.
National Archives of Canada, PA 31615

the fate of the buffalo, passenger pigeon, and other species was raised up as a lesson to twentieth-century sportspeople and legislators.[6]

From the 1890s to the First World War, prominent Americans led campaigns against commercial and meat hunting. Their message was soon heard in the Canadian west. During a period when westerners were claiming superabundant populations of wildlife, outsiders were directing pressure on governments to initiate more stringent conservation measures. In the new province of Alberta, members of the Campfire Club of America, one of the most powerful conservation lobbies in the United States, pressured the Canadian government in 1910 to enlarge Waterton park, in part to preserve bighorn sheep populations.[7] In 1888, the Texan C.J. "Buffalo" Jones gained notoriety in Manitoba when he purchased Samuel Bedson's domesticated buffalo herd at Stony Mountain, some of the last buffalo in North America. By the mid-1890s, Jones was "rescuing" musk-oxen and other big game from the Mackenzie region; he also opposed the subsistence hunting of Chipewyan and Cree hunters at Fort Smith and Lake Athabaska in what is now northern Alberta.[8] In the 1880s, William T. Hornaday's writing on the American bison and his impressive taxidermy displays formed a devastating critique of the Red River hunt, by then stopped. Now a conservation leader, Hornaday condemned the memory of this subsistence hunt. His criticisms were easily redirected to still popular forms of meat and "pot" hunting, and they supported the aim of sport hunting lobbies to preserve wild animals for sport. In the first decade of the twentieth century, Hornaday began pressing Canadian federal and provincial governments to restrict Amerindian hunting freedoms in British Columbia.[9]

Conservation advocacy in Canada was, not surprisingly, directed at British Columbia, the sportsperson's "Eden." Bryan Williams, the chief game guardian, was well versed in the ethics of nineteenth-century sportsmanship and maintained correspondence with leading American conservationists. The League of American Sportsmen, of New York, having formed "for the purpose of protecting the game and game fishes, the song, insectivorous and other innocent birds," invited Williams at the turn of the century to annual meetings that brought together "the brightest and best game protectors in the country." The National Association of Audubon Societies asked Williams whether he had noticed "any increase in public sentiment favoring the better protection of wild birds and animals." Whatever the implications of outside conservationists stepping into local game matters, the popularity of such ideas and the conviction that without action wildlife would disappear in the last wilderness regions trickled into western communities. There the notion of conservation mingled with the local interests of rod and gun clubs, which began appropriating the philosophy of conservation – based on efficient use of animals and careful limits on hunting – to welcome the growth of local conservation associations.[10]

Many conservation clubs were soon encouraged by a surging interest in natural resource conservation supported by national bodies. The Canadian Commission of Conservation, established by Wilfrid Laurier in 1909, followed Theodore Roosevelt's initiatives in the United States to begin a science-led planning of resource use. The Canadian commission formally took up the issue of fish and game conservation in the war years. Hoping to supplement the new preservation policies of the national parks, the commissioners encouraged the creation of local fish and game conservation associations in order to take the "gospel of efficiency," as the progressive movement has been termed, into local settings.[11] The postwar Essex County Wild Life Conservation Association proved its value to game wardens, who thought that behind them stood "a body of men, members of an association, who pledge themselves to observe the laws and to do everything they can to see that others observe them." The Commission of Conservation eventually recommended that provincial governments encourage the formation of such organizations.[12]

But unlike the broader American and eastern Canadian conservation movements, which saw virtue in the expert planning of resource use, fish and game associations in western Canada continued to look to common citizens and their expertise. These associations upheld a tradition in which community members looked after resources for the benefit of their community. Numerous divergences in the aims of conservation were soon apparent when community members, alarmed by social and economic problems in their midst, enthusiastically began conserving wildlife to safeguard their own access to it and to control the suspicious activities of marginal groups.

In the western Canadian context at the turn of the century, pressing concerns of community members were indeed the hordes of newcomers arriving almost every year and the development of heavy resource extractive industries. Swelling numbers of ethnic groups arrived either as itinerate labourers or as hopeful patent farmers. To those who witnessed the first land rushes and the arrival of Clifford Sifton's "men in sheepskin coats" from Europe, immigration now threatened to change the Anglo-Canadian character of western communities. This heavy immigration added distinctive cultural, religious, and dietary traditions to townships originally established by Anglo-Ontarians. Certainly, new immigrants hunted and fished differently than better established westerners. The first fish and game associations usually consisted of a community's charter members, settlers "making good,"[13] who took up conservation and attempted to divert the dietary priorities of newcomers. By regulating the diets and the hunting practices of a diverse patchwork of ethnic groups, these associations tried not only to preserve sporting pastimes for their members but also to conserve core British values in communities perceived as being inundated by eastern European settlers, Asian labourers, or "papist" sodbusters.

Even more associations appeared immediately after the Great War, when westerners witnessed a second demographic phenomenon of the settlement period. While many conservationists still banded together to control and assimilate foreigners in their communities, many associations now formed when a town's population stagnated. Residents were alarmed at the perceived growth of rival settlements while growth in their own community slowed. Communities, then, became xenophobic not only toward "non-British" outsiders trammelling quarter sections and stream frontages but also toward citizens of rival towns and cities carrying away the wealth of nearby lakes, streams, and fields. These associations sought to restrict their hunting and fishing freedoms.

This analysis of community associations suggests that in pioneer settings wildlife conservation was in many ways interwoven with local concerns to protect a community's central character and safeguard the land's wealth for local use. When local residents were most unable to claim nearby resources or felt that outsiders were competing for control of those resources, wildlife became a matter of pressing civic importance. Such an interpretation of the role of fish and game associations arises from a reading of surviving provincial game guardian files and possibly the most complete record base still extant, the federal Department of Marine and Fisheries, which reveals some ninety associations forming throughout the west before 1930, many being established in the 1920s (see Appendix). Estimating the actual number of these independent associations is impossible. Game guardian files in most provinces have been poorly preserved, and the records of many associations that lobbied provincial authorities have simply been destroyed in archival purges. There were likely numerous associations in Saskatchewan and Manitoba that have vanished without a trace.

These associations were distinct from earlier rod and gun clubs long established in provincial and territorial towns. As I have noted, these clubs periodically formed to have laws changed, often in regard to treaty hunting freedoms and season dates. In 1893, rod and gun clubs formed in towns along the CPR line – Medicine Hat, Moose Jaw, Calgary, Lethbridge – and in Edmonton. They were largely social clubs, however, bringing together sportspeople who enjoyed open access to nearby game.[14] The clubs in Calgary, a town that Bailley-Grohman claimed was the "sportiest little town in the west,"[15] provided convivial meeting places for visitors arriving by train. Club members met visitors in the lobby of the Alberta Hotel, shared a few drinks, later introduced them to trustworthy guides and outfitters, and gave them information about the best game haunts.

Conservation associations beginning to form in the late nineteenth century differed in purpose from these social clubs. Their members pledged to act as voluntary guardians and enforce the game laws. They were confident that they could determine or at least influence the writing of ordinances. They also undertook projects to introduce game birds, animals, and exotic sport fish to their locales. Colin Inkster's Winnipeg Game Protective Association, established in 1884, marks the beginnings of this conservation tradition. Inkster, testifying at the Senate inquiry into western food sources, stated that club members had encountered "great difficulty in carrying out the law on account of not being able to prevent the Indians from killing [moose, deer, and other large animals] during the close[d] season in their reserves."[16] Little is known of the Macleod Game Protective Association, which formed in 1889, soon after completion of the CPR. The association was formed at a "well attended meeting of sportsmen on Saturday evening,"[17] the town paper, the *Gazette,* reported. Its secretary-treasurer, Dr. George DeVeber, published a letter in the following newspaper issue asserting that "The buffalo and elk are extinct; the antelope, mountain sheep and goat, black and white tail deer, are fast approaching the same state, and are only to be found semi-occasionally in some remote and favored locality."[18] He blamed this bleak situation on Amerindian hunters and settlers who killed and egged out of season and urged the newspaper to regularly publish the game laws. He then appealed "to sportsmen in each and every district in the territories to form sister societies."[19] Fits and starts of enthusiasm usually decided the outcome of such game protection. The Macleod newspaper did not bother to publish accounts of the association. There probably was not much news to report. Town conservationists rallied again in 1896, this time to debate game laws more appropriate in the first land rushes.

The larger association of "sister societies" that DeVeber proposed finally began to appear when the Southern Alberta Fish and Game Protective Association (SAFGPA) formed in 1906. It coalesced, not by accident, immediately after Alberta's provincial autonomy, when wildlife management fell under the control of the government's new game office, then part of the agriculture department. Besides taking a leading role in determining exactly what the new game ordinances would be – and continuing to do so long into the province's history – its members almost immediately began introducing game birds to replace dwindling native pheasant populations. They also attempted to raise funds to introduce Swiss chamoix into the foothills to replace disappearing antelope.

The proactive role taken by the SAFGPA in maintaining and protecting a sporting environment distinguished it from traditional, quite complacent, rod and gun clubs. The differences became clear in 1919 when the Edmonton Rod and Gun Club asked conservationists in Calgary to introduce the organizational form of a "game protective association" to its members. They, too, wanted to undertake similar lobbying, restocking, and enforcing.[20]

Edmonton sportspeople, like others across the west, were turning to this form of organization for a reason. Significant environmental changes were occurring in the first decades of the twentieth century. Local fish and game environments were being dramatically degraded. Westerners now appreciated the ease with which western natural resources could be exhausted. Besides antelope, now disappearing in its last ranges in ranching frontier, game birds from Manitoba to British Columbia were declining. On Vancouver Island, blue pheasant populations seem to have been eradicated immediately after construction of the railway. Once widely inhabiting the lush valleys and coulees of Vancouver Island's rainforests, the birds were now thinning in number. Clubs in Vancouver and Victoria soon joined in an effort to introduce European and Asian birds to replace these disappearing native birds.

On the prairies, farmers and sport hunters alike saw declining numbers of sharp-tailed grouse and, with its northern migration into Manitoba in the 1880s, pinnated grouse, both regarded as native "prairie chickens." The chicken population seems to have been reduced by generous bag limits and the bird's central place in settler diets. Large swatches of the foothills and prairie were empty of braces. As early as 1890, the Northwest Territories government heard from all quarters about the problem. Settlers near Red Deer complained that neighbours were exporting the birds to Calgary's meat markets. Edmonton, Red Deer, and Calgary residents were signing petitions "That prairie chicken are now being destroyed wholesale and at all seasons of the year in the said Territories by Indians and others."[21] Saskatchewan's game branch noted dramatic population declines by 1906. When brace numbers revived after ordinances were tightened, the Saskatchewan government netted and transferred some birds to depleted British Columbia in 1908. But in 1910, W.M. Van Valkenburg, of the newly formed Saskatchewan Game Protective Association, vigorously objected to any further exports until the bird's population became more stable. The government thereafter debated whether it should outlaw all shooting or merely reduce the season by half, from two months to one. In 1910, it opted for a shortened season and prohibited all market sales of chickens. Tellingly, game ordinances were now being printed in Cree, English, German, and French. Criticism of all types of commercial bird hunting meanwhile increased. Sunday shooting was now disallowed. Concurrently, game offices coped with the decline of the "graceful" antelope as more and more of its grazing land was converted into farmland.[22]

During these first boom years of immigration, Fred Bradshaw, the chief game guardian in Saskatchewan, sensed a crisis. He argued that these birds should be hunted for sport rather than food. "The great value of game birds is not so much as an article of food, although that is considerable in itself, and a practical way of reducing the high cost of living," he pointed out in his annual report for 1912, "but as an inducement that attracts farmers from the monotony of their daily work, and clerks, tradesmen and merchants of the cities to the prairie and the woods."[23] Bradshaw's office had already stated that the taking of meat "should be looked upon as merely incidental to a successful hunting trip." By the war years, his department could not lessen the impact of settlers on bird populations. Bradshaw made numerous speeches to sportsmen's groups, schoolchildren, and the students of the province's teachers' college. His message of conservation became at times almost lyrical: "The embers of hope still smolder and we now look to the education of the masses as the means of fanning them into a flame so bright and glaring as to arrest the attention of all our citizens to the importance of this great movement of protecting and conserving our wild life in a sane and reasonable manner" – this stated in a government blue book![24] He worked diligently with sportspeople in the province and encouraged associations to form both to create a voluntary body to enforce regulations and to gauge public opinion about needed regulations. But in promoting the "more game" movement in Saskatchewan, to which "scientist, nature lover, sportsmen, farmer, game guardian, boys and girls" would contribute, he saw an ideal cooperative movement taking place, akin to that uniting the politics of prairie farmers. Bradshaw's vision of pioneer society included the almost utopian end of the farm movement, whereby humans using rational gifts might transcend their competitive nature. His province would be a place where game would abound, where "conditions will be such as to permit the true sportsman to bag sufficient game to satisfy his needs without giving rein to his baser animal instincts to kill every living thing that crosses his path."[25]

A pressing problem for Bradshaw and the associations soon forming in Saskatoon and Regina was nevertheless the notable decline in prairie chicken populations. Season reductions, limits on their sale, and absolute prohibitions on chicken exports seemed to briefly reinvigorate the bird's numbers. In 1914, the game guardian and most sportspeople put aside, momentarily, their earlier drive to have foreign birds introduced to replace chickens. But by 1916, radical measures seemed to be inevitable when the game guardian admitted that his office now heard a commonly asked question, "Where are the prairie chickens?" J.P. Turner, of the Manitoba Game Protective Association, published through the province's Department of Agriculture and Immigration a pamphlet on the subject detailing the bird's estimated distribution and need for protection. He deemed the prairie chicken "typical" of the west, "as characteristic of the prairies as the buffalo formerly was among the animals." He said that no bird deserved more "serious thought and attention" since now looming was its "extermination over the length and breadth of the broad grasslands and stubbles of the Canadian West."[26]

Turner cited spreading settlement as the chief cause of depletion. But it was likely the scale of subsistence hunting among farmers that was extirpating native wild game populations. Demographic changes prompted more conservation associations to form, many appearing in the middle of the Laurier-era land booms. Now westerners were anticipating new onrushes of immigrants who, in nearby lands and streams, would scramble for yet more protein. Residents joined these associations in droves as town populations rose or, more often the case, nearby rival settlements did. In the case of the prairie chicken, its near disappearance during the land boom prompted locals to ask new questions about the finite nature of other western resources and, more importantly, their ability to grab their fair share of them.

With wildlife closely associated with terrestrial wealth, conservation gained impressive support among westerners coping with the havoc of the settlement boom. After the turn of the century, British Columbia's resource industries were spreading so rapidly that local residents in the province's hinterlands thought that they had lost control to outside interests: to large American capitalists or, more simply, droves of newcomers who seemed to be taking wealth from residents. To charter members of communities, game associations played a central role in protecting nature's heritage for deserving first settlers. Not surprisingly, perhaps, the first intensive conservation activity began in areas of the province where mining resources were most hotly contested. In 1906, the Fernie Game Protective Association began work in the southeastern portion of the province, where community members claimed that "the feeling about the protection of game is stronger than [in] any other part of the province." Local residents were particularly concerned about Stoney band members who made the long journey from their reserve in the Alberta foothills on the Bow River. The first resolutions of the club demanded that the region be incorporated into the province's game ordinances and that a game reserve, off limits to Stoney hunters, be established nearby.[27]

The members of this association were well versed in conservation. Mayor Tuttle was said to be an old friend of Theodore Roosevelt and was "a great sportsman and hunter, having lived on the frontier all of his life," as one letter to the province's chief game guardian pointed out.[28] He claimed to have witnessed the slaughter of the buffalo and was "now an ardent game protector." But the story of conservation near Fernie has complex roots in the region's resource development. Mining was attracting newcomers, American investment, and ethnic workers. These developments concerned community members already living in the region. They were alarmed by the numerous outside interests now vying for resources to which they claimed some right. Fernie was undergoing a short-lived boom in population growth, and regionally the town was competing with outsiders for access to local resources. Mining leases were being quickly bought up by local and foreign companies. American branch lines were being built nearby. The Montreal-based CPR was vying for a share of the mining traffic by establishing its Crow's Nest link. Victoria businessmen, too, were bidding for what became a failed railway scheme to connect the region directly to their coastline and control.

In this setting, community members became suspicious of outsiders, whom they saw as robbing forests of game and streams of fish. It probably helped that the Fernie association was led by J.B. Turney of the Crows Nest Pass Coal Company. Turney also organized the Fernie Tourist Association, which sought to exploit the region's bountiful big-game populations. In the context of contested metropolitan control, these local conservationists mobilized against foreigners and interlopers "stealing" wealth from original town members or besmirching the region's reputation as a bountiful game haunt. The association's leading concerns were controlling Native hunters, issuing licences to foreigners, and denying miners their traditional freedom to kill anything they needed for subsistence. The association claimed that most "miners" were actually foreigners with unhampered access to game.[29]

Here the issues of access to game and rights to coal resources became linked. For example, Fernie conservationists soon locked horns with some of the most prominent and politically influential American activists. After launching similar conservation campaigns in Montana, Theodore Roosevelt and William T. Hornaday became interested in the region's game populations after the turn of the century. Both renowned conservation advocates, they pressed the province's chief game guardian to establish a regional game reserve. The Fernie association, undertaking its conservation initiatives at the same time, originally enjoyed Hornaday's blessing. In 1907, the director of the New York Zoological Society published *Camp Fires in the Canadian*

Rockies. In it, Hornaday described the region's threatened bighorn sheep populations and underscored the valuable work of the Fernie association. With the Canadian Pacific Railway in Calgary, J.S. Dennis later referred Hornaday to the provincial game guardian, Bryan Williams, noting that Hornaday "has become enthusiastic for a game reserve in that part of the Province." Hornaday was soon writing on the need to establish such a game and forest reservation in the "territory between the Elk and the Bull Rivers, British Columbia."[30]

Hornaday had already involved himself with local conservation initiatives. He believed that, on the western side of the Rockies, "So many persons are now planning to go hunting next season in that region, it seems to me very necessary that immediate steps should be taken to protect it." He claimed to know of at least half a dozen parties planning to visit the area. "The area referred to is so small that the game which now abounds in it could easily be frightened out of it, and the proposed reserve as a whole very greatly damaged. The mountain sheep within it are not sufficiently numerous to stand being hunted any more, and it will be a great pity for even one more sheep to be killed there." He promised that such a game preserve would "become a veritable wonderland for observations on big game, wild animal photography, and the enjoyment of natural scenery, both with the camera and without." He also pointed out that the area was accessible by two railways, reached from both Michel and Fort Steele. "As I have several times pointed out, there are no commercial interests at stake concerning the area in question. It contains neither coal, gold nor valuable timber."[31]

At about the same time, *Forest and Stream*, in New York, was convinced that "with proper protection British Columbia should for many years offer the best hunting to be had on this continent."[32] But here ways and means differed. Hornaday's lobby was strongly supported by Pennsylvanian coal company interests since the projected reserve did not interfere with existing coal leases. The proposed reserve land sprawled directly over the Stoney people's traditional hunting paths into the Kootenay region. Given its location, the reserve would chiefly protect bighorn sheep. Fernie sportsmen, however, disagreed with such a proposal. They wished to have a better guardian system created to restrict Stoney pot hunting and an enforced bag limit to protect sheep, goats, and bears. They wanted a reserve to protect elk.[33]

These fundamentally different points of view on conservation strategies soon divided national opinion. In 1908, Hornaday rallied a Toronto meeting of the North American Fish and Game Protective Association with an executive committee drawn from mostly eastern cities. He delivered a lecture on his projected "Goat Mountain Reserve" in British Columbia and showed a map of its location, claiming that the location was "too valuable to be any longer left open for hunting purposes."[34] He undoubtedly communicated at the meeting what he wrote to the BC game guardian – that the president of the Fernie association "must be simply crazy to oppose it!"[35] When the Toronto-based association approved Hornaday's plan and printed a brochure to gather public support for the reserve, the brochure dismissed the Fernie proposal with the comment "A fine country, that, for a game preserve! The Fernie Association is to be congratulated on the far-seeing wisdom of its choice!"[36]

Although a Cranbrook newspaper applauded Hornaday's work, his circular, later appearing in the *Calgary Herald*, caused some residents there to protest. The Hornaday initiative "smacks of unfairness," one individual wrote to the BC game guardian. It had been dreamed up by someone who has "never visited the ground on which the Fernie people base their contention," the letter writer argued.[37] The chief game guardian eventually situated the Kootenay reserve according to local opinion despite Hornaday's protests. There seems to have been considerable pressure on him to do otherwise, for Hornaday told Arthur Williams that he had even discussed such matters over breakfast with Roosevelt and communicated the American president's deep concern over wildlife populations in British Columbia.[38]

The Fernie association had coalesced to protect local interests in a period of rising uncertainty over resource development. Local conservation initiatives gained urgency when it was not clear who rightly owned and profited from the region's vast mineral wealth. First Nations, American capitalists, and "foreign" miners all seemed to undermine the rights of squatters. Indeed, in this coal-rich region of British Columbia, so close to the American border, associations were created to try to prevent outsiders from carrying away local fish and game populations. The Michel and District Anglers Association was formed in 1910, as was a Cranbrook association. These towns experienced brief population explosions. Other towns and settlements in the region also experienced sharp population surges. The Kootenay region's overall population jumped from 31,962 to 50,772 between 1901 and 1911. Mining development was attracting hordes of newcomers. The Yale and Cariboo District, which comprised the Similkameen Valley, Lillooet, Kamloops, and Grand Forks areas (all having game protective associations by the end of the decade), doubled in population. Significantly, these regions now had larger ethnic and American communities. Yale and Cariboo had as much as 50 percent of their populations designated "non-British born" in this decade, compared with Vancouver, New Westminster, and Burrard, communities with two-thirds to three-quarters of their populations "British born."[39] Even if populations remained predominantly British in certain localities, rapidly rising ethnic populations in neighbouring areas seemed to directly threaten local game. The large appetites of neighbouring mining communities likely prompted the Coldstream Gun Club to form in Vernon in 1906. By 1911, with the Kettle Valley attracting legions of outside hunters, Grand Forks sportsmen formed their own association, their letter-head reading "Shoot not for Gain but Sport and all that may be in it, and let honour, sportsmanship and good fellowship prevail."[40]

With immigration booming in the first decade of the twentieth century, urban areas recruited impressive populations, and new associations formed. When the populations of New Westminster and Vancouver rose precipi-tously, an association appeared in Richmond by 1907 to represent the inter-ests of a largely rural membership. A Delta organization appeared in 1912. Residents of Richmond and Delta believed that urban sport hunters from Vancouver were shooting out their local pheasant populations. Richmond's new conservationists urged the provincial game guardian to have trolley car drivers search under coats of passengers for illegally shot wildfowl. Mean-while, Vancouver had an association by 1901 in a period when urbanites were concerned about declining wildlife populations nearby. One city asso-ciation devoted its work to having foxes and wild turkeys reintroduced to Stanley Park in 1912.[41]

New conservation clubs organized elsewhere in BC mining and forestry frontiers. On Vancouver Island, sport hunters had become dismayed by the rising pressure of hunting near town and city, and they began to introduce game birds. A hunter from Pincher Creek, Alberta, wrote home in 1907 that he "was very much disappointed with the sport here, there is absolutely none, all the game is either frightened to death or left maimed in some way, fishing, there is none, perhaps if one went hundreds of miles, it might be had, but this is out of the question ... Even near Victoria the country is still in its natural state, hundreds of sportsmen swarm out of Victoria on every possible occasion and run amuck over anybody's land. They don't know what the word sport means."[42] Up the island's coast, where mines and for-ests attracted newcomers, the Cumberland Gun Club (1906), the Nanaimo Gun Club (1906), and the Ladysmith Gun Club (1908) formed to urge more comprehensive game ordinances. Residents were concerned that enlarging electoral bases were becoming predominately "foreign." The Nanaimo dis-trict had some 25,000 "British-born" citizens and 7,000 "foreigners," many of them Chinese. Many of these newcomers were hunting and fishing to alleviate the cost of living in inflationary resource hinterlands. Nanaimo's rich mining resources were now attracting miners, who used the province's free mining licence to hunt for subsistence without restriction. Miners, in-deed, became the special concern of conservationists. On mine paydays, conservation association leaders showed up at the town bank to make speeches to miners cashing their pay. They even managed to make some converts. Indeed, association leaders signed up everyone they could – even known poachers – to inculcate newcomers with the sportsman's ethics and express their disapproval of larder hunting.

Specific, sometimes unrecoverable, local concerns motivated citizens to create many of these organizations. Most attempted to curtail the activities of "non-British" immigrants and restrain the pot hunt. With these efforts often failing and members believing that too many freedoms were given to "miners," conservationists tried to advance more radical measures. Members of the "protective" association at Duncan, for instance, voted to have their district left unorganized and therefore unregulated when the province's game ordinances seemed to grant too many hunting freedoms to miners. From the start, members of such associations wanted to safeguard their own access to species. In the Duncan case, local sportsmen believed that ordinances were ineffective and that the sportsman's own conservation measures gave outsiders and newcomers even more opportunities for pot hunting. Others were also leery of exactly who benefited from conservation. In Cumberland and nearby Nanaimo, the provincial game guardian encountered stiff opposition among sportsmen toward his proposal to extend the game laws to their region. Although the professional ranks in associations welcomed the work of Williams, those in need of meat on the table believed him to be a CPR agent protecting game for tourists. Local sportsmen imagined a conspiracy when the game guardian arrived in town selling his ordinances at the same time that the railway was building its luxurious hotel in Nanaimo. Indeed, gun clubs from numerous communities circulated petitions against the game laws since their members believed that the CPR planned to change its land grant into a game preserve and "to prevent anybody shooting anywhere for a number of years and then open it only to tourists."[43] Having travelled to many towns up the coast, Williams found a few "absolutely uneducated socialists" who filibustered his discussion meetings. "They professed themselves in favour of protection but said they did not want the C.P.R. to do it."[44]

Alberta and British Columbia shared a resource frontier in the Crow's Nest region, where game and fish were being eaten by hungry miners – often migrant wage labourers taking seasonal jobs in mining, forestry, and farm work. In the coal-mining community of Coleman, poorly paid miners were fishing to supplement their diets. An association of sport fishers soon formed to stop them. Its leaders seem to have successfully recruited numerous ethnic newcomers. But it is not clear exactly how doing so helped to curb enormous appetites. The Department of Marine and Fisheries knew that the Coleman association was largely composed of "miners of foreign extraction, and they are more difficult to be made to observe the laws than the average English speaking person," one reason that the department encouraged the association in any way possible.[45] But the poverty driving newcomers to pot fishing and hunting became all the more apparent as settlement populations increased. It was not that original inhabitants themselves had not fished and hunted for food; rather, they no longer required this source of protein as badly. Members of associations argued that too many impoverished newcomers would eat everything available. As early as 1908, the Bow River winding through Calgary was "lined with pot hunting fishermen from morning till night," and anglers believed that their waters were depleted of trout before open season even began.[46] These anglers did not hesitate to identify the source of the problem. The ethnic makeup of pot hunters and fishers was revealed when, farther upstream, the parks commissioner translated fishing regulations in 1913 into Polish, Danish, and Italian. In 1919, the *Calgary Herald* accused Italian miners of salting down barrels of fish at Spray Lakes.[47]

The hunting and fishing activities of Amerindians and ethnic groups within park boundaries now vexed administrators. The priority of restocking the parks with fish arose in the last decade of the nineteenth century after railway construction and coal mining at Canmore and Anthracite devastated lakes and streams. By 1897, Howard Douglas, the parks commissioner, was fielding information on how to make Rocky Mountains National Park "more attractive to sportsmen" after Devil Lake and many of the streams within the park were virtually depleted by construction workers and miners.[48] When a British angler headed out from the Banff Springs Hotel to the Spray Lakes for an unsuccessful five days of fishing, he saw firsthand the effects of subsistence fishing: five miners, "Italian I think, from the Canmore coal mine," were dynamiting the lake by day, spearing fish by night, and netting bays and creeks. The visitor reported that "it appears to be a regular practice of these men."[49] The parks department followed up on the report and arrested miners who had left the shores of the lake littered with "fine trout." The incident did not end there. It created panic among CPR officials, who, contrary to the advice of the Department of Marine and Fisheries and Calgary fishers, sent a special railcar filled with five hundred brook trout from Nipigon, Ontario, to Banff to be placed in the Bow River.[50]

Throughout Alberta, game birds and fish were rapidly disappearing as settlement increased. Anglers were dismayed by the amount of pot fishing by the new settlers. This concern was apparent in the conservation movement begun by Richard A. Darker, who travelled through the settled areas of the province to create the Southern Alberta Fish and Game Protective Association. He called an organizational meeting in Calgary and drew no fewer than eighty delegates, many from the southern towns of the province. A representative of the Department of Marine and Fisheries attended the meeting and judged the group to be made up of the "best settlers in the country and principal men of the towns and villages."[51] Over three days in 1907, the delegates decided the best fishing times on rivers and a number of game matters. Among their concerns were "that the foreigners be prevented from getting access [to dynamite] for illegitimate purposes" and prohibiting the barter, sale, or trade of trout.[52]

Such associations drew members from a town's professional and wealthy ranks. Often physicians, lawyers, and wealthy ranchers formed their executives. Darker, himself a sales manager of Canada Life in Calgary, was an ardent sportsman closely connected to other civic associations, particularly the auto club. He lived in Mount Royal and participated in both the Rotary Club and the Alizar Temple. Darker pursued hunting as a cherished leisure activity when he could get away from his many civic duties and hard work. He and his friends often headed out on the CPR to be dropped off at a siding, to which they would return days later "bearded and smelling of fish." His company's in-house magazine profiled him after the success of a sales program in southern Alberta and described him as a paragon of sportsmanship: "seven feet of muscular manhood."[53]

Darker's association appeared, not coincidentally, with the province's establishment. Its members wanted to influence the writing of game ordinances. The association's letterhead soon reached the office of the provincial game guardian and the federal Department of Marine and Fisheries, which administered provincial fisheries until the transfer of resources in 1930. The association immediately shaped an agenda to make Alberta's foothills, meadows, and prairies into a sport hunting and fishing paradise. The province's minister of agriculture attended the first meetings and promised to incorporate proposals regarding game into the regulations for the following year. The group vigorously pursued restocking programs. In 1907, Calgarians Fred Green and George Wood undertook a failed experiment to introduce bobtailed quail to the nearby prairie. Austin B. de Winter, who assisted Darker and ran the Calgary chapter of the association, was himself a wealthy Mount Royal resident who subsequently attempted to introduce Hungarian partridge and Chinese ringnecks and Mongolian pheasants. Winter, in fact, raised his broods in his backyard in Mount Royal. In 1910, the association actively sought to reduce bag limits allowed to anglers, lower than the twenty-five trout a day; to establish nearby a fish hatchery to restock depleted streams; and to develop strategies to maintain and enhance the local stream's sport fishing reputation. In 1912, Winter urged the elimination of grayling in the Bow River to make room for more sporting cold-water trout varieties.[54]

These associations increased their work with the further sweep of settlement. Ranks mustered in obscure settings such as Wetaskiwin. There a branch of the SAFGPA was created in 1910 with no fewer than fifty members. The Calgary *Eye Opener* found the amount of pot fishing and hunting by then remarkable. It reported one party of fishers getting away with a hundred undersized trout from a local stream. The Department of Marine and Fisheries overseer in southern Alberta believed that a guardian should be appointed

Table 3

Incorporation dates of sample fish and game associations compared with local population changes, 1901-21

Town or city	Year of Association's creation	1901 population	1911 population	% change from 1901	1921 population	% change from 1911
Ladysmith, BC	1908	n/a	3295	–	9634	192
Nanaimo, BC	1906	n/a	8168	–	8877	9
Fernie, BC	1907	n/a	3146	–	4353	38
Cranbrook, BC	1908	n/a	3090	–	2725	-12
Similkameen Valley, BC	1912	n/a	3721	–	7457	100
Vancouver, BC	1907	27010	60104	123	60879	1
Blairmore, AB	1925	231	1137	392	1552	36
Coleman, AB	1925	n/a	1557	–	1590	2
High River, AB	1920	153	1182	673	1198	1
Macleod, AB	1921	796	1844	132	1723	-7
Okotoks, AB	1925	245	516	111	448	-13
Pincher Creek, AB	1920	335	1027	207	888	-14
Stavely, AB	1919	n/a	245	–	292	19
Drumheller, AB	1928	101	583	477	668	15
Calgary, AB	1919	4392	25125	472	32188	28

in each town, "for it is in proximity of the town that most reckless fishing is done."[55]

But while many associations formed in the context of rising western populations in the first decade of the century, many more coalesced when initial population booms could not be sustained. This demographic development of the Great War appeared clearly in the 1921 federal census. Association leaders reacted to the perceived threat posed by residents of other communities who were invading their locales and killing their wildlife. Table 3 shows a sample of the many associations that formed during periods of population crisis. As regional populations continued to climb, local community members were under the impression that rival settlements were drawing more settlers, who were now carrying away bird, fish, and game species from their own locales. This was hardly a trivial matter given the rising concern in communities to make their region appear particularly blessed by nature. Boosters were anxious that a community's natural resources appeal to outside investors and prospective settlers. Now there was an all-out race for rail links and branch lines to sustain infant communities. And new capital projects could only be paid for by newcomers, who would bolster a town's population and swell tax rolls.

Many associations formed immediately after the First World War, when townspeople became concerned by the number of fishers visiting streams. By 1919, Charles Hayden, the *Calgary Herald* editor (who went on to form the Alberta Fish and Game Association in 1929), was certain that without protection angling might become "a lost science" as far as Alberta was concerned.[56] The letterhead of the Claresholm Fish and Game Protective Association spread the new watchwords: "Be a Sport – Don't Be a Hog."[57] With the end of the First World War, indeed, as sufficient settlement took place, serious competition was setting in between anglers and pot fishers. Edmonton's population shot from a mere 2,600 to almost 35,000 in the decade before 1920. The Northern Alberta Game and Fish Protective League, following the lead of Calgary conservationists, formed shortly after the war in the opulent Macdonald Hotel "to further the interests of sportsmen by planting game birds and fish in local fields and waters, giving all game protection during closed seasons and to advocate legislation that will be helpful toward the end of increasing game and fish."[58] From Edmonton to Macleod, town and farming populations increased sixfold to sevenfold in the same period. Most anglers believed that poaching out of season and ordinance violations in season were on the rise.[59]

But even more problematic to these local observers was the foreign poacher. The Coleman Rod and Gun Club in 1925 joined the nearby Bellevue club largely to protect Crow's Nest Pass waters when the Alberta government completed highway work.[60] Not surprisingly, the measure that most interested such communities was tributary closure, aimed directly at deterring outsiders from local streams. The stream closure movement eventually prompted the Department of Marine and Fisheries to rewrite ordinances. The Coleman Rod and Gun Club urged stream closure, as did the Pincher Creek Board of Trade. Both communities faced difficulties maintaining town populations in the brisk settlement period. Both associations were adamant that tributaries of the Old Man and Crow's Nest Rivers should be closed to the hordes of outsiders now using automobiles to drive into the region. These motorists were particularly intrepid, driving along roads to their ends and thereafter rocky floodplains to reach favourite fishing holes. Most associations therefore complained a great deal about anglers gaining access to the river and stream frontage on privately leased ranch- and farmland, where they caused a "nuisance." The local conservationists even claimed that outsiders did not bother closing gates behind them and left rubbish at their campsites. One fisheries official queried whether "there may be a personal reason for these farmers wishing to have the streams closed, other than for the protection of fish."[61]

It was in the context of massive infusions of auto and rail visitors that the tributary closure took effect in 1927. Then Alberta streams tributary to the Old Man, Crow's Nest, and Waterton Rivers, comprising some eighteen streams, were closed to fishing. But there was little unanimity among associations on this issue. These associations, after all, had been created locally, and many were not affiliated with a central organization. When Calgarians first proposed tributary closure on their own streams in 1920, the Pincher Creek conservation association balked, complaining that the action would be imposed by outsiders and that many homesteaders in the area needed fish for food during the summer, when the tributaries in question were usually open. What the Pincher Creek association really wanted, as did most in the Canadian west, was protection of fish and game for local use. So did anglers in Okotoks, struggling with stagnant population growth. They formed the Foothills Angling Association in 1921 largely to pressure the federal government to open nearby Willow Creek for their use.[62]

When fishing remained an important mainstay of subsistence for some, and a dearly held sport for others, the Department of Marine and Fisheries looked to these associations for advice and realized that few bodies of fishermen held the same opinions. In boomtown Calgary, conservation associations could adamantly oppose each other's proposals. Those affiliated with the Calgary Anglers Association (CAA), created in 1920, wanted liberal regulations mostly to suit a tourist industry that would offer visitors open access to the Bow River during the summer months. Although its first executive had lobbied for stream closure, it urged the measure only for northerly streams flowing into the Red Deer River – presumably because tourists visited mainly the southerly streams. Members meanwhile believed that the closures demanded by smaller towns to the south were too restrictive, would create too much congestion on open waters, and would encourage too much illegal fishing.[63]

The CAA had obvious connections to railway and booster groups for which angling figured as an important city attraction and revenue generator. By 1917, Calgary anglers had made sure that season opening dates on the Bow River were pushed back in blatant contradiction of the season dates in Rocky Mountains National Park, dates previously decided by Darker's association in 1907.[64] Wartime anglers simply wanted to catch fish as soon as the weather permitted. Some CAA members advocated even earlier summer angling seasons to benefit the tourist industry, one reason why a local businessman running a sporting goods store was able to get no fewer than 171 signatures on a petition for earlier open seasons.[65] The same anglers held radical views on the numbers of fish that ordinances allowed. Approving of the existing limit of twenty-five trout a day, the CAA wanted the government to allow open and unlimited fishing for the unattractive Dolly Varden (bull trout). Anglers not only believed that this measure would eventually make more room for more sporting fish but also knew that visitors would enjoy catching the Dolly Varden for its sheer size. These anglers wanted the fishing season to remain open, with a prize for the person who caught the largest number of fish, with proceeds going to Calgary hospitals.[66]

Far different aims prompted the activities of the Southern Alberta Fisherman's Association, which formed in 1919. Its origin as an angling association seems to trail to 1915, when John F. Eastwood reported to the Department of Marine and Fisheries that the association was interested in having its membership "act as a protector" of fish.[67] Eastwood had ambitious plans for the group. They included providing the federal department with an annual blue book report on the association, gathering data on the habits of fish in Alberta, and even creating a breeding pond to stock depleted streams. Its members were far more possessive of local piscine resources. Immediately after its formation, ranchers and prominent Calgary businessmen joined. Starting correspondence with the "flourishing" Coleman Angling Club, these anglers became some of the more ardent advocates of tributary closures. They could also appear the most comical in communities because of the evangelical edge of early conservation. One frequent letter writer to Ottawa reported his activities as a volunteer ordinance enforcer, hiding in bushes to capture Calgary "fish hogs" who went over the limit. The watchdog said that some of the poachers, such as a couple and their child, who were taking some eighty fish from the Bow River, laughed at him when he asked to see their licence.[68]

The case of High River, Alberta, perhaps illustrates how local social and economic concerns determined the priorities of such early protective associations. Richard A. Darker had visited the town as early as 1909 to encourage the locals to join his game protective association, though it is unclear how successful he had been.[69] In these heady years of town building, residents were wildly optimistic about the future: between 1901 and 1911, town population rose over 600 percent. In 1906, the High River *Times* was certain that "the natural advantages combined with the sagacity of her people make that town certain to reach metropolitan proportions in a few years."[70] A settler anonymously wrote in the paper that the town was "at the very heart of Alberta, if not the hub of the universe," having attracted settlers from all quarters. They had "merely touched the fringe of available agricultural land and mineral resources."[71] By 1909, the *Times* editor, Charles Clark, stated that "a pessimist of the worst type is he who would say that High River's prospects at the present time are not the greatest."[72] That year, when new trout-fishing regulations were introduced, the High River *Times* appropriated the optimism of the townspeople. Noting the new, shortened angling season (the open date moving from March 1 to May 1) and the limits on selling trout, the editor wrote that "A true sportsman will not go out of his way to help in the destruction of what is a great asset to the country."[73]

But between 1911 and 1921, the town's expectations were seriously undermined by a disappointing one percent population growth. The war, of course, affected population growth. But town leaders suspected other forces at work. The *Times* editor now harped on the need for townspeople to keep streets clean, chided those who did not boost the reputation of the town, and began campaigning for incorporation. The Highwood River, flowing through town, soon nourished rivals such as Claresholm and Carmangay down the Little Bow diversion. By 1908, Claresholm was already outshining High River after building an electric light plant and beginning to plan a waterworks. Stavely, too, was making plans for a waterworks.

It was in the context of slowing development in 1919 that townspeople became concerned about fish depletion. Town anglers estimated that during the previous season some one thousand undersized trout had been poached in closed periods. In 1920, the Highwood River Angling Protective Association (HRAPA) formed, firmly independent of Calgary groups and championing "the interest of fish culture and protection in High River."[74] Its executive included many of High River's most prominent citizens, such as H.D. Elliot, a local bank manager and the president of the group. A.A. Ballachey, a High River lawyer and an active member and executive officer, replaced Elliot as president in 1928. At the first meeting in 1920, George Lane, horse breeder and town patriarch, was elected as honorary vice president. The membership also made Edward, Prince of Wales (at that time an avid angler on his stocked lake on the E.P. Ranch), honorary president. Nonexecutive members included the Count de Foras and town lawyer A.Y. McCorquodale. By 1922, the association had gathered some fifty members, "representatives of all walks of life in this community from farmers to ranchers to barristers, and bankers," all united to have the Highwood River's natural bounty preserved.[75]

In High River's case, members of the local association rallied around a community myth suggesting that the Highwood River was traditionally a stream teeming with cutthroat trout, the "king" of sport fishes, which was now losing its place to rival species. The association therefore began urging eradication programs or regulations to fish out graylings. As the association wrote to Ottawa, "we are anxious to see everything done that can be done to preserve it [as a cutthroat trout stream] even if it has to be at the expense of the grayling."[76] This would not have been an isolated case in which a local movement formed to purge streams of unattractive fish to make room for more sporting varieties. Although the first fishing laws had not protected "nuisance" fish such as the Dolly Varden, by the 1920s local opinion was that it was good to take as many of them, as well as suckers, as possible so that streams could be improved. Fisheries guardians had to counter the agitation of members of the Calgary Fish and Game Protective Association in 1928, seeking permission to take bull trout at any time, when streams were frequented by rainbow and cutthroat trout.[77]

In High River, the "problem" of "nuisance" fish continued to motivate association members, who actually attempted to estimate how far suckers, grayling, and bull trout were invading the river's upper reaches and tributaries. They concurrently enumerated the outsiders visiting their backyard fishing holes. Dave Blacklock, a local angling authority, urged the High River citizen to become "a member of a club whose main object is 'clean sport' and plenty of it." In his lecture sponsored by the Highwood River Angling Protective Association, he noted "the amounts of cars bearing men and women, old and young, coming from the cities with tents, frying pans, and fishing rods." The lecturer charged the community to be on its guard – and he was confident that, through the association's vigilance, in years to come, the Highwood River and others nearby could become "the mecca for thousands of visitors, who, *along with members of this club*, enjoy this great sport, in this, one of the greatest countries the Lord has ever allowed a man to cast a hook."[78]

The tributary closure movement had much of its genesis in High River, where it was taken up as a popular grassroots cause in the war years. Theoretically, tributary closure would take fishing pressure off breeding fish and allow smaller fish, believed to inhabit smaller streams, to grow to sufficient size before they migrated to main rivers, where controlled fishing would occur. Throughout the First World War, community anglers noted fish depletions in the Highwood River. They became advocates of stricter regulations for the next decade. Telegrams and letters postmarked High River often landed on the desks of bewildered Ottawa bureaucrats demanding that the Highwood's tributaries be off limits to anglers. Ranchers, farmers, lawyers, and even bedridden convalescents at the High River hospital voiced their disapproval of officials who foolishly tampered with "natural law" in this respect or implemented what were perceived as unsound conservation policies in their town's river.[79]

H.D. Elliot, the first president of the Highwood protective association and one of the town's most skilled fly fishermen, eventually established links with American angling groups such as the powerful Isaac Walton League of America, whose national secretary visited the Highwood River in the mid-1920s. At that time, H.J. Morgan called it one of the greatest trout streams in the world. Through American protective association newsletters, Elliot kept abreast of US conservation policies. He probably learned of "natural hatcheries" from this source. One newsletter in his possession, published by the American Game Protective Association, carried a story describing the closed tributary system in place in Quebec's Rowley Hunting and Fishing Preserve. "The little fish keep to the small waters; the big naturally drift to the larger," the story claimed. "Even in waters which are heavily fished a constant supply of new stock may be obtained by closing to all fishing the feeder streams."[80]

The 1919 petition of town anglers for tributary closure, these "natural breeding grounds" of the Highwood River, requested two years of closure.[81] Elliot and other anglers reacted when in 1920 the local fish guardian noted a startling downturn in the number of trout entering the river via tributaries. Their new association's lobbying that year led to the first tributary closures. Frank Watt, another local angler and secretary of the association, reported on the program. Closed tributaries would "serve as more or less natural breeding places for trout who when they come to a certain size will probably go into the main stream and help to keep it stocked."[82]

As a solution to fish depletion, the "natural hatchery" idea applied on the Highwood River spread to other foothills communities. Fish Creek anglers demanded the closing of Bow and Elbow tributaries, and Walter E. Robi, of the Calgary Angling Association (formed largely to pressure the government for stream closures), asked for Fish, Bragg, and all creeks "that flow into the Bow from the north" to be closed.[83] By November 1920, Richard A. Darker and his affiliates in the Southern Alberta Angling Association pushed for the closure of all tributaries in southern Alberta for two years. Overwhelmed by the outcry for the measure, the Department of Marine and Fisheries complied in 1921 and closed virtually all foothills tributaries.[84]

Throughout the decade, a debate ensued about how long such streams should remain closed. Darker's association moved for permanent closure of Highwood tributaries or at least until 1925. By 1927, Coleman and Pincher Creek associations successfully closed feeder streams of the Old Man, Crow's Nest, and Waterton Rivers "indefinitely" – a large watershed including eighteen significant streams.

Behind such conservation initiatives, however, were economic developments and the turmoil of settlement. A new railway branch line and – likely more significant – a network of new road systems built in southern portions of the province increased access to remote reaches of river systems. The 2A Highway south from Calgary to the western portions of the Highwood River soon brought anglers out by the carload. Rambling into remote and picturesque reaches, they pulled out fishing rods stored under rumble seats whenever a promising stream appeared. Contemporaries gravely viewed the increasing number of fishers who now appeared along stream frontages and sloshed through spawning beds. Back in High River, Elliot wrote to the department that "owing to good roads ... and new bridges built by the Alberta government ... tourist traffic on the river was greater [in 1922] than in any previous year, and the river fished to a greater extent than ever before."[85] Watt wrote to the department that automobiles allowed anglers to venture into remote reaches of the river; their driving along the rocky riverbed meant "that the trout are very scarce and very wary."[86]

High River citizens were not the only foothills residents witnessing the onrush of angling tourists. The Bow, Elbow, Old Man, and Red Deer Rivers, Bragg Creek, and tributaries were favoured by tourists, who were soon a nuisance to ranchers. Along Willow Creek, "hundreds" of outsiders from Nanton, Stavely, Champion, and Carmangay camped and fished, leaving gates open and rubbish strewn over the countryside. Not surprisingly, ranchers supported Watt's and Elliot's proposed tributary closures. A Willow Creek rancher sought stream closure to protect his fish from such bothersome campers. Bragg Creek community members asked for "protective" tributary closures of the Elbow River after Calgary anglers proved to be irksome on their riverside properties.[87] Near Pincher Creek, a Todd Creek "conservationist" wanted to close a stream that ran through his property to allow him to "have fishing for himself" and "to keep others out," as one overseer reported.[88] Along Highwood tributaries, cattlemen had to "put up broken fences, shut gates, catch and remove tin cans from the lower jaw and hoofs of cattle, due to careless campers."[89] As early as 1918, George Stanley pointed out that the river's tributaries were being camped by people from Calgary, Lethbridge, Vulcan, Okotoks, and other towns, "endangering the fishery."[90]

The High River association had statistics to prove its point. In 1926, its members took a count of cars and anglers. They reported 33 anglers from Okotoks, 181 from High River, 16 from Longview, 73 from Black Diamond, and no fewer than 1,968 from Calgary. On a single Sunday afternoon, they counted 300 cars of anglers passing the first rancher's gate some thirty kilometres west of town, deep in tributary country. The association claimed that all of these people were tourists who "visit our enticing pools and beautiful runs to be found along the course of the alluring Highwood River."[91]

Ever protective of their resources, High River anglers showed little charity toward tourists suspected of injuring their sport fisheries. Visitors caught on closed waters were consistently given the highest fines in the province. Two anglers caught on Pekisko Creek – a closed tributary of the Highwood River – were given fines of fifty dollars, and the following year four others received the same judgment, the highest fines in the province. The local association in fact wanted a fine of a thousand dollars handed out for such an offence (tin signs nailed to nearby trees ominously announced "You're liable to a fine of $1,000 and imprisonment if apprehended fishing illegally. BEWARE").[92] Members became vocal watchdogs at poachers' trials, insisting on high fines or approving of fines being waived if the visitor promised to leave the area and never come back. Calgary newspapers noticed the lynch-mob quality of such trials, particularly one in 1926 where two Calgary anglers were tried for fishing at Pekisko Creek. HRAPA members present at the trial unsuccessfully pressured the magistrate to give the offenders thousand-dollar fines. "High River anglers," the *Calgary Herald* noted dryly, "are taking their fishing propensities seriously."[93]

The association's close ties to the Department of Marine and Fisheries led to one of the most sensational trials for poaching in the province's history. In 1929, the local fish guardian arrested two Turner Valley sportsmen who had rented a cabin near the Highwood River for day-hunting trips. An over-the-limit cache of trout found in the cabin landed the two in a courtroom, where both the fisheries department and the HRAPA sought to prove their guilt. The fish guardian gave testimony. The Calgary overseer drove to the trial to join the proceedings and act as court stenographer. A.A. Ballachey, by then president of the HRAPA and a prominent High River lawyer, represented the Crown (free of charge!). Meanwhile, other High River anglers and townspeople crowded into the courtroom for the four-hour trial. It became "the most important and impressive hearing that has occurred in my district," the Calgary fisheries officer reported to Ottawa. Even though he lost the case, he said that the public attention generated during the trial had helped the conservation cause.[94]

Another association had earlier launched a similar high-profile case. In 1928, the Didsbury Fish and Game Protective Association took up the case of four town youths suspected of dynamiting a trout stream. The association rented a movie theatre for a capacity-audience trial, which the Crown won. "The general public is now realizing that strict enforcement of the Regulations is necessary," the Calgary overseer wrote, "and that the public sentiment is against such offenses."[95]

Much of this conservation work grew from local concerns about outsiders' access to local resources. Riparian lessees and ranchers were experiencing a "serious amount of damage through persons camping on their hay meadows which are situated along the banks of the river."[96] As a fisheries overseer believed, the stream closure movement and much of the protection offered by associations were motivated by these local concerns. A good number of ranchers supporting stream closure felt "more disposed to tell a fisherman to go elsewhere than they would to examine a creel or to check up on a man's catch if the creeks were open."[97] The federal fisheries department itself knew that, in the case of the High River association, local and foreign anglers were treated differently. The association, for instance, asked magistrates not to fine local farmers for abusing the regulations, and it objected when only small fines were given to outsiders committing the same offence.

Conservation grew from a settler's concern for the land and its bounty. Biota, we have seen, could easily be transformed by boosters into valuable symbols of wealth. Westerners investing their future in the soils and grasses near townships were, in the early pioneer period, easily led to doubt the land's capacity to provide equally for themselves and newcomers. Whether town or city populations rose rapidly or stagnated chronically, citizens turned to fish and game protection as a means of preserving a stake in the wealth that others seemed to be tapping. Westerners undoubtedly estimated and understood that wealth differently than outsiders. But many demanded the rewards promised to them in a frontier setting, one reason why fishing and hunting were recounted so often in pioneer reminiscences. When Dr. W.A. Bigelow wrote his life story as a physician in western Canada, it was tellingly entitled *Forceps, Fins, and Feathers*. He devoted much space to his duck hunting in marshlands and his fishing in Rocky Mountains National Park (Banff).[98] Sport was an important part of his social life. But fish and game enthusiasts were also using wildlife as a means of estimating the profits of their western experience. They imagined wealth within reach when they saw spawning runs jamming nearby tributaries. Perhaps understandably, they sought to protect their own access to that resource through conservation efforts. In this respect, the creeks and rivers running through their land or directly through towns had powerful meaning.

Most alarming to residents, indeed, was the possibility that outsiders might preempt local resources. Their concerns were realized when land speculators seized and drove up prices on vacant town lots or when townships remained sparsely populated because of abandoned homesteads. Entire farming communities became angry about railway companies whose choice lands provided the best river and lake access. It was probably in the context of such jealousy that settlers grew uneasy when tourists came to view, hunt, or purchase as souvenirs wildlife. By the turn of the century, many railway visitors, intent on seeing nature, considered wild animals a leading attraction in the west. Wild animals, indeed, certified a back-to-nature visit. For that reason, Arthur Wheeler, soon leading the Alpine Club, in 1904 pressured the Department of the Interior to increase its wildlife protection, even of bears, in Rocky Mountains National Park. "The protection of goat, caribou and other deer should be made something more than mere legislation," he wrote to the department, "and bear should be included in the list."[99] Wheeler himself was an ardent sportsman, and his work suggests the dilemma confronting a larger settler society. Although he promoted western visits, particularly to the mountain parks, he feared the impact of visitors on these natural places. He opposed the building of amenities within the parks, viewed by administrators as necessary when tourists' visits increased. Wheeler meanwhile believed that wildlife so integral to a nature visit should be protected from overexploitation. "If it could only be realized how greatly the sight of a bear, sheep or goat, or even of one of the smaller fur-bearing mammals in its native home adds to the pleasure and excitement of a Tourist's visit," he said, it stamps the experience "as the 'real thing', and how it is talked about and spread abroad." Wheeler believed that "it would soon be made apparent that there is more money in these animals alive than in a temporary value derived from their pelts."[100]

What Wheeler and other westerners were realizing about wildlife was that exploitation, beginning with promotion, often led to exhaustion. Indeed, many early conservationists recognized the possibility that wildlife, like other features of the raw land, could be transferred easily into the outsider's possession. Wildlife protection was therefore identified as an important new priority by tourism industries. In Depression-era Alberta, when the government sought tourist revenue to supplement a badly sagging economy, the provincial publicity commissioner, Colin G. Groff, began urging that "specially qualified agents" be placed in American cities to advertise the national parks and "to develop and direct tourist traffic to Canada with particular reference, of course, to Alberta."[101] In his memos to the parks department, he stressed the need to protect "many of the animals in the parks which are part of the parks' attractive features."[102] By the early twentieth century, it was accepted largely without debate that wildlife was integral to any representation of true wilderness, one reason why a New York travelogue speaker, Thomas Travis, insisted on including wildlife in his slide and motion picture shows. When he began making arrangements to visit Banff in 1928 by writing to guide Pat Brewster, he explained that his programs were intended "directly to advertise your part of the country, and a great deal depends on our getting the pictures. I had in mind not only scenery, but the small game and fish, and would like to get some good pictures of the Ptarmigan, Gopher, or Whistling Marmot, the Water Weasel and all such things as nests and birds and of course a few bear or porcupine if they happen along. Then too the fish will be very important."[103]

Zoos were one way to share rights to such a resource. Western inhabitants had long recognized that wild animal zoos could attract and please visitors. In 1884, Alexander Begg suggested that the Department of the Interior build a "zoological branch" at Banff that would make "this beautiful and interesting locality still more attractive."[104] Begg suggested that it build a zoo to keep moose, elk, caribou, black-tailed, and other varieties of deer. Most necessary of all was the maintenance of a buffalo herd "which but a few years since roamed in hundreds of thousands over the prairie and along Bow River."[105] To tourists, wildlife animated the natural world and helped to "harmonize with and embody the mystery of our wilderness," as Maxwell Graham once said when he urged greater protection of birds in park areas.[106] At Banff, in particular, a "game park," once created, quickly became one of the most popular places in the park. The zoo comprised some three miles of fenced area to the north of the townsite. In 1907, twelve thousand people visited the compound, which by then contained seventy-nine buffalo, fifteen moose, eleven elk, seven mule deer, four Persian sheep, six angora goats, and two mountain lions.[107]

Many western efforts to protect wildlife were based on the fear that, outside zoo limits, a resource integral to western representation could be quickly overexploited. In 1905, the *Vancouver Daily Province* reported that Jim Brewster, one of the "best known mountain pioneers," who ran an outfitting service in Banff and escorted hunters to game locations in the foothills region, was blaming Stoney hunters for game population downturns. "Where big game hunters a few years ago could get grizzlies, silver tips, mountain sheep, elk, moose and deer without a particle of effort," the Banff outfitter said, "to-day much time and trained guides are necessary."[108] The story was relevant to newspaper readers who shared an interest in the region and who would have been alarmed that individuals – outsiders – were exhausting the land's wealth. Brewster indeed attributed the changes in game populations to "the Indians from the prairies," whom he claimed were making about twenty-five dollars for each bighorn sheep head sold to tourists. Brewster was not entirely candid about the amount of pressure exerted on these animal populations through sport hunting. A New York newspaper credited the mountain man with killing over 150 grizzly bears.[109] But Brewster's report well captured the western concern that a resource might be lost to outside interests, and the guide well understood the great foreign demand for wildlife souvenirs. The accounts of Brewster Trading Company, owned and operated by the Brewster brothers, suggest that tourists offered lucrative sideline profits. For 1907 alone, the company prepared 112 bighorn sheep heads at ninety-five dollars each; 4 deer heads at twenty-five dollars each; a moose valued at one hundred dollars; an elk at one hundred dollars; and an antelope at twenty dollars. There were also a number of unmounted sheep heads, caribou, and a host of other specimens, including the hides of four large grizzlies and three black bears.[110]

For all the economic benefits of tourists' visits, then, their demand for animal souvenirs revealed the problematic issue of resource exploitation. Rail and then road travellers were buying a sheep or goat head, animal pelt, or antler set while in the west. The phenomenal growth of the "head trade" after the building of the CPR sheds light on the value that these visitors, often from urban settings, placed on animals as souvenirs. Western sportspeople were among the first to object to this trade, and they began campaigning against it by 1900, when train travellers were buying heads from tourist shops and curio dealers, many of them specializing in buying heads from Amerindians and reselling them at or near train depots. John McDougall seems to have encouraged Stoney hunters to take up the trade, much to the anger of sport hunters in the late 1880s. Stoneys at Exshaw and Morley sold heads long after the provincial government banned their sale in 1905. Continuing infractions reported in courts suggest that Amerindians were selling the pelts and heads of animals that they were probably hunting for food to travellers and urban businesspeople far into the 1920s.

Even after ordinances prohibited sales of heads, visitors took advantage of loopholes to procure these prizes. Alberta's regulations allowed a hunter to sell a trophy directly to a buyer with a signed affidavit. Heads in a raw state were often legal to ship, but mounted heads were not. By 1908, the Department of Agriculture had to rush a supply of affidavits to the Exshaw Trading Company, in the shadow of the Rockies, "as there are a number of heads arriving at that point daily," Benjamin Lawton, the chief game guardian, reported.[111] Many of those heads were later sold through dealers in the United States and western Canada from stores such as Norman Luxton's Sign of the Goat curio shop in Banff. Luxton was a self-described wilderness man, taxidermist, newspaper editor, and town promoter. He opened his crowded curio shop in Banff at the turn of the century. At one point, he kept a live bear tied up near his store entrance. Travellers were enthralled by the wild animal pelts, heads, furs, and Native curios crowding shelves and covering walls.[112]

Most of Luxton's wares were supplied by his brother-in-law, D.M. McDougall, who ran a taxidermy outlet called the Morley Trading Company. Luxton's business correspondence and ledgers suggest the dimensions of demand for wildlife keepsakes at both stores. Luxton recorded selling to a Philadelphia businessman one grizzly bear skin, one wolf head, three coyote skins, and three goat skins in 1905. To another American tourist, Luxton supplied two wolverine skins, one cross fox skin, one grizzly bear skin, and a fox muff. Tourists in Banff, stepping off the train platform into a romanticized wilderness, "Walhalla" as some liked to imagine it, looked to Luxton to supply some of the most important relics of what they considered a spiritual journey. Meanwhile, he received from Morley hunters and nearby settlers massive quantities of wares that he later sold to tourists. A farmer and hunter from Brooks, Alberta, in 1907 sent Luxton two foxes, offered the skulls of coyotes, and promised to send on some antelope heads. The same year, a hunter from Vernon, British Columbia, sold Luxton a mountain lion skin.[113]

The head trade in British Columbia disconcerted the provincial warden, Arthur Williams, along with numerous fish and game associations. Williams found the sale of trophies and wild meat explicitly at odds with the plan to have wealthy sport hunters find big game in the province. Even after laws prohibited trophy sales to nonhunters, far too many means existed to support this exploitation of wildlife. In 1909, the chief game guardian encouraged, without much success, station agents to inspect permits for each head being shipped out of the province by rail. "A great many animals and heads of animals find their way out of East Kootenay every year," he said in one letter to the CPR, requesting that its agents be vigilant. He also ordered Victoria and Vancouver taxidermists to obtain a licence before they exported trophies. He even investigated the origins of taxidermy adorning the prestigious Union Club in Victoria, where sportsmen met, played pool, and discussed hunting.[114]

Governments in Alberta, Saskatchewan, and Manitoba recognized that travellers and city dwellers were buying big-game specimens as souvenirs. Under the direction of the chief game guardian, Charles Barber, Manitoba began compiling statistics of exported heads in 1902. Seventy-seven mounted heads were reported by the department that year, including moose, deer, elk, and caribou. Over the next decade, Barber statistically monitored the hundreds of heads, hides, antlers, and scalps of animals – including moose, elk, deer, jumping deer, black-tailed deer, caribou, and antelope – exported from the province.[115]

A further element of pioneer fish and game protection, however, appeared in interwar restocking efforts and wildlife preservation programs. The development of wildlife preservation in the national parks system has already been studied by Janet Foster. However, the interest among western settlers in wildlife reserves and restocking activities has largely gone unnoticed in environmental history. By the time that federal entomologist Gordon Hewitt was writing his *Conservation of the Wild Life in Canada* (which appeared in print in 1921 after his death), game reserves had been established throughout the west. Joined with the growing national park reserves and sometimes created in the vast forestry lands transferred to provincial control, these game reserves totalled some twenty thousand square miles by 1921. That amount constituted about two-thirds of the area reserved for wildlife across Canada. By 1911, a reduction of "forest reserve parks" had created a system of "national" parks such as Waterton and Yoho. Glacier, Elk Island, Jasper, Mount Revelstoke, and Kootenay were formed or in the making in the same period.[116] These "breeding" areas were by no means supported only by federal officials. The seventy residents of Edmonton who originally urged the territorial government to establish what became Elk Island National Park in 1904 – to preserve a small herd of elk east of the city – were reacting to the visible decline of wildlife populations nearby. In 1906, Fort Saskatchewan residents began building an enclosure in the Cooking Lake Forest Reserve.[117] Meanwhile, the news in 1907 that the federal government had purchased buffalo for Alberta reserves prompted the Saskatchewan Game Protective Association to demand that its province too "should receive a portion of the herd" for a reserve. The same sportsmen were interested in Manitoba's plans to reserve areas at Riding Mountain.[118]

Westerners who took up fish and game conservation usually looked forward to establishing a local game or "breeding" area near their towns and cities. Such spaces would be legislated as either game preserves or public shooting areas. Whether as an area for controlled hunting or as an area for the "spillover" of game to adjacent regions, the game preserve was, by the end of the First World War, an important public matter. Lethbridge townsfolk were proud to have some of "the last of the antelope" protected near their community in the federal Nemiskam Antelope Park; settlers near Wainwright were equally enthusiastic that buffalo were being preserved on federal land nearby. Communities also built local reserves or zoos. The Moose Jaw game park has already been described. Throughout the 1920s, individuals set aside some property for wildlife. Along the Highwood River, Archie Hogg dedicated considerable portions of his farm for wildfowl habitat. He was influenced by the memory of his father, who had conserved prairie chicken habitat at the turn of the century. Many of these individual efforts at game preservation went unrecorded. Gordon Hewitt described R. Lloyd, at Davidson, Saskatchewan, who reared antelope on his farm. Hewitt encouraged other farmers to convert some of their land into private reserves of this type.[119] The "protection of game and wild life on the farm requires neither special knowledge nor great expense," he wrote, believing that wildlife would enhance the attractiveness of farms and "retain some portion of the youth that now finds farm life too uninteresting, and migrates to the cities."[120]

By the early 1920s, the concept of a game preserve had been popularized by Jack Miner in Ontario and American conservationists such as William T. Hornaday. In theory, the game reserve offered numerous benefits to nearby communities. Primarily, it acted as a breeding area – that is, it protected animals from hunting pressure and controlled as much as possible the damaging effects of natural predators. The offspring of game animals, in return, would multiply and naturally expand their range beyond reserve boundaries to offer game to nearby communities. Western Canadian commentary on reserves suggests that such theoretical ends were considerably extended by pioneers. Westerners saw wild animal reserves sustaining nature's wealth and even influencing the character of nearby settler communities. Fundamentally, the settler believed that a game preserve made wildlife both "abundant and fearless." By protecting wildlife species within a geographical space, humans could ensure the continued abundance of wild animals. By removing human hunting pressure and predatory animals, these regions reestablished an ideal, if not pre-Fall, concord in nature whereby peace between animals and humans could be restored. Such an outcome in game preservation was, not surprisingly, extremely important for settlers building their new western society.

It seems to have been intentional, too, that westerners imagined such ideal ends of game preservation after the Great War. Undoubtedly, the sacrifice of war prompted western Canadians, like Europeans and other North Americans, to hope that the darker aspects of competitive Darwinian nature could be better controlled. Following the war, western farmers who adopted radical farm politics were converts to the belief that humans could and should undertake such ambitious projects. At the least, they should remove inefficiencies that were restraining the region's productivity. They believed that the land's wealth could be better tapped through more just and reasonable transportation agreements and the scrapping of unnatural protective tariffs. Such simple, common-sense solutions could, in turn, unfetter nature's potential superabundance. The war years had proven that, when farmers applied proper, scientific agriculture and mechanization, almost unbelievably high yields could be drawn from western soils. Before the environmental disaster of the dustbowl decade, the farmer was still confident that all this and more was possible. Indeed, the westerner imagined his or her own hand in God's creation: as an agent in a process of improvement, the farmer literally willed wheat from weeds.

Farming communities also tended to look at wildlife populations as harvest commodities. To communities so reliant on natural resources, this living aspect of the land's wealth had to be prudently and rationally managed. Most farmers, loggers, and miners saw themselves as agents in a naturally productive design. They believed that nature required some degree of human cultivation, and the wild beasts of the field were no exception. From this perspective, Alberta sportsmen saw themselves "civilizing" nature. The Alberta Fish and Game Protective Association had taken up the task of not only protecting game but also "bringing in new species which will flourish in this country," as the *Calgary Herald* reported in 1927.[121] The association boasted about its earlier introduction of Hungarian partridge and later pintailed grouse. These birds, "which accompany Civilization," had been introduced while the native prairie chicken had predictably receded "before Civilization."[122]

Others imagined that humans were providentially mandated to improve and utilize resources that otherwise would be wasted in their wild state. Frank Oliver, newspaper man, government administrator, and farm promoter, certainly shared a pioneer's opinion that expanding commercial fishing on lakes near Edmonton during the war years was improving the fish stocks there. He told the Department of Marine and Fisheries that these lakes required fishers so that fish would not become overcrowded, consume existing food supplies, and starve. He claimed that Lake Wabamun, intensively fished during the land boom years and again during the war, "has been continually fished for nine years and that the fish are now of better quality."[123] The very notion that wildlife *could* be conserved was based on an understanding that relatively simple measures, similar to those taken by a farmer tending crops or applying dry-land farming techniques, could maintain perpetual bounty in animal populations. The farmer knew the lesson of fallow farming. The ease with which nature could be controlled through relatively simple human intervention led, in turn, to optimistic futures in local cereal and quadruped crops. The *Lethbridge Daily Herald* in 1909, then, forecast that "Game [Was] Increasing in Southern Alberta," reporting the efficacy of game ordinances, the very day after it announced that "Alberta Crops [Were] Looking Good."[124]

The proactive role that westerners assumed they should play in increasing nature's wealth was usually directed to underwater wildlife reserves. Department of Marine and Fisheries officers contended with settlers who believed that flagging local streams could be revived. By the 1920s, these officers had the almost impossible task of dealing with local demands for a share of the rainbow trout fry and fingerlings being reared at the Banff hatchery, established in 1913. In Ottawa, the department was overwhelmed by letters from farmers, ranchers, and schoolteachers asking for fry to stock lakes, streams, sloughs, and salty cattle baths. Even the owner of a Medicine Hat hotel with an eye for publicity potential requested trout fry for a pond in which he hoped to stage a "fish show."[125] Most requests were summarily rejected. Other applicants paid the $1.20 for a hundred fry and released them in farm ditches and sloughs to meet certain death in water far too warm for their survival.

The sixty to eighty fish and game protective associations throughout the west in the interwar years, however, could not easily be mollified in their demands for fry. Albertans, having some thirty associations by 1929, were confident that water bodies of all description could become thick with trout. The High River association alone demanded some 1.5 million cutthroat trout fry just after the war, an impossible request considering Banff's capacity of a few hundred thousand a season. At least the Highwood River was considered a high priority by the department.

Government decisions regarding other potential fry locations had to be made, in part, according to answers given by an association on a printed survey. The Macleod association answered the department's questionnaire in the following way:

Is Water Clear or Muddy? – Clear
Is it suitable for drinking purposes? – Yes it's fine
What natural fish food does it contain? – All natural fish food usual in mountain water
Is this food scanty or abundant? – Abundant[126]

The answers to such questionnaires aside, these associations had considerable influence in determining fry locations because their members usually did the leg work for the department when planting was undertaken. Banff fry were sent by train to a location specified by an association. Its members provided the department's employee with the necessary manpower and a car or horse transportation to get the milking cans filled with junior fish into remote streams – rushing to do so before these cans overheated.

Many of these first plantings were likely ineffective. At the time, however, association members believed that they were doing more than merely compensating for angling pressure on western rivers. They believed that hatcheries made stream environments more efficient. By releasing fry or fingerlings, association members were correcting problems in nature: spawning fish procreated "inefficiently" because eggs were lost, milt was washed downstream, and small fry were eaten by carnivorous competitors. Ideally, such hatcheries helped fry to "fight their own battles" in hostile stream environments and transform even the best western streams into teeming trout beds.[127]

Such had been the philosophy of fish culture for some time. But new farmers were particularly sure that humans had a role to play in making streams more efficient. Indeed, in a land where the "single crop" philosophy was beginning to place a monotone carpet of wheat across western Canada, westerners were supporting a similar planting philosophy in streams running through their townships. Believing that predators and "coarse" fish were crowding out superior game fish, townspeople were purging streams of bull trout in the hope that the superior cutthroat trout would at last find the room it deserved. Associations legally unable to do so themselves were urging fish guardians to rid streams of ling, suckers, and other unwanted varieties. Others pressured the Department of Marine and Fisheries to allow them to introduce exotic fish marketed in the United States. For instance, the loch leven was the trout of choice for Pincher Creek anglers. The department rejected almost all applications to introduce exotic fish. It did, though, implement a single-crop policy of stocking fish in Alberta's mountain watersheds. As J.A. Rodd, the aquaculturalist for the Banff hatchery, explained to the Pincher Creek angling association in 1913, "fish culture or aquiculture in its relation to water is somewhat similar to agriculture in its relation to land." Farmers avoided introducing root crops in grain or grazing districts, Rodd explained, and the "aquiculturalist" knew that, as some soils prove best for certain crops, "so are certain types of water best adapted for certain species of fish."[128] Rodd was likely anxious to nix demands for exotic fish that E.E. Prince, the department's fisheries expert, adamantly opposed. Such officials likely attempted to justify fry allotments that never really satisfied town and city angling clubs. By the mid-1920s, however, the direction in fish plantings was to supply a single "crop" of fish species for western watersheds, including rainbow, brown, loch leven, and cutthroat trout, depending on the stream and watershed.[129]

These initiatives were taken up with enthusiasm at a local level because settlers were certain that they had a role to play in making western nature more productive. For the same reason, they took up fur farming. With fur fetching high prices on the market, farmers believed that they could raise wildlife as easily as domesticated livestock. Farmers in the western provinces rushed to place fox-breeding stock in wire mesh pens and reap what was initially believed to be bonanza profits from silver and cross fox furs. They tried raising muskrat and eventually mink, believing that wild animals could be raised better in human-controlled conditions than in nature. Indeed, the very genesis of fur farming and its real popularization occurred not on large, specialized fur farms but on mixed and small farms. These farmers believed, as did the conservation commission, which backed up fur farming in the war years, that the controlled conditions on a farm could create a better fur for market than a trapper could capture in the wild. Although the reality of fur farming was far different – often small in scale, rife with disease, and generating poor-quality furs – western farmers remained convinced that some wild animals could be raised better in controlled breeding environments than in the competitive and violent conditions of nature.[130]

These matters might seem to be unrelated to game reserves, but they are not. Westerners saw the establishment of such reserves as part of a rational configuration of wild and improved areas, one space granting vitality and abundance to the other. The Manitoba government set aside Turtle Mountain and Spruce Woods Game Preserves in well-settled regions as well as Riding Mountain; game department officials believed by 1913 that "we have made the longest step in a sure and right direction towards perpetuating and ensuring a good supply of our game animals and birds to the use of the present and rising generations."[131] Manitoba eventually set aside ten game areas by the end of the war, six in 1916 alone.

Throughout the period, commentators judged the success of wildlife preservation according to both the numbers of animals increasing yearly – itself an appropriation of farm accounting – and how "fearless" animals were becoming of humans. In this latter reckoning, the western game preserve suggested that nature was righted within its borders. Predators that threatened harmless and defenceless species were removed from the sanctuary. Both criteria were critical to westerners' understanding of the Edenic society that they wished to establish.

It was by these criteria that the Jasper Park superintendent, R.S. Stronach, assessed wildlife protection. He pointed out not only that game was showing a "considerable increase" immediately after the war but also that "owing to the strict protection afforded they are becoming extremely tame. Deer are sometimes seen walking through townsites and sheep are also very tame. There is a flock of the latter which can be seen at almost any time ... along the railway line. Beaver are also very numerous and tame, and tourists take a great deal of interest in watching them at work."[132] Waterton Lakes Park's superintendent saw the same merits in his office's preservation initiatives. That they have "been very satisfactory is proved by the large numbers of game which are from year to year becoming tamer and are more frequently visible to the tourists."[133] J.B. Harkin believed that wildlife in Yoho Park had increased and that "bear, moose and deer roam the park at will and seem to know that no harm will befall them."[134] He seemed to be sure that sanctuaries such as those in the parks showed "how readily wild animals will accustom themselves to the presence of man, once they are convinced there is nothing to be feared."[135] Gordon Hewitt reported the success of Banff's wildlife reserve, where "during the winter the deer overcome their natural shyness and may be seen constantly in the streets of Banff."[136]

This hope for wildlife preserves – that animals would lose their fear of humans within them – was reiterated in park advertisements and newspaper coverage. In the immediate postwar years, such news held out the marvellous potential of bringing humans back into an ideal state of nature before the Fall. Few, indeed, wanted to allow the savage competition of Darwinian nature to run its course in these natural areas. The divided reaction to the parks department's hiring of American professional hunter E. "Cougar" Lee in 1935 is a case in point. He was hired after publicity mounted concerning mountain lions in the parks system. Norman Luxton's *Craig and Canyon* first demanded action when cougars began killing deer. The paper printed the account of a couple who had watched a cougar stalk a mountain goat near their car. "One cry came from the goat," Luxton wrote, "and the killer rolled with it under some bushes ... perhaps to suck the blood of the carcass."[137] W.C. Fisher, the new president of the Calgary Fish and Game Association, soon demanded bounties on cougars. Although Calgary naturalist and writer Dan McCowan objected in the *Calgary Albertan* to the hiring of Cougar Lee, believing that survival of the fittest "is the only law that will preserve a balance among wild life,"[138] many observers believed that cougars, like other predators, should be removed from game preserves. The *Toronto Star Weekly* ran the headline "War Declared on Predatory Animals to Save Game in National Park."[139] The parks service eventually discontinued Lee's contract, not because of the poor publicity that it generated but because the warden service was removing more cougars from the parks system than the high-priced hired gun.[140]

Westerners, however, wanted predators removed from the garden of their own making. The *Calgary Herald* found it enthralling in 1923 when it reported that "Wild Game [Are] Visiting Waterton Lakes Park," with the subhead "Big Horn Sheep and Bear Are Unafraid of Residents at Resort." The story highlighted the regular visits of these animals "around the buildings and seemed quite at home and unafraid, although several persons were close by."[141] The new Banff-Windemere road, meanwhile, offered access to wildlife: "moose and other big game can be seen daily along the route," the *Herald* noted.[142] Mabel B. Williams, who wrote a series of books on the parks system and facilities for auto tourism just after the First World War, saw animals becoming tame in these areas. She considered this one of the appeals of wildlife protection. Kootenay National Park, Canada's first "national highway park," allowed the auto tourist to be "swept at once into an enchanted world." She stated that animals inside parks were not afraid of humans since they innately realized that "within these boundaries" humans have "laid aside" their "ancient enmity," and the animals were "quick to offer in return the gift of equal friendship."[143]

But there was yet another side to protection in these areas. Maynard Rogers, the superintendent of Jasper Park, succinctly stated that the real benefit of reserves was to augment wildlife populations. His 1920 report pointed to rapidly increasing wildlife populations within the park. Year by year, he wrote, "the increase has brought about the beneficial result that the surplus is gradually moving outside of park boundaries thus furnishing to the legitimate sportsman good shooting in the areas adjoining." BC sources informed him that on the eastern slopes of the Rockies, approximately two thousand bighorn sheep were found by sport hunters, able to fill their bags quickly. He wrote about a Mrs. Mead, of Chicago, and her sixteen-year-old son, who "procured their four heads in the first twenty-four hours, one especially large head over 18 inches among the number," and about a Miss Foster, her brother, and a friend, with guides, who shot ten sheep and seven goats. "Mr. Foster shot a very fine caribou," he said. "This all goes to prove that the protection afforded by our warden service has been satisfactory."[144]

The notion that animal preserves served as "breeding areas," each affording abundance to nearby settlements, was widely circulated by the time that Rogers wrote his report. Gordon Hewitt believed that "this is one of the great advantages of such natural reserves," that the preserves linking Waterton, Rocky Mountains, and Jasper Parks served as "an unrivalled breeding ground for the big-game animals of the Rocky Mountains region, and the surplus wild-life population will afford a constant supply of big-game and fur-bearing animals for the adjacent unprotected regions."[145]

As "refuges," these game preserves assisted western society caught up with the notion that humans could master social problems and dominate the natural environment. Westerners likely read with enthusiasm reports of the *Medicine Hat News* in 1925 that elk populations were increasing so rapidly in areas north of Banff that they were driving out bighorn sheep in the region. "The elk, a few years ago, had been driven almost to extinction on the North American continent," the newspaper wrote, and were now so plentiful that "the government will have to take measures to decrease their numbers."[146] In other ways, the success of the Wainwright reserve suggested that human planning had not only saved buffalo in Canada but had also maintained them in such abundance that Hollywood moviemakers by 1923 were using them to re-create the great buffalo hunts of the earlier era. So plentiful were the buffalo now that twenty-four were shot – humanely, a newspaper report pointed out – during filming of *The Last Frontier*.[147] Newspaper readers in Medicine Hat seemed to see the surplus of such reserves changing nearby topography. A tourist map, printed in the paper in 1925, showed highways, railways, natural parks and reserves, bird sanctuaries, and historical sites. The wildlife reserves throughout the west were plainly highlighted, for instance, at Wainwright, Namaskam, and the national parks. The map showed farming regions – by then covered with wheat crops – surrounding such reserves, which appeared as abundant with wildlife.[148]

Settlers confronting the problem of fish and game depletion were in some measure confronting a larger uncertainty in their pioneer experience. Given their problematic financial and political situation, westerners wished to attract more settlers, increase tax rolls, and encourage town and city growth. However, when promotions seemed to succeed, settlement booms brought "foreigners," new cultures, and different customs to the settler's doorstep. And the booms sometimes seemed to benefit rival settlements, a critical issue given the increasingly competitive spirit between communities. Early fish and game protection took place in the same microcosm of pioneer rivalry and uncertainty. Westerners boasted about local wildlife abundance and exaggerated the unending supply of this resource. But just as quickly they sought to secure this wealth when it appeared to benefit newcomers more than themselves. The chaotic pace of population expansion, each stage bringing enormous needs for food and greater demands on the environment, undermined the confidence of even the well-established farmers "making good."

Numerous social concerns motivated conservation movements within the context of immigration and contested proprietorship. It was no coincidence that early century newspapers reported the "Celestial" who was caught with eggs and game out of season. The report usually reprinted a conviction and heavy fine for the infraction. Newspapers described impoverished eastern Europeans, whether sodbusters or itinerate miners, salting barrels of fish from mountain streams or consuming moose in summer. And they reported Amerindians appearing before magistrates for eating antelope after it was protected by law. Beyond new environmental sensibilities, conservation had a social background. Indeed, it is telling that a high proportion of convictions for fishing abuses fell on the "foreigner" in settlement communities.[149] Through such conservation activities, charter groups controlled in some measure the influx of newcomers within town limits and regulated the marginalized members among them.

More fundamentally, though, conservation stopped the depletion of a local resource, and in this pioneers likely saw wildlife as providing much more than merely food or sport. Their interest in game conservation suggests that they sought to maintain superabundant wealth in their new land. The game reserve's abundance, indeed, would spill into neighbouring settler societies. Wild animals were thought to belong to the settler, and they symbolized a western natural heritage that pioneers were anxious to claim as their own.

Conclusion

At first glance, a social history of wildlife in western Canada is as complex as the societies that have developed in the region. First Nations people thought about animals differently than did eighteenth-century Europeans; in turn, liberal-era farmers viewed wildlife in other ways and used wild animals for new purposes. Attitudes toward these animals indeed varied according to cosmological assumptions, local needs, and changing historical necessities emerging in the course of western development. Nevertheless, this history has highlighted elements of continuity. Amerindians and fur traders, despite their very different views of the natural world, looked to wild animals for their survival. They exchanged wild meat and, in doing so, built an interdependent society according to ongoing problems of subsistence in western regions. The social organization of the fur trade era was always oriented toward the harsh realities of a northern environment. Fur trade society itself was constrained by the limitations of a closed economy in which finite quantities of wild meat circulated as currency. Attitudes toward nature, social relations, and subsistence strategies, then, were regulated not according to "original affluence" but according to a very uncertain food supply.

Newcomers in the mid-nineteenth century – farmers, expansionists, government agents, and administrators – joined efforts to replace fur trade society with model agricultural communities. Their activities were shaped by ethics of individualism and a belief that both the natural world and human nature could be improved. Wild meat, though important in settler diets, was of secondary interest in subsistence strategies introduced in the farming era. In fact, early in the territorial period, newcomers tended to view wildlife as animate representatives of a wilderness being pushed away by the agricultural frontier. After settlers became less dependent on wild meat protein, they transformed wild animals into symbols of western forests, climates, soils, and rivers. If the fur trader had a pessimistic appraisal of the land, nineteenth-century farming communities grounded in principles of mid-Victorian liberalism saw nature's economy as open-ended, its productive potential limited only by the farmer's resolve of "making good."[1]

By the turn of the century, after the first land booms further buoyed confidence in development, westerners used wildlife to represent the region's supposedly unbounded natural resources. Wild animals, birds, and fish seemed to be as abundant and inexhaustible as the land's wealth. By the end of the First World War, wildlife was crucial to booster campaigns, immigration fairs, and taxidermy displays in local natural history museums. Now the optimism about western Canada's environment and the potential of its resources contrasted with pessimism developing in the United States. The sobering lessons of environmental crisis were being taught elsewhere, and the progressive era's solution of maximum sustainable yield had little use among westerners promoting their land as superabundant. Moreover, with close associations with untainted natural wealth, wildlife became important for the identities of nearby communities. In his study of the planning of nineteenth-century Ontario parks, Gerald Killan identified utilitarianism as initially guiding park policies. Park developers justified these land reserves because they protected forests and rivers for industry and economic development.[2] In the Canadian west, pictorial representations, wildlife descriptions, and conservation initiatives were shaped by similarly utilitarian considerations long into the twentieth century. The abundance of western wildlife maintained a regional understanding of the land as Eden.

It was, indeed, the issue of natural plenitude that chiefly motivated the first wildlife conservation in the Canadian west. Wild biota assured farm bounty, enriched the region, and determined the social tenor of new communities. Local interest in rationally planning wildlife resources, whether fish populations or bird species, hints at the ideal, almost utopian, ends of interwar game reserves established near communities. Especially after the human tragedy of the First World War, westerners hoped to solve modern problems by drawing on nature and managing its wild animals. Westerners believed in animal preserves not only because they raised speculative interest in the potential wealth of a nearby community but also because, bringing wild animals into concord, they suggested an alternative course of development for the region.[3] The wolf, cougar, and coyote bounties both inside and outside park boundaries were, for that reason, part of a wider pioneer program aimed at correcting nature's worst elements and eliminating competition – issues important to visionaries planning their communities.[4]

The way that wildlife protection could contribute to social questions also explains the timing of interest in fish and game conservation. Town and city elites who led protective associations had encouraged immigration and now hoped to control its social and economic impacts on their communities. They rallied around conservation campaigns in order to safeguard nature's wealth for their citizens. They also used game ordinances to stop outsiders from invading regions most vulnerable to poaching. Throughout the territorial and early provincial periods, westerners jealously guarded fish and game resources, as they did the land's most precious resources. When they were uncertain about their own fortunes, they joined associations that promised to control the incursions of outsiders and foreigners. These associations, then, directed their protective measures toward outsiders from rival towns and cities who were carrying away local wealth or marginalized individuals not yet incorporated into the society developed by charter groups.

The period of study in this book ends before the Second World War, when western Canadian society faced profound economic changes and farmers and city dwellers emerged from their pioneer roots. But evidence suggests that western orientations to wildlife survived the war. The protest against the federal government's closure of the Wainwright buffalo reserve in 1939 illuminated the continuing popularity of progressive-era ideas. The government had received reports of ill health and tuberculosis in the herd and made the decision to transfer some of the animals to Elk Island and Wood Buffalo National Parks. The rest would be slaughtered, and the land would be turned over to the military. Westerners reacted immediately. Here was the dashing of a dream: a sanctuary supporting wild animals would literally be overrun by tanks, the ugly machines of war. The Telegraph Social Credit Group No. 481, of Clandonald, Alberta, protested the reserve's closure and the herd's destruction. J.R. Hoad, president of the Saskatchewan Fish and Game League, advanced the widespread protest of sportsmen and nature lovers. Meanwhile, the Clearwater and West Country Fish and Game Association offered to move the herd to the nearby forestry reserve, if only to save the buffalo from destruction. Henry Stelfox, one of the association's leaders, even offered to move the herd with or without tuberculosis. Even W.J.S. Walker, of the Canadian National Parks Association in Calgary, was outraged at what he called a "blunder" by the government. Although he did not want to embarrass the country during wartime, "the method in which this Wainwright business was carried out created more correspondence from our members, even from far away Prince Edward Island and Vancouver Island, than anything since the Spray Lakes," a reference to an earlier decision to allow hydroelectric development in what was then national park space. Given western understandings of wildlife, the closure of a game preserve, not surprisingly, brought immediate responses from westerners who saw wild animals as symbols of local wealth. Nearby towns had promoted the establishment of the Wainwright reserve. They saw it and other regions abundant in wildlife as providing tributary benefits of nature's wealth to farms and towns. Many were disappointed, then, to learn that some 1,226 buffalo, 113 moose, and 242 deer had been slaughtered.[5]

The protest against Wainwright's closure grew from attitudes toward wildlife that had developed in western subsistence traditions and later economic hopes. Promotional campaigns and numerous maps, illustrations, narratives, and handbooks depicted the west as the last wildlife refuge in North America. The value of this "resource" and its place in recreational areas continue to be debated. Opposition to development permits, which threaten to incrementally extirpate wildlife, mounts from a grassroots understanding that wildlife raises assessments of western wealth.[6] Wildlife management issues, indeed, move with ease between rural and city populations that see value in the west's reputation as abundant with wild animals. The overwhelming public response in Alberta to a recently proposed Spray Lakes recreation project in Kananaskis Country, feared to affect grizzly populations there, suggests some ways that wildlife can quickly become an unexpected rallying point in local and provincial politics. Government private bills aimed at protecting grizzlies in remote areas of British Columbia also indicate how seemingly obscure wildlife questions can be turned into extremely popular politics. The utilitarian argument that westerners used to protect wildlife, then, continues to have relevance. But it gains its power only in relation to the affluent ends of an economy planned around an abundance of natural resources. There is little appraisal of the ways in which human and "natural" areas are separated and managed for productive ends. Nature recreation is, indeed, often undertaken as a means of coping with, not questioning, the industrial age and aspects of urban growth that ultimately make the land unlivable. Nature preserves and glimpses of wildlife might strengthen an individual. But he or she undertakes recreation of this sort to increase productivity in a modern workplace. Many an overburdened office worker or business manager finds inspiration in nature in order to survive urban life, much like a turn-of-the-century clerk found the resolve to return to his office after spending a weekend shooting grizzlies and deer.

Utilitarian understandings of wildlife are, indeed, guided by fundamental assumptions about humans, the natural world, and its wild animals. With other communities attempting to find new approaches to environmental issues, those in western Canada are beginning to question dated environmental assumptions. Western Canadians are also searching for ways to incorporate, rather than separate, groups that are marginalized within the whole. Undoubtedly, new environmental attitudes will form the beginning point in such a search. Historically, wild animal products linked people. The end of subsistence needs among settlers widely separated newcomers and First Nations. Early conservationists aimed to preserve specific populations of fish and game and, in doing so, to exclude certain groups from fishing or hunting them. As westerners appreciate wildlife as part of a living landscape, they will find opportunities to appraise existing land use and real human needs in the western environment. Western Canadians will also revise romantic understandings of "wild" and "domestic" animals that continue to dominate approaches to range management, park policies, and urban planning. As most environmental lobbyists are well aware, much of their public support is generated among people who observe only in passing the virtues of biodiversity. Westerners do not see wildlife as part of a world in which they live, and, in fact, they believe that habitat reduction is at times both necessary and inevitable for further municipal, agricultural, or industrial progress.

Ecologists advance a far more complex argument for wildlife protection that will gain popularity in time. The populations and varieties of wildlife – and the intricacies of energy flows between the animate and inanimate worlds – provide critical indices of the land's ability to sustain life. According to this ecological model, the viability of western life rests, indeed, on the degree to which wildlife populations remain robust inside and outside human settlements. The western frontier of the next millennium will certainly include new understandings of wild animals. And humans will search for new accommodations with other living biota – in a western land allowed to nourish life.[7]

Appendix: Independent Conservation Associations in Western Canada

The following list of fish and game protective associations was generated from correspondence files of the federal Department of Marine and Fisheries and from game guardian files in provincial archives of British Columbia, Saskatchewan, and Manitoba. Other references appear in the surviving papers of associations held in Glenbow Archives, Calgary, and in the Provincial Archives of Alberta, Edmonton.

An asterisk behind the year indicates the association's first reference in correspondence.

Alberta Fish and Game Protective Association (1907), Calgary, AB; R.A. Darker, President; 1908, Arthur G. Wolley Dod, President of Calgary chapter. By 1927, called Alberta Fish and Game Protective and Conservation Association; reorganized into Alberta Fish and Game Association in 1928; Charles A. Hayden, President.

Alberta Gun Club (1893), Lethbridge, NWT.

Association for Importation of Game Birds (1908*), Victoria, BC.

Banff Fish and Game Protective Association (1925*), Banff, AB; W.L. Mitchell, Secretary.

BC Forest and Stream Club (1901), Vancouver, BC; A.F. Beasley, Honorary Secretary.

Bellevue Fish and Game Protective Association (1925*), Bellevue, BC; James Fisher, Secretary.

Calgary Anglers Association (1920), Calgary, AB; David Keir, Secretary-Treasurer.

Calgary Rod and Gun Club (1890*), Calgary, NWT; Edward Hodder, President (1893); W.H. Heald, President (1904).

Camrose Fish and Game Association (1928*), Camrose, AB.

Cardston Rod and Gun Club (1927), Cardston, AB; S. Baxter, Secretary-Treasurer.

Central Saskatchewan Game Protection Association (1923), Saskatoon, SK; D. Stewart, President; F.A. Blain, Vice President; Rupert W. Neil, Secretary-Treasurer.

Chilliwack Game Association (1907*), Chilliwack, BC.

Claresholm District Angling Club (1921*), Claresholm, AB; D.A. Anderson, Secretary-Treasurer.

Claresholm Fish and Game Protective League (1926).

Coldstream Gun Club (1906*), Vernon, BC.

Coleman Angling Association (1918), Coleman, AB; William Rees, President.

Coleman Rod and Gun Club (1925).

Cragmyle Fish and Game Association (1928*), Cragmyle, AB.

Craik Game Protective Association (1924), Craik, SK; Frank Parks, President.

Cranbrook District Fish and Game Protective Association (1908*), Cranbrook, BC; C.M. Edwards, Secretary-Treasurer.

Cumberland Gun Club (1906*), Cumberland, BC.

Cypress Hills Angling and Protective Association (1927), Cypress Hills, AB; B.S. Walters, Secretary-Treasurer.

Delta Game Association (1912), Delta, BC.

Didsbury Fish and Game Association (1928*), Didsbury, AB.

Drumheller Fish and Game Association (1928), Drumheller, AB; W. Guterson, Vice President.

Edmonton and District Rod and Gun Club (1890*), Edmonton, NWT; Richard Hardisty, Superintendent; A.H. Griesbach, C.F. Strange, members (1893).

Edson Fish and Game Protective Association (1930), Edson, AB.

Fernie District Game Protective Association (1907*), Fernie, BC; R.C.S. Randall, Secretary-Treasurer; H.W. Herchmer, President; Mayor Tuttle, J.B. Turney, members.

Foothills Angling Association (1921), Nanton, AB; W.C. Ebbert, President.

Golden Game Association (1908*), Golden, BC.

Hanna Fish and Game Association (1928*), Hanna, AB.

Highwood River Angling and Protective Association (1920), High River, AB. By 1926, known as High River Fish and Game Protective Association; Frank Watt, Secretary; H.E. Elliot, President (1922); A.A. Ballachey, President (1928).

Kettle Valley Rifle Association (1911*), Grand Forks, BC; Sergeant-Major Charles G. Wheeler, Secretary.

Killam Rod and Gun Club (1928*), Killam, AB.

Kokanee Game Protective Association (1907*), Kokanee, BC; Charles W. Busk, President.

Ladysmith Gun Club (1908*), Ladysmith, BC (Vancouver Island).

Lethbridge Rod and Gun Club (1922), Lethbridge, AB.

Luscar Fish and Game Protective Association (1928*), Luscar, AB; John Richmond, President.

Macleod Angling Association (1921*), Macleod, AB; R.A. Hamilton, Secretary.

Macleod Gun Club (1893*), Macleod, NWT.

Manitoba Game and Fish Association, Winnipeg branch (1920s), later became Winnipeg Game and Fish Association.

Manitoba Game Protective League (1882), Winnipeg, MB; Colonel John Walker, President (1882); Colin Inkster, President (1884); R.H. Hunter, Vice President; F.S. Simpson, Secretary-Treasurer; Justice Miller, W.H. Hood, W. Peter Price, J. Hingston Smith, committee members. Known as Manitoba Game Protective Association by 1906.

Manitoban Audubon Society (1915), Winnipeg, MB. Created "to arouse in a greater degree the public conscience in the important subject of preserving the wild birds and the game animals of the province" (constitution by-laws).

Maple Creek Rod and Gun Club (1893*), Maple Creek, NWT.

Medicine Hat Fish and Game Association (1928*), Medicine Hat, AB.

Michel and District Anglers Association (1910), Michel, BC; George Wilde, Secretary.

Moose Jaw Rifle Association and Gun Club (1893*), Moose Jaw, NWT.

Nanaimo Gun Club (1906), Nanaimo, BC; George B. Brown, Secretary.

Nanaimo Rod and Gun Club (1908).

Nelson Game Association (1906), Nelson, BC.

Nordegg and District Fish and Game Protective League (1929), Nordegg, AB; A. Opley, Secretary-Treasurer.

Northern Alberta Fish and Game Protective League (1920), Edmonton, AB; Walter Holmes, Secretary.

Pincher Creek Anglers' Association (1920), Pincher Creek, AB; J.J. Gillespie, Secretary.

Prince Albert Fish and Game Association (1926), Prince Albert, SK.

Red Deer Rod and Gun Club (1893*), Red Deer, NWT.

Revelstoke District Fish and Game Protective Association (1906), Revelstoke, BC; John H. Jackson, Honorary President.

Richmond Game Protective Association (1907*), Richmond, BC (Lulu Island); Austin Harris, Deputy Game Guardian.

Rocky Mountain House Rod and Gun Club (1922), Rocky Mountain House, AB; G. Candy, Secretary.

Saskatchewan Game Protective Association (1906), Regina, SK; W.R. Motherwell, President (1924); W.M. Van Valkenburg, Secretary (1910), President (1930); A.E. Etter, Secretary-Treasurer (1924). By 1943, known as Saskatchewan Fish and Game League.

Saunders Fish and Game Protective League (1930*), Saunders, AB; A.E. Williams, Secretary-Treasurer.
Sheep Creek Branch of the Alberta Fish and Game Club (1925*), Okotoks, AB; Dave Blacklock, Secretary.
Similkameen Valley Game Protective Association (1912), Similkameen Valley, BC.
Southern Alberta Angling Association (1919), Calgary, AB. Also known as Calgary Fishing Society, Southern Alberta Game Fishermen's Association. Walter E. Robi, Secretary; R.A. Darker, President.
Stavely Fishing Club (1919), Stavely, AB; E.C. Webster, President.
Vancouver Forest and Stream Club (1907), Vancouver, BC; Francis Miller Chaldecotte, President.
Vancouver Island Fish and Game Club (1906), Victoria, BC; J. Musgrave, Honorary Secretary.
Victoria Fish and Game Club (1906*), Victoria, BC.

In 1928, the Department of Marine and Fisheries listed the following towns in Alberta as also having fish and game protective associations (not chapters of the Alberta Fish and Game Association): Bassano, Bentley, Brooks, Cadogan, Carbon, Carsland, Carstairs, Castor, Claresholm, Delia, Drumheller, Hillcrest, Jasper, Lacombe, Midnapore, Stavely, Strathmore, and Vulcan.

Notes

Introduction

1 George Altmeyer, "Three Ideas of Nature in Canada, 1893-1914," *Journal of Canadian Studies* 11, 3 (1976): 21-36.

2 I.S. MacLaren, "The Metamorphosis of Travellers into Authors: The Case of Paul Kane," in *Critical Issues in Editing Exploration Texts: Papers Given at the Twenty-Eighth Annual Conference on Editorial Problems, University of Toronto, 6-7 November 1992*, ed. Germaine Warkentin (Toronto: University of Toronto Press, 1992), 67-107; see also MacLaren's "Literary Landscapes in the Writings of Fur Traders," in *Le Castor Fait Tout: Selected Papers of the Fifth North American Fur Trade Conference, 1985*, ed. Bruce Trigger, Toby Morantz, and Louise Dechêne (Montreal: Lake St. Louis Historical Society, 1987), 566-85.

3 "Fur and the Fur-Trade," *Saturday Magazine*, January 1842: 48.

4 Ibid.

5 H.M. Robinson, *The Great Fur Land: Or, Sketches of Life in the Hudson's Bay Territory* (Toronto: Coles Publishing, 1972).

6 On Romanticism and nature visits, see Patricia Jasen, *Wild Things: Nature, Culture, and Tourism in Ontario, 1790-1914* (Toronto: University of Toronto Press, 1995).

7 Lisa Mighetto, *Wild Animals and American Environmental Ethics* (Tucson: University of Arizona Press, 1991), 2-7.

8 "Wildlife" was used in 1879, and "Wild Animals" was used by Macaulay in the early nineteenth century. J.A. Simpson and E.S.C. Weiner, eds., *The Oxford English Dictionary*, vol. 20, 2nd ed. (Oxford: Clarendon Press, 1989), 336, 330.

9 John R. Stilgoe discusses the term and the idea of wilderness in *Common Landscape of America: 1580-1845* (New Haven: Yale University Press, 1982), 7-12.

10 See John Wadland, *Ernest Thompson Seton: Man in Nature and the Progressive Era 1880-1915* (New York: Arno Press, 1978).

11 The Earl of Southesk, *Saskatchewan and the Rocky Mountains* (Edinburgh: Edmonston and Douglas, 1874), 216-17.

12 Incident recorded in J.S. Woodsworth, *Strangers within Our Gates: Or, Coming Canadians* (Toronto: Missionary Society of the Methodist Church, 1909), 37-38.

13 See Alan MacEachern's impressive analysis of predator control in "Rationality and Rationalization in Canadian National Parks Predator Policy," in *Consuming Canada: Readings in Environmental History*, ed. Chad Gaffield and Pam Gaffield (Toronto: Copp Clark, 1995), 197-212.

14 Janet Foster, *Working for Wildlife: The Beginning of Preservation in Canada* (Toronto: University of Toronto Press, 1978); Robert G. McCandless, *Yukon Wildlife: A Social History* (Edmonton: University of Alberta Press, 1985); Paul-Louis Martin, *La Chasse au Québec* (Québec: Boréal, 1990); Harriet Ritvo, *The Animal Estate: The English and Other Creatures in the Victorian Age* (Toronto: Penguin Books, 1990); David Elliston Allen, *The Naturalist in Britain: A Social History* (Princeton: Princeton University Press, 1994); Keith Thomas, *Man and the*

Natural World: A History of the Modern Sensibility (New York: Pantheon Books, 1983); James Turner, *Reckoning with the Beast: Animals, Pain, and Humanity in the Victorian Mind* (Baltimore: Johns Hopkins University Press, 1980).

15 Hermann Hartwig, *Animals and Men*, trans. Richard and Clara Winston (Garden City, NY: Natural History Press, 1965); Foster, *Working for Wildlife*. See Robert Craig Brown, "The Doctrine of Usefulness: Natural Resource and National Park Policy in Canada, 1887-1914," in *Canadian Parks in Perspective*, ed. J.G. Nelson (Montreal: Harvest House, 1970), 46-62; Leslie Bella has approached Canadian preservation as a conservation movement in *Parks for Profit* (Montreal: Harvest House, 1987).

16 Samuel P. Hays, *Conservation and the Gospel of Efficiency: The Progressive Conservation Movement, 1890-1920* (Cambridge: Harvard University Press, 1959). Scientific planning in Canada has been the subject of much work. See Suzanne Zeller, *Inventing Canada: Early Victorian Science and the Idea of a Transcontinental Nation* (Toronto: University of Toronto Press, 1987); W.A. Waiser, *The Field Naturalist: John Macoun, the Geological Survey, and Natural Science* (Toronto: University of Toronto Press, 1989); Carl Berger, *Science, Nature, and God in Victorian Canada* (Toronto: University of Toronto Press, 1982).

17 For exceptional work devoted to uncovering "the complicated motivations for preservationism that were specific to the culture and economy of the late nineteenth and twentieth centuries," see Andrew C. Isenberg, "The Returns of the Bison: Nostalgia, Profit, and Preservation," *Environmental History* 2, 2 (1997): 180. See also Allen, *The Naturalist in Britain*; McCandless, *Yukon Wildlife*; and Ritvo, *The Animal Estate*. A valuable contribution to social attitudes and the environment is provided by Turner, *Reckoning with the Beast*.

18 Valerius Geist, *Buffalo Nation: History and Legend of the North American Bison* (Saskatoon: Fifth House Publishers, 1996), 102-19.

19 On the buffalo's decline, see Dan Flores, "Bison Ecology and Bison Diplomacy: The Southern Plains from 1800 to 1850," *Journal of American History* 78, 2 (1991): 465-85.

20 Karen Wonders, *Habitat Dioramas: Illusions of Wilderness in Museums of Natural History* (Uppsala, Sweden: Uppsala University Press, 1993), 114-43.

21 Prominent examples are Frank Graham, Jr., *The Audubon Ark: A History of the National Audubon Society* (New York: Alfred A. Knopf, 1990); and David Evans, *A History of Nature Conservation in Britain* (London: Routledge, 1992).

22 John F. Reiger, *American Sportsmen and the Origins of Conservation* (Norman: University of Oklahoma Press, 1986).

23 Keven Wamsley connects conservation with statism in "Good Clean Sport and a Deer Apiece: Game Legislation and State Formation in 19th Century Canada," *Canadian Journal of History of Sport* 25, 2 (1994): 1-20. A regional approach is offered by J.G. Nelson, *The Last Refuge* (Montreal: Harvest House, 1973), 126-52.

24 Andrew C. Isenberg addresses some aspects of local context in "The Wild and the Tamed: The Destruction of the Bison," paper presented at the Themes and Issues in North American Environmental History Conference, University of Toronto, May 1998.

25 John A. Livingston, *The Fallacy of Wildlife Conservation* (Toronto: McClelland and Stewart, 1981).

Chapter 1: Amerindians, Voyageurs, and the Animal Exchange in the Western Fur Trade

1 Eric W. Morse, *Fur Trade Canoe Routes of Canada: Then and Now* (Toronto: University of Toronto Press, 1989), 24-25.

2 Andrew Graham, "Observations on Hudson's Bay, 1767-8-9," Hudson's Bay Company Archives (hereafter HBCA), E.2/6.

3 Milan Novak et al., *Furbearer Harvests in North America, 1600-1984* (Toronto: Ministry of Natural Resources, Ontario, 1987).

4 Ibid. Wentzel's journal is quoted by Shepard Krech III, "The Trade of the Slavey and Dogrib at Fort Simpson in the Early Nineteenth Century," in *The Subarctic Fur Trade: Native Social and Economic Adaptations*, ed. Shepard Krech III (Vancouver: UBC Press, 1984), 107.

5 See catalogues of HBC auctions, HBCA, A.54/1-348, reel 489; HBC importations, HBCA, A.53/1, reel 488; and 22 October 1771 entry in Memorial Books of the HBC, HBCA, A.9/4.

6   Harold A. Innis, *The Fur Trade in Canada* (Toronto: University of Toronto Press, 1999), 298-99.
7   Excerpt from *London Times,* 19 March 1914, printed in J. Walter Jones, *Fur Farming in Canada* (Ottawa: Commission of Conservation, 1914), 186-88.
8   Elizabeth Vibert, *Traders' Tales: Narratives of Cultural Encounters in the Columbia Plateau, 1807-1846* (Norman: University of Oklahoma Press, 1997), 94, 173-74.
9   A.R. McLeod letter, 31 May 1825, McCord Museum Archives (hereafter McCord), M2783, Robert McVicar Fonds.
10   William MacIntosh letter to John McDonell, 8 May 1833, McCord, M2799, HBCA Fonds.
11   Donald Southerland letter, 21 July 1803, Archives nationales du Québec, Southerland Letterbook, 0-526.
12   See State of Provisions at York Fort 1761 compared with 1766, HBCA, ff. 96-98.E.2/6, microfilm reel 4M1.
13   William Auld to Colin McDonnel, 1 October 1811, National Archives of Canada (hereafter NAC), Selkirk Papers, vol. 1, p. 99.
14   John Long, "Voyages and Travels of an Indian Interpreter and Trader" (London, printed for the author, 1791), 119.
15   Long, *Voyages and Travels,* 117-18.
16   H.M. Robinson, *The Great Fur Land: Or, Sketches of Life in Hudson's Bay Territory* (Toronto: Coles Publishing Company, 1972), 94-95, 348.
17   James Parker describes the *dépouille* in *Emporium of the North: Fort Chipewyan and the Fur Trade to 1835* (Regina: Canadian Plains Research Center, 1987), 53; Brian J. Smith, "The Historical and Archaeological Evidence for the Use of Fish as an Alternative Subsistence Resource among Northern Plains Bison Hunters," in *Aboriginal Resource Use in Canada: Historical and Legal Aspects,* ed. Kerry Abel and Jean Friesen (Winnipeg: University of Manitoba Press, 1991), 41; on red deer and bear flesh, see Arthur J. Ray, *Indians in the Fur Trade* (Toronto: University of Toronto Press, 1998), 222-23.
18   See Barry Potyondi, *In Palliser's Triangle: Living in the Grasslands, 1850-1930* (Saskatoon: Purich Publishing, 1995), 14-15; Don Gayton, *The Wheatgrass Mechanism: Science and Imagination in the Western Canadian Landscape* (Saskatoon: Fifth House Publishers, 1990); and John Milloy, "'Our Country': The Significance of the Buffalo Resource for a Plains Cree Sense of Territory," in *Aboriginal Resource Use in Canada: Historical and Legal Aspects,* ed. Kerry Abel and Jean Friesen (Winnipeg: University of Manitoba Press, 1991), 55-56.
19   W. Dease, 19 July 1825, McCord, M2761, Robert McVicar Fonds.
20   McLeod's Lake Post journals, 1845-48, Glenbow Archives (hereafter GA), M165.
21   Fort Resolution journal, 1861, Cornwall Files, GA, M272.
22   Letter to John MacDonald, 10 April 1833, McCord, M2798, HBCA Fonds. On the issue of starvation, see Mary Black-Rogers, "Varieties of 'Starving': Semantics and Survival in the Subarctic Fur Trade, 1750-1850," *Ethnohistory* 33, 4 (1986): 353-83.
23   J.B. Tyrrell, ed., *Journals of Samuel Hearne and Philip Turnor between the Years 1774 and 1792* (Toronto: The Champlain Society, 1934), 136-37.
24   4 November 1778 entry, Robert Longmoore journal, Hudson House, Upper Canada, HBCA, B.87/a 1, 1M63.
25   Philip Turnor, at Henley House in 1779, recommended that eight men be posted there: "two or three of them might be employed in hunting and they might find a Winter fishery which cannot be managed under three hands which cannot be spared out of five men as their [sic] would be only two men left at the House." See Tyrrell, *Journals,* 272.
26   Cocking diary, at Cumberland House, 19 August 1777; 7 December 1789 entry, Lower Hudson House journal, 1780-81, HBCA, B.87/a3.
27   E.E. Rich, ed., *Cumberland and Hudson House Journals, 1775-1782,* vol. II (London: Hudson's Bay Record Society, 1951), 27.
28   William Tomison revealed in a candid journal entry in 1779, following Longmoore to Hudson House, "embarked on my Journey with a female Indian for my canoemate," and when he reached Longmoore he found the men all well and wrote down the welcome news that one of the Indians living in the settlement had killed a moose that would serve three days of provisions. William Tomison journal, 22 and 27 September 1779, HBCA,

B.87/a 2. For the role of women in the fur trade, see Sylvia Van Kirk, *Many Tender Ties: Women in Fur-Trade Society in Western Canada, 1670-1870* (Winnipeg: Watson and Dwyer, 1980).

29   Tyrrell, *Journals*, 190; see the account of Fulton's wintering party and the cannibalism attending it in Long, *Voyages and Travels*, 120-21.

30   Edward J. McCullough, *Prehistoric Cultural Dynamics of the Lac La Biche Regions*, MA thesis, University of Calgary, 1977, 149-50. See my article "'Victuals to Put into Our Mouths': Environmental Perspectives on Fur Trade Provisioning Activities at Cumberland House, 1775-1782," *Prairie Forum* 22, 1 (1997): 1-22.

31   See James Isham's description of meat preparation and its term of "*Ruhiggan*" in *James Isham's Observations on Hudsons Bay, 1743*, ed. E.E. Rich (Toronto: The Champlain Society, 1949), 155-56. Hearne described the rationing of a "handfull of Dry'd beat meat call'd Thewhagon." Tyrrell, *Journals*, 136.

32   Walter Robert Bown, testimony in "Report and Minutes of the Select Committee of the Senate on the Existing Natural Food Products," in Appendix no. 1 of the *Journals of the Senate of Canada, 1887* (Ottawa: Maclean, Roger and Company, 1887), 111; for a discussion of this committee, see the following chapter.

33   These prices are drawn from Cumberland House Accounts 1810-30, HBCA, B.49/d/2-40.

34   Humphrey Marten told the Cumberland House factor that "Mr. Cocking also says that the Natives will send Spies to pry into your Situation in regard to Provisions. If they find you in want their demands are extravagant, if other ways moderate; you will do well therefore to appear always well stocked tho' You should not be so in reality." Letter of September 1776, in *Cumberland House Journals and Inland Journal, 1775-82*, ed. E.E. Rich (London: Hudson's Bay Record Society, 1951), 88.

35   Krech, "The Trade of the Slavey and Dogrib," 114.

36   On trading territories, see Shepard Krech III, *The Ecological Indian: Myth and History* (New York: W.W. Norton, 1999); "The Old Moose and Brother came in, brought nothing having burn't all their Furrs, one of their wives being dead," in Charles A. Bishop, *The Northern Ojibwa and the Fur Trade: An Historical and Ecological Study* (Toronto: Holt, Rinehart and Winston, 1974), 248; Calvin Martin, *Keepers of the Game: Indian-Animal Relationships in the Fur Trade* (Berkeley: University of California Press, 1978).

37   Vibert, *Traders' Tales*, 113.

38   Jennifer S.H. Brown and Robert Brightman, eds., *"The Order of the Dreamed": George Nelson on Cree and Northern Ojibway Religion and Myth, 1823* (Winnipeg: University of Manitoba Press, 1988), 8-9.

39   Duncan McGillivray, *The Journal of Duncan McGillivray of the North West Company at Fort George on the Saskatchewan, 1794-5*, ed. A.S. Morton (Toronto: Macmillan, 1924), lx.

40   See ibid., lvii, 41; Cumberland House journal, 2 September 1784, HBCA, B.49/a15. Krech, *The Ecological Indian*, 132, offers daily rationing figures.

41   Morse, *Fur Trade Canoe Routes of Canada*, 24-25.

42   A.S. Morton's introduction to *The Journal of Duncan McGillivray*, vii.

43   I am using the Henday journal as it appears in Andrew Graham's journal of 1767, HBCA, E.2/6.

44   See Milloy, "Our Country," 54-61.

45   On Amerindian cosmology and animal mythology, see Brown and Brightman, eds., *"The Orders of the Dreamed*," 119-24.

46   Henday journal, 30 July 1754; on Amerindian hunting customs and rituals, see Krech, *The Ecological Indian*, 128-29.

47   Henday journal, 14 September 1754.

48   Calvin Martin, "Subarctic Indians and Wildlife," in *Old Trails and New Directions*, ed. Carol M. Judd and Arthur J. Ray (Toronto: University of Toronto Press, 1980), 73-81.

49   J. Baird Callicott, "Traditional American Indian and Western European Attitudes toward Nature: An Overview," in *Defense of the Land Ethic: Essays in Environmental Philosophy* (Albany: State University of New York Press, 1989), 182-84; Thomas L. Altherr, "'Flesh Is the Paradise of a Man of Flesh': Cultural Conflict over Indian Hunting Beliefs and Rituals in New France as Recorded in the *Jesuit Relations*," in "Notes and Comments," *Canadian Historical Review*

64, 2 (1983): 267-76; and John Foster, "The Métis and the End of the Plains Buffalo in Alberta," in *Buffalo*, ed. John Foster, Dick Harrison, and I.S. MacLaren (Edmonton: University of Alberta Press, 1992), 62.

50 Isham, *James Isham's Observations*, 81.

51 William Walker's journal from Lower Hudson House, 9 October 1781, HBCA, B.87/14.

52 McGillivray journal entry, 20 September 1794, *The Journal of Duncan McGillivray*, 33.

53 E.E. Rich, *Cumberland and Hudson House Journals, 1775-1782*, vol. I (London: Hudson's Bay Record Society, 1951), 157-58.

54 W. Ferdinand Wentzel diary entries for 15 and 18 November and 5, 10, 11, and 18 December 1804, NAC, Masson Collection, MG 19, C1, vol. 8.

55 Ray, *Indians in the Fur Trade*, 130.

56 Ray provides an important analysis of trade goods use in ibid., 72-93.

57 See Charles M. Grant's introduction to A.N. McLeod's post journals in *Five Fur Traders of the Northwest: Being the Narrative of Peter Pond, and the Diaries of John Macdonnell, Archibald N. McLeod, Hugh Faries, and Thomas Connor* (Minneapolis: University of Minnesota, 1933).

58 Ibid., 133.

59 Journal of Qu'Appelle Lake Post, 1857-58, GA, M889.

60 *Fort Pelly Journal of Daily Occurrences, 1863* (Regina: Regina Archaeological Society, 1987).

61 Ray, *Indians in the Fur Trade*, 130-31.

62 Bishop, *The Northern Ojibwa and the Fur Trade*, 11-12, 228-62; Ray, *Indians in the Fur Trade*, 117-65; Arthur J. Ray, "Periodic Shortages, Native Welfare, and the Hudson's Bay Company 1670-1930," in *The Subarctic Fur Trade: Native Social and Economic Adaptations*, ed. Shepard Krech III (Vancouver: UBC Press, 1984), 6-7; J.C. Yerbury, *The Subarctic Indians and the Fur Trade, 1680-1860* (Vancouver: UBC Press, 1986), 14, 70-73, 79-81, 102-5, 113-16.

63 GA copy of *Tait's Edinburgh Magazine for 1838*, 5 (1838): 648, 654.

64 Norman McLeod diary, 15 December 1800, in *Five Fur Traders of the Northwest*, ed. C.M. Grant, 139-40.

65 Wentzel diary, 9 October 1804.

66 28 October 1781, Lower Hudson House journal, HBCA, B.87/a/4.

67 James Sutherland journal at Escabitchewan Post for 27 January 1793, HBCA, B.64/a/1.

68 Sutherland journal entries for 30 January and 1 February 1793; Escabitchewan Post journal.

69 Diary of John Macdonnell, 1793, in *Five Fur Traders of the Northwest*, ed. C.M. Grant, 107, 109.

70 Sutherland journal at Escabitchewan Post, 18 December 1792.

71 See, for instance, the work of James Isham and Alexander Light, who in the mid-1740s began submitting naturalist collections from their posts at Hudson Bay. James L. Baillie, Jr., "Naturalists on Hudson Bay," *Beaver*, 14 (1946): 36. Also, Grace Lee Nute points out Karl A. Geyer's contribution in the *London Journal of Botany*. See Nute, "A Botanist at Fort Colville," *Beaver*, 14 (1946): 28. See also HBCA, A9/4 Memorial Books, entry for 22 October 1771, reel 54, and ibid., A9/5, 107.

72 Robert Brown, "The Present State of Science on the North-Western Slopes of the Rocky Mountains," *Journal of Travel and Natural History* 1, 3 (1868): 176-78. Roland H. Alden and John D. Ifft provide a more general account of early naturalists in "Early Naturalists in the Far West," *Occasional Papers of the California Academy of Sciences*, 20 (San Francisco: California Academy of Sciences, 1943). Debra Lindsay directs attention to the Smithsonian Institution's work in *Science in the Subarctic: Trappers, Traders, and the Smithsonian Institution* (Washington: The Smithsonian Institution, 1993).

73 Bernard R. Ross, "An Account of the Botanical and Mineral Products, Useful to the Chipewyan Tribes of Indians, Inhabiting the McKenzie River District," *Canadian Naturalist and Geologist*, 7 (1862): 133-37; Bernard R. Ross, "List of Mammals, Birds, and Eggs, Observed in the McKenzie's River District, with Notices," *Canadian Naturalist and Geologist*, 7 (1862): 137-55; Roderick Ross MacFarlane, "Land and Sea Birds Nesting within the Arctic Circle in the Lower Mackenzie River District," *Historical and Scientific Society of Manitoba Transaction*, 39 (1888-89): 1.

74 Andrew Murray, "Contributions to the Natural History of the Hudson's Bay Company's Territories," *Edinburgh New Philosophical Journal* (1858): 5. Copy held at HBCA, Winnipeg.

75 Murray's questionnaire can be found in HBCA, "Queries Connected with the Natural History of the Honourable Hudson's Bay Company's Territories and the Indian Territories of British North America; Addressed to the Gentlemen in the Interior," PP1828-1. In the same collection, see the circular published by the Smithsonian, 1869, PP1869-4. John Richardson said that "the quadrupeds or birds may be skinned by opening their own belly, taking away the body, and leaving the skulls, and legs and wing bones." GA, memo from John Richardson to Murdoch McPherson, 1825, box 1, file 16, M941.
76 Ray, "Periodic Shortages," 1-19.
77 Correspondence between Davis, Macfarlane, and Dewdney, Indian Affairs Correspondence, NAC, RG 10, vol. 3808, file 53,556.
78 Ibid.

Chapter 2: The Territorial Period, Game Crisis, and the Western Domestication Movement
1 On the transition into the Canadian period, see Arthur J. Ray, *The Canadian Fur Trade in the Industrial Age* (Toronto: University of Toronto Press, 1990), 37-46. See W.L. Morton's use of the term in "The Old Order and the Transfer," in *Manitoba: A History* (Toronto: University of Toronto Press, 1967), 94-120. The following works provide new understandings of earlier social and economic changes: Gerhard J. Ens, *Homeland to Hinterland: The Changing Worlds of the Red River Métis in the Nineteenth Century* (Toronto: University of Toronto Press, 1996); Irene Spry, "The Great Transformation: The Disappearance of the Commons in Western Canada," in *Man and Nature on the Prairies*, ed. Richard Allen (Regina: Canadian Plains Institute, 1976), 21-45; Gerald Friesen, *The Canadian Prairies: A History* (Toronto: University of Toronto Press, 1987), 195-96.
2 For an overview of western images, see R. Douglas Francis, *Images of the West: Changing Perceptions of the Prairies, 1690-1960* (Saskatoon: Western Producer Prairie Books, 1989).
3 Doug Owram discusses views of the fur trade in *Promise of Eden: The Canadian Expansionist Movement and the Idea of the West, 1856-1900* (Toronto: University of Toronto Press, 1980). See also R. Douglas Francis, "From Wasteland to Utopia: Changing Images of the Canadian West in the Nineteenth Century," *Great Plains Quarterly* 8, 3 (1987): 178-94.
4 Allusions to the west as a breeding ground for animals are found in "Canada and the Hudson's Bay Company," *Saturday Review*, 27 March 1869: 416; and Alexander Morris, *The Hudson's Bay and Pacific Territories: A Lecture* (Montreal: John Lovell, 1859), 7. William Hooker attempted to chart "the most southern possessions of British North America," disregarded by previous natural histories. See Sir William Jackson Hooker, *Flora Boreali-Americana; Or, The Botany of the Northern Parts of British America* (London: Henry G. Bohn, 1840).
5 Thomas Rawlings, *What Shall We Do with the Hudson's Bay Territory? Colonize the "Fertile Belt," Which Contains Forty Millions of Acres* (London: A.H. Baily, 1866), 26-27; "Fur and the Fur-Trade," *Saturday Magazine*, January 1842: 48; G.O. Corbett, Red River letter, *Times*, 10 September 1868; "Canada," *Illustrated London News*, 18 December 1858.
6 John M. MacKenzie, *The Empire of Nature: Hunting, Conservation, and British* (Manchester: Manchester University Press, 1988); Robert A. Stafford, *Scientist of Empire: Sir Roderick Murchison, Scientific Exploration and Victorian Imperialism* (Cambridge: Cambridge University Press, 1989). The implicit imperialism of botanical and zoological surveys is gaining new attention. Amerindians did not see these collectors as neutral agents. Henry Yule Hind encountered Indians who were suspicious of the work behind his botanical collections and stated bluntly at Muskeg River, in present-day Ontario, that "The white man looks at our flowers and trees and takes away the Indian's land." Henry Yule Hind correspondence, in *British Parliamentary Papers, Colonies: Canada,* 22: 464. Charles Messiter, a companion of Milton and Cheadle, had difficulty gaining access to the Saskatchewan buffalo grounds because of the suspicions that his hunting raised among Cree bands near Fort Carleton. Charles Alston Messiter, *Sport and Adventures among the North-American Indians* (London: R.H. Porter, 1890), 63, 90. See also John Palliser, *Solitary Rambles and Adventures of a Hunter in the Prairies* (London: John Murray, 1853); John Palliser, *The Journals, Detailed Reports, and Observations Relative to the Exploration, by Captain Palliser of That Portion of British North*

America (London: George Edward Eyre and William Spottiswoode, 1863), 56, 97. See also E.E. Rich, *The Fur Trade and the Northwest to 1857* (London: Oxford University Press, 1968), 1.

7 On Mill's view of the homestead farmer, see Eugenio F. Biaginin, *Liberty, Retrenchment, and Reform: Popular Liberalism in the Age of Gladstone* (Cambridge: Cambridge University Press, 1992), 87, 89-91. Chester Martin provides an overview of the Dominion Lands Survey policy in *"Dominion Lands" Policy* (Ottawa: Carleton Library, 1973). On liberalism in the west, see W.L. Morton, *The Progressive Party of Canada* (Toronto: University of Toronto Press, 1950); David Laycock, *Populism and Democratic Thought in the Canadian Prairie: 1910-1945* (Toronto: University of Toronto Press, 1990); Lewis H. Thomas, *The Struggle for Responsible Government in the North-West Territories* (Toronto: University of Toronto Press, 1956); Lewis G. Thomas, *The Liberal Party in Alberta: A History of Politics in the Province of Alberta, 1905-1921* (Toronto: University of Toronto Press, 1959); and D.J. Hall, *Clifford Sifton*, 2 vols. (Vancouver: UBC Press, 1976).

8 Department of the Interior, *Western Canada: Where and How and All about It, Information and Facts,* 1915. Copy held at Glenbow Library, Calgary.

9 Brown quoted in Vernon C. Fowke, *The National Policy and the Wheat Economy* (Toronto: University of Toronto Press, 1957), 35.

10 Morris, *The Hudson's Bay*, 7.

11 Vankoughnet to E. Dewdney, 5 December 1884, GA, Dewdney Papers, p. 1106, vol. 5, M 320. An excellent overview of the growing food crises affecting Indian nations is offered by Blair Stonechild and Bill Waiser, *Loyal till Death: Indians and the North-West Rebellion* (Calgary: Fifth House Publishers, 1997), 27-84.

12 Ens, *Homeland to Hinterland*, 38-40.

13 *The Nor'-Wester,* 15 November 1860.

14 See Father André's comments sent from St. Laurent to the North West Council in response to inquiries about the buffalo herds. Father André wanted the hunt restricted to the summer months and an end to the wintering camps that would "greatly induce them becoming civilized." NAC, RG 10, vol. 3641, file 7530.

15 "Game Laws Discussed," *Edmonton Journal,* 6 March 1907.

16 John Macoun, *Manitoba and the Great North-West: The Field for Investment, the Home of the Emigrant* (London: Thomas C. Jack, 1883), 575. "Cut off the supply and nature asserts her wants and necessity causes action." Ibid., 551.

17 Selwyn to Minister of Interior, 21 April 1874.

18 Memorandum by A. Meredith, 1874, NAC, Indian Affairs Files, RG 10, vol. 3609, file 3229.

19 Wildlife extinction is cited in a letter to the Department of the Interior, 7 January 1875, NAC, RG 10, vol. 3609, file 3229; "Notes," *Medicine Hat Times,* 29 July 1886; "Another Opinion," ibid., 2 October 1886.

20 Dufferin's speech is quoted at length in Macoun, *Manitoba and the Great North-West,* 514.

21 1818 petition, NAC, Selkirk Papers, MG 19, Series E1(1), vol. 13; and Bird's report from Red River and the comments of Pat Quinn to Anthony Gillaspy, NAC, Selkirk Papers, vol. 2, p. 192.

22 "Report of the Select Committee of the Senate Appointed to Inquire into the Resources of the Great Mackenzie Basin, 1888 (hereafter "Report of the Select Committee"), in *Appendices to the Twenty-Second Volume of the Journals of the Senate of Canada* (Ottawa: Brown Chamberlain, 1888), 246. On Macoun and his western promotional work, see W.A. Waiser, *The Field Naturalist: John Macoun, the Geological Survey, and Natural Science* (Toronto: University of Toronto Press, 1989), 35-39; on the Mackenzie inquiry, see 146-47.

23 See "Map Showing Geographical Distribution of the Principal Canadian Mammals," appended to "Report of the Select Committee," 246; *Lethbridge News,* 12 January 1888. The *Report of the Minister of Agriculture of the Province of Manitoba for the Year 1880* (Montreal: Gazette Printing, 1881), 3, stated that the "capacity to support life" of Manitoba soils and the "variety and abundance of wild animals" in the province proved its great farming potential. Copy held at Provincial Archives of Manitoba (hereafter PAM). Later Department of the Interior brochures discussed wildlife as a food resource. See *The Lac La Biche District, Alberta: A Guide for Intending Settlers* and *The Last Best West,* the department's popular brochure. NAC, RG 76, vol. 389, file 541601.

24 Quoted in Stonechild and Waiser, *Loyal till Death*, 55.
25 Alexander's speech, 20 April 1888, *Debates of the Senate, of the Dominion of Canada, 1888* (Ottawa: A.S. Woodburn, 1888), 352.
26 See Abbott's reply, ibid., 354.
27 Notes taken from the meetings are in John Schultz Files, PAM, MG 12, E1, file 7820.
28 Schultz's remarks in the Senate on 18 May 1887 are noted in *Debates of the Senate, of the Dominion of Canada, 1887* (Ottawa: A.S. Woodburn, 1887), 76.
29 See Schultz's notes of questions and answers arising from these proceedings in "Select Committee Appointed for the Purpose of Collecting Information Regarding the Existing Natural Food Products of the North-West Territories, and the Best Means of Conserving or Increasing Them," John Schultz Files, 43.
30 Evidence from the inquiry appears in *Debates of the Senate ... 1887*; "Report and Minutes of Evidence of the Select Committee of the Senate on the Existing Natural Food Products of the North-West Territories, and the Best Means of Conserving and Increasing Them," Appendix 1 of the *Journals of the Senate of Canada, 1887* (Ottawa: Maclean, Roger, 1887), 3-151.
31 Fort Edmonton factor quoted in William A. Dobak, "Killing the Canadian Buffalo, 1821-1881," *Western Historical Quarterly* (1996): 48; see also Dan Flores, "Bison Ecology and Bison Diplomacy: The Southern Plains from 1800 to 1850," *Journal of American History* 78, 2 (1991): 465-85.
32 As reported in *Les "Métis,"* 9 August 1877.
33 Walter Robert Bown provides valuable food prices in "Report and Minutes of Evidence," 111. See Red River accounts, Department of Indian Affairs, July-August 1871, NAC, RG 10, vol. 3580, file 676.
34 See Bown, "Report and Minutes of Evidence," 111-14. Cf. H.M. Robinson, *The Great Fur Land: Or, Sketches of Life in Hudson's Bay Territory* (Toronto: Coles Publishing Company, 1972), 165. Robinson confirms Bown's prices for 1870.
35 Bedson testimony, "Report and Minutes of Evidence," 67; price series are based on accounts from Cumberland House, HBCA, B.49/d/115-132, and prices appearing in accounts of the Department of Indian Affairs, some of which are found in NAC, RG 10, vol. 3751, file 30249, and accounts, NAC, RG 10, vol. 3580, file 676.
36 Frank Tough, *"As Their Resources Fail": Native Peoples and the Economic History of Northern Manitoba, 1870-1930* (Vancouver: UBC Press, 1996), 61.
37 Prices are taken from expenditure tables found in reports of the Department of Indian Affairs for the years 1872 (33), 1879 (188-89), and 1881 (254-55) (Ottawa: Government Printer, 1873, 1880, 1882); fresh venison had the most remarkable volatility in pricing. Cumberland House Accounts show that fresh moose and deer obtained the following prices: in 1889, eight and five cents a pound; in 1892, seven and five cents a pound. See HBCA, Cumberland House Accounts, B.49/d/138-141.
38 1884 bill of lading, HBCA, Cumberland House Accounts, B.49/d/135.
39 See 1893 outfit listed in Cumberland House Accounts and Press Books, HBCA, B.49/d/140.
40 Tough, *"As Their Resources Fail,"* 61, 67.
41 Provencher to Minister of Interior, 20 April 1877, NAC, Indian Affairs Correspondence, RG 10, reel C-10113, file 8110; see Ray, *The Canadian Fur Trade*, 46; John J. Van West, "Ojibwa Fisheries, Commercial Fishers Development, and Fisheries Administration, 1873-1915: An Examination of Conflicting Interest and the Collapse of the Sturgeon Fisheries of the Lake of the Woods," *Native Studies Review* 6, 1 (1980): 30, 34-35.
42 Whitcher to Burgess, 26 March 1884, NAC, Game Preservation File, Northwest Territories, RG 15, vol. 317, file 73055.
43 "Report of the Select Committee," 23.
44 Morton, *Manitoba*, 94-120, 150; *Manitoban and North-West Herald*, 29 October 1870. By 20 November, the paper had added "Rupert's Land" to its masthead.
45 See John E. Foster, Dick Harrison, and I.S. MacLaren, eds., *Buffalo* (Calgary: University of Alberta Press, 1992), in particular Foster's essay, "The Métis and the End of the Plains Buffalo in Alberta," 61-78, and MacLaren's essay, "Buffalo in Word and Image: From European Origins to the Art of Clarence Tillenius," 95. MacLaren's essay deals with literary and artistic renderings of the buffalo and Paul Kane's artistic contribution to expansionism.

46 The *Nor'-Wester* editor accompanied and described the buffalo hunt; see the issues of 14 July
    and 14 and 28 August 1860. Alexander Begg, *Seventeen Years in the Canadian North-West*,
    paper read on 8 April 1884 at the Royal Colonial Institute (London: Spottiswoode, 1884), 5.
47 The Campaigner, "An Old Time Buffalo Hunt," *Great West Magazine* 13, 2 (1898): 69-77.
    Donald McIvor, a Manitoba farmer, testified at the Mackenzie District inquiry that HBC
    employment as "boatmen and servants" had been beneficial to the Indians and that the
    employment had helped to "civilize" them. "Report of the Select Committee," 302. See
    also Dobak, "Killing the Canadian Buffalo," 43; Archer Martin, "The Hudson's Bay Com-
    pany and Mr. Julian Ralph," *Manitoban* (1892), CIHM, 134.
48 Robinson, *The Great Fur Land*, 135-50, for the code of law. See Frederick Verner's buffalo
    paintings, especially *The Last Buffalo* (1893), reprinted in Francis, *Images of the West*.
49 Robert Miller Christy, *Manitoba Described: Being a Series of General Observations upon the
    Farming, Climate, Sport, Natural History, and Future Prospects of the Country* (London: Wyman
    and Sons, 1885), 83-84; W.L. Morton, "Agriculture in the Red River Colony," in *Contexts of
    Canada's Past: Selected Essays of W.L. Morton*, ed. A.B. McKillop (Toronto: Macmillan, 1980).
    In 1877, David Laird reported that twenty-three "destitute" bands had arrived at his office
    to receive 8,000 pounds of pemmican. Meanwhile, Treaty Six and Treaty Four bands were
    given rations, including over 4,000 pounds of pemmican but only 243 pounds of beef.
    David Laird, report for the year 1878, Report of the Department of the Interior Part I, *Senate
    Papers*, Tabulations (Ottawa, Government Printer, 1879), 56-58. Robinson, *The Great Fur
    Land*, 68, recognized that the transfer "had served to dissipate the quiet content of the
    Company's officers." *Les "Métis,"* 18 January 1877; editorial, *Les "Métis,"* 19 April 1877;
    "Les Traiteurs," *Les "Métis,"* 12 July 1877.
50 See reports of the buffalo hunt in "Écho du Nord-Ouest," *Les "Métis,"* 8 February 1877; *Les
    "Métis,"* 12 April 1877; and ordinance to protect Manitoba game, *Les "Métis,"* 26 April 1877.
    The Manitoba Game Protective League formed in May 1882, with Colonel John Walker as
    president; Colin Inkster later succeeded him. PAM, box P 3611, file 7, Winnipeg Game and
    Fish Association. See McKay's buffalo park mentioned in *Les "Métis,"* 9 August 1877.
51 *Les "Métis,"* 15 March 1877.
52 See Morris to Minister of Interior, 4 April 1874, Preservation of Buffalo in NWT file, Indian
    Affairs Letterbooks, NAC, RG 10, vol. 3609, file 3229; and David Laird, "Report of the Sub-
    Committee of the NW Council re: Preservation of the Buffalo in the NW, 1877," NAC, RG
    10, vol. 3641, file 7530. Charles Bell pointed out that, should the Indians "see the game all
    killed out by strangers, and the government doing nothing to prevent it when it was in
    their power to do so, is it likely they will quietly go onto reserves"? Charles Bell, letter, 4
    April 1874, NAC, RG 73, vol. 3609, file 3229. Lewis H. Thomas missed the importance of
    this legislation in his classic study of the North West Council's struggle for self-
    determination. Lewis H. Thomas, *The Struggle for Responsible Government in the North-West
    Territories* (Toronto: University of Toronto Press, 1956).
53 Morton, *Manitoba*, 193, 227.
54 See "Historical and Scientific Society of Manitoba," Deputy Minister, Game Branch of Mani-
    toba Files, PAM, box 34, file 36.1, RG 17, B1.
55 *Macleod Gazette*, 7 March 1889.
56 See "La Question des Indiens," *Le Manitoba*, 14 juin 1888; "President's Inaugural Address,"
    Annual Report of the Historical and Scientific Society of Manitoba for the Year 1888 (Winnipeg:
    Manitoba Free Press, 1889), 5; John Schultz, "The Old Crow Wing Trail," *Transactions* 45
    (1884), Canadian Institute of Historical Microfilm: 3.
57 Lieutenant Governor Schultz's plan to domesticate caribou in Keewatin, Schultz to Haytor
    Reed, NAC, RG 10, vol. 3950, file 130, 405. William Christie's testimony at the Mackenzie
    Basin inquiry mentions HBC buffalo domestication, "Report of the Select Committee," 103.
58 This is according to William Cullen Bryant, unpublished manuscript, "Bedson and His
    Buffalo," PAM, Norman Bedson Files, P4255/16.
59 Mentioned in "Domestication of the Buffalo" and quoting Sam Bedson, *Canada: A Memo-
    rial Volume* (Montreal: E.E. Biggar, 1889), 193. The *Manitoba Free Press* stated that Smith had
    the last "few" of Bedson's herd by 1889 at his farm at Silver Heights. *Manitoba Free Press*,
    "Buffalo Crosses," 4 January 1889.

60 Bedson's history can be traced in his warden letterbooks. See NAC, Register 2, Bedson Letterbooks, RG 73, vol. 19, microfilm reels T-11079 to 11084, 81.
61 Ibid. His report on the Sioux, whom he believed had reformed during three years of incarceration, is found in Bedson Report, *Sessional Papers*, Department of Justice Annual Report, Paper No. 14 (Ottawa: Government Printers, 1876), 138.
62 Bryant, unpublished reminiscences, PAM, Norman Bedson Files, P4255/16. Newspaper obituary in ibid.
63 Bedson Letterbooks, 14 July 1879, Register 1, RG 73, vol. 19, 559-60, regarding rationing; Bedson to Indian Affairs, 6 April 1876, Register 1, 528. His letterbooks show the location of the land that he registered in 1874. Register 1, 244, 294.
64 The *Winnipeg Free Press* reprinted the American piece entitled "Bedson's Buffaloes," 3 December 1883.
65 See damaged newsprint notice "Les Deux origna ... croisés de M. Bed ... expédiés à Mont ... ils figureront dans le grand carnaval du mois de février," *Le Manitoba*, 3 January 1889.
66 *Manitoba Free Press*, 21 February 1885; and Bryant memoir, Norman Bedson Files, 2.
67 See Colonel Henry Inman, *Buffalo Jones' Forty Years of Adventure* (London: Sampson Low, Marston and Company, 1899), 246-50, in which one reference to Bedson is made. The *Manitoba Free Press* correctly called Jones "more pronouncedly ... a showman than breeder," 4 January 1889.
68 To the Philadelphia parks commissioner, Bedson wrote on 7 April 1880, "I have several Buffalo which have [unreadable] from the plains ... I wish to dispose of a couple of them." Bedson Letterbooks, Register 1, 567.
69 Edward Roper, *By Track and Trail: A Journey through Canada* (London: W.H. Allen, 1891), 53.
70 "The Last of the Mohicans," reprinted from the St. Paul paper in the *Nor'-West Farmer*, 7, 6 (1888): 147.
71 Jones pondered one night "upon the contrast between the qualities of the white man's domestic cattle and those of the red man's cattle [buffalo] ... Why not domesticate this wonderful beast which can endure such a 'blizzard,' defying a storm so destructive to our native cattle?" Cited in Inman, *Buffalo Jones*, 48; see also "Domestication of the Buffalo," 192-93.
72 Ernest Thompson Seton, "A List of the Mammals of Manitoba," *Transactions* 23 (1886): 10-11.
73 Bedson sent the Mackenzie Basin inquiry the newspaper clipping describing the skin. See "Report of the Select Committee," 227-28.
74 The company's capital stock had been greatly increased, but few details of who had been involved in the scheme appeared in the report. "The Buffalo Breeding Company," *Nor'-West Farmer and Manitoba Miller* 5, 7 (1886).
75 "The Last of the Mohicans," *Nor'-West Farmer* 7, 6 (1888).
76 See L.V. Kelly, *The Range Men: The Story of the Ranchers and Indians of Alberta* (Toronto: William Briggs, 1913), 200-3, 377-98; *Lethbridge News*, 19 July 1888.
77 Bedson was not yet making much effort to take his stock to market and was "getting only 18 cents a pound" for flesh. "Mr. Bedson's Ranche," *Lethbridge News*, 19 July 1888 (reprinting a story carried in the *Chicago Times*); "Proposition to Resuscitate the Supply of Buffalos," *Lethbridge News*, 18 June 1886; "The Departing Buffalo," *Lethbridge News*, 29 March 1888.
78 "The Breeding of Buffalo," *Lethbridge News*, 10 October 1888.
79 Ibid., in which both *Bulletin* stories are reprinted.
80 *Lethbridge News*, 23 February 1888.
81 Charles Bell testimony, in notes from Senate Inquiry into Existing Natural Food Products of the North West Territories, John Schultz Files, PAM, MG 12, E1, file 7820.
82 See *Le Manitoba*, 22 September 1887, which discussed the history of the French voyageurs on the plains, "now almost all disappeared." See coverage of the departure in Inman, *Buffalo Jones' Forty Years*, 236-37; and "Buffalo Crosses," *Winnipeg Free Press*, 4 January 1889.
83 Macoun, *Manitoba and the Great North-West*.
84 David H. Breen, *The Canadian Prairie West and the Ranching Frontier, 1874-1924* (Toronto: University of Toronto Press, 1982), 33.
85 Kelly, *The Range Men*, 11; ibid., photographs on 27 and 35.

86 On the settler's collection, see Jennings to Harkin, 3 February 1936, NAC, RG 84, vol. 2155, file u318, part 2.
87 Major Robert Larmour, *Canada's Opportunity: A Review of Butler's "Great Lone Land" in its Relation to Present Day Conditions and Future Prospects* (Toronto: William Briggs, 1907), 26.

Chapter 3: From Meat to Sport Hunting

1 "Game Protection," *Macleod Gazette*, 24 May 1887.
2 Frank Gilbert Roe, *The North American Buffalo: A Critical Study of the Species in Its Wild State* (Toronto: University of Toronto Press, 1951). Roe identified aspects of a "tradition" distorting the accuracy of pioneer, Amerindian, and scientific accounts of the buffalo in chapters devoted to its range, population size, trail making, origins, et cetera, but particularly on 12-24, 26-33, 75, 80-81, and 180.
3 This is the title of Walter Walsh's reminiscence, "Once a Monarch of the Prairie," *Owl*, November 1893: 115-17.
4 "Ancient Blackfeet Legend Has Historical Counterpart," *Lethbridge Daily Herald*, 27 December 1913.
5 The Lumsden photographs of the Saskatoon bone heaps appear in plate X, C. Gordon Hewitt, *The Conservation of Canadian Wildlife* (New York: Charles Scribner's Sons, 1921).
6 "Notes," *Medicine Hat News*, 2 October 1886.
7 Ibid., 21 August 1886.
8 Achilles Daunt, *In the Land of the Moose, the Bear, and the Beaver* (London: T. Nelson and Sons, 1885), 112-13.
9 Colonel Henry Inman, *Buffalo Jones' Forty Years of Adventure* (London: Sampson Low, Marston and Company, 1899), see 300-1, 307-8, and photograph on 302.
10 Charles Mair, "The Last Bison," in *Dreamland and Other Poems: Tecumseh: A Drama*, ed. Norman Shrive (Toronto: University of Toronto Press, 1974), 149; on Charles Mair's ideas about buffalo in the West, see his article, "The American Bison," *Transactions of the Royal Society of Canada*, Section II (1890): 106-7. Norman Shrive, *Charles Mair: Literary Nationalist* (Toronto: University of Toronto Press, 1965), xxiv. Doug Owram provides biographical information in *Promise of Eden: The Canadian Expansionist Movement and the Idea of the West, 1856-1900* (Toronto: University of Toronto Press, 1980), 64.
11 Charles Short interview, GA, RCT 1, Knupp Family Fonds; on the pioneer era in the region, see Lillian Knupp, *Roots of the Medicine Tree Country, High River, Alberta* (High River: Highwood Heritage Books, 1997), 27.
12 Ord's narrative, in *Reminiscences of a Bungle: By One of the Bunglers*, ed. R.C. Macleod (Edmonton: University of Alberta Press, 1983), 14.
13 Cassell's diary entry, 11 April 1885, in ibid., 126.
14 William Francis Butler, *The Great Lone Land: A Narrative of Travel and Adventure in the North-West of America* (Edmonton: M.G. Hurtig, 1968), 217; "The Lone Land," *Calgary Herald*, 23 November 1883.
15 "A Big Bear Hunt," *Macleod Gazette*, 26 August 1898.
16 "Bears," *Calgary Herald*, 5 October 1883.
17 "Bear Chase," *Calgary Herald*, 26 October 1883.
18 *Mainland Guardian*, 20 October 1888.
19 See "Antelope" and "Bear Chase," *Calgary Herald*, 26 October 1883.
20 See Karen Wonders, "A Sportsman's Eden," *Beaver*, October-November 1999: 31.
21 "Big Game and Wolves about Killing Cattle in Magrath," *Lethbridge Herald*, 16 January 1913.
22 *Calgary Herald*, 24 April 1928.
23 H.W. Seton Karr, *Shores and Alps of Alaska* (London: Sampson Low, Marston, Searle and Rivington, 1887), 5.
24 Newton H. Chittenden, "Settlers, Miners, and Tourists Guide from Ocean to Ocean by the C.P.R.," 1885, CIHM 3051, 4; see also John Prince Sheldon, *From Britain to British Columbia: Or, Canada as a Domain for British Farmers, Sportsmen, and Tourists* (Ottawa: Government of Canada, 1887), 9.
25 Clive Phillipps-Wolley, *A Sportsman's Eden* (London: Richard Bentley and Son, 1888), xii, xiii.

26 J.H. Hubbard, "Sport in the Canadian North-West: A Paper on the Game Birds and Animals of Manitoba and the North-West Territories," 29 July 1886, pamphlet collection of the Public Archives of British Columbia (hereafter PABC), 33.

27 Arthur Bryan Williams, *Game Trails in British Columbia: Big Game and Other Sport in the Wilds of British Columbia* (London: John Murray, 1925).

28 A. Bryan Williams, "Annual Report of the Chief Game Guardian for the Year 1911," *Sessional Papers*, BC legislature (Victoria: Queen's Printer, 1912), 5.

29 Williams to Herchmer, 23 March 1906, Letterbook 5, Game Guardian Files, PABC, RG 446.

30 Frank I. Clarke, "Hunting Big Game in British Columbia," *Man-to-Man Magazine*, 9 October 1910: 777.

31 Mrs. Clive Phillipps-Wolley, in Clive Phillipps-Wolley, *A Sportsman's Eden*, 33, 37.

32 Sheldon, *From Britain to British Columbia*, 39.

33 Harold Bindloss, *Prescott of Saskatchewan* (Toronto: McLeod and Allen, 1913), 16.

34 *The Sportsman's Map of Canada and the Northwest Territory*, 1908, Canadian Pacific Archives (hereafter CPA), X186.

35 Frederick Lort-Phillips, *The Wander Years: Hunting and Travel in Four Continents* (London: Nash and Grayson, 1931), 213.

36 H. Somers Somerset, *The Land of the Musket* (London: William Heinemann, 1895), xiv.

37 CPR "Annotated Time Table," Westbound Edition, 5 November 1902, pamphlet collection of the National Library of Canada.

38 *Summer Tours by the Canadian Pacific Railway* (Montreal: Passenger Department, 1887), 12.

39 *The Sportsman's Guide to the Hunting and Shooting Grounds of the United States and Canada* (New York: Chas. T. Dilingham, 1888), 190-92.

40 Thomas Martindale, *Sport Royal, I Warrant You!* (Philadelphia: H.W. Shaw, 1897), 18, 43, 57-58; this book was republished under the title *Sport Indeed* (Philadelphia: George W. Jacobs, 1901).

41 T.R. Patillo, *Moose-Hunting, Salmon-Fishing, and Other Sketches of Sport* (London: Sampson Low, Marston and Company, 1902), 104, 114, 138.

42 The "beef famine" was identified in Calgary newspapers by Alfred Frederick Sproule, *The Role of Patrick Burns in the Development of Western Canada*, MA thesis, University of Alberta, 1962, 57.

43 See *Mainland Guardian*, 5 September 1888; the account of deer appears in the "Brief" section, ibid., 17 October 1888; Vianen's feathered game is also in the "Brief" section, ibid., 7 November 1888.

44 Ibid., 8 September 1888.

45 Photograph NA-3462-24, GA.

46 History of Protective League, "Winnipeg Game and Fish Association," PAM, box P 3611, file 7.

47 Minister of Interior to Manitoba Provincial Secretary, 9 June 1885, NAC, and Game Preservation, NWT, NAC, RG 15, vol. 317, file 73055.

48 See sec. 2, cap 85, An Ordinance for the Protection of Game, 1898, Ordinances of the North-West Territories.

49 Sec. 4, Wild Animals, *Acts of the Legislature of the Province of Manitoba, 1890* (Winnipeg: Queen's Printer, 1890).

50 Cap. 95, Game Act, 1911, see Schedule B.

51 Cap. 88, Game Act, 1897, sec. 27.

52 F.W. Godsal, "The Game Laws," *Macleod Gazette*, 30 August 1887.

53 General Population Tables, 1881 Census, vol. 1 (Ottawa: Maclean, Rogers and Company, 1882), Table 1; taxidermists are listed in Occupations of the People, ibid., vol. 2, Table 14; and comparative data from 1885 Census of Manitoba and 1891 Census.

54 "On calcule que le marché aux bestiaux comprend à l'heure qu'il est plus de 3000 têtes de bétail. Les prix sont tombés et en conséquence il se vend de bonnes vaches à lait pour $25.00. Quand donc les bouchers diminueront-ils le prix de la viande?" Les "*Métis*," 12 July 1877.

55 *Debates of the Senate, of the Dominion of Canada, 1887* (Ottawa: A.S. Woodburn, 1887); "Report and Minutes of Evidence of the Select Committee of the Senate on the Existing

Natural Food Products of the North-West Territories, and the Best Means of Conserving and Increasing Them," Appendix 1 of the *Journals of the Senate of Canada, 1887* (Ottawa: Maclean, Roger and Company, 1887), 67, 145, 180; Thomas McKay testimony, ibid., 149; prices of prairie chickens and partridges were confirmed by Samuel Bedson, who claimed that a pair fetched twenty-five cents on the market. See Bedson testimony, ibid., 74.

56 Sproule, *The Role of Patrick Burns*, 31.

57 *Herald* quoted in Beulah May Barss, *Pioneer Food Patterns in the Western Interior of Canada*, MA thesis, University of Calgary, 1979, 62-63.

58 Mining region prices appear in the report of John Ash, the minister of mines, regarding Cassiar district in *Journals of the Legislative Assembly of the Province of British Columbia*, vol. 4 (Victoria: Government Printer, 1876); see his description of the district, and his price lists of other foodstuffs, 545-70.

59 For Burns's marketing, see Sproule, *The Role of Patrick Burns*, 76.

60 Quoted in Edith Rowles, "Bannock, Beans, and Bacon: An Investigation of Pioneer Diet," *Saskatchewan History* 5, 1 (1952): 42.

61 Mrs. George Lane Memoirs, GA, file M 652.

62 J.R. Romer to K.W. McKenzie, 12 April 1909, NAC, Department of Marine and Fisheries Files, RG 23, vol. 344, file 2995, part 1.

63 Solmundson to Department, 1909, NAC, RG 23, vol. 365, file 3216, part 1.

64 35th Annual Report of the Department of Marine and Fisheries for the year 1902 (Ottawa: Government Printer, 1903), 116.

65 See overseer report from District 2 of Northwest Territories, in 37th Annual Report of the Department of Marine and Fisheries for the Year 1904 (Ottawa: Government Printer, 1905), 209-10.

66 32nd Annual Report of the Department of Marine and Fisheries for the Year 1899 (Ottawa: Government Printer, 1900), 186.

67 MacFarlane to Department, 14 November 1910, NAC, RG 23, vol. 344, file 2995, part 1.

68 *Regina Leader*, 23 April 1889.

69 C.E. Radclyffe, "The Canadian Poacher," *London Times*, 2 April 1908.

70 Letter, *Macleod Gazette*, 11 October 1895.

71 Petition to Lieutenant Governor, 1889, Northwest Territories, Bills and Unpublished Sessional Papers, Provincial Archives of Saskatchewan, Regina (hereafter PAS-R), R.2.92.

72 Letter from Richmond Game Protective Association, 1907, PABC, Game Guardian Files, GR 446, box 2, file 100-3.

73 See T.N. Willing, *Report of the Game Branch, Department of Agriculture of the Province of Saskatchewan* (Regina: Government Press, 1907), 126.

74 *1911 Report of the Chief Game Guardian, Department of Agriculture of the Province of Saskatchewan* (Regina: Government Printer, 1912), 171.

75 Kreh to Bradshaw, 26 January 1919, Provincial Archives of Saskatchewan, Saskatoon (hereafter PAS-S), NR 3, box 1 Big Game – General, 1918-39, file 21.

76 Crawford to Winkler, 22 November 1915, PAM, files 1127-28.

77 Ibid.

78 Bradshaw correspondence, 1920, PAS-S, NR 3, box 1, Big Game – General, file 21.

79 Hewitt, *Conservation*, 8-9.

80 *1907 Report of the Chief Game Guardian, Department of Agriculture of the Province of Saskatchewan* (Regina: Government Printer, 1908), 527.

81 "A Bill for the Passage of an Act for the Preservation of Game," *Victoria Gazette*, 23 April 1859; see also clipping file of published game ordinances in PABC, GR 961, box 1.

82 "Vict. Bill to Prevent the Careless Distribution of Poison with Attempt to Destroy Wild Animals," 22 March 1875, *Journals of the Legislative Assembly of the Province of British Columbia*, vol. 4 (Victoria: Government Printer, 1876), 19.

83 For legislation, see *Acts of the Legislature of the Province of Manitoba*, Game Laws and Amendments, 1890-1900 (Winnipeg: Government Printer, 1891-1901).

84 An Ordinance for the Protection of Game, 1903, *The General Ordinances of the North-West Territories in Force Sept 1 1905* (Regina: Government Printer, 1907).

85 See Kearn's advertisements in the *Qu'Appelle Vidette*, 28 May 1885.

86 See Petition to Department of Marine and Fisheries, 24 February 1899, NAC, RG 23, vol. 292, file 2241, part 1.
87 "The Game laws," *Regina Leader*, 30 November 1886; "The Right of the Public to Shoot," *Edmonton Journal*, 1 March 1907.
88 "Game Laws Discussed," *Edmonton Journal*, 6 March 1907.
89 Petitions in the correspondence of Deputy Superintendent General to Regina Indian Commissioner, 13 November 1893, NAC, RG 10, vol. 6732, file 420-2.
90 "Game Laws Discussed," *Edmonton Journal*, 6 March 1907.
91 Second Report of the Provincial Game and Forest Warden of the Province of British Columbia, *Sessional Papers, 1906* (Victoria: Government Printer, 1907), F10.
92 Fourth Report of the Provincial Game and Forest Warden of the Province of British Columbia, *Sessional Papers, 1908* (Victoria: King's Printer, 1909).
93 W.H. Heald's report, 1909, to Williams, PABC, GR 446, box 3, file 2.
94 Seventh Report of the Chief Game Guardian of the Province of British Columbia, *Sessional Papers, 1911* (Victoria: Government Printer, 1911), 15; for the year 1912, 6.
95 "Report of the Chief Game Guardian," in *Annual Report of the Department of Agriculture of the Province of Saskatchewan* (Saskatoon: Government Printer, 1907), 61.
96 Meiklijohn to Bradshaw, 19 December 1918, PAS-S, NR 3, box 1, file 21.
97 Frank Parks to Bradshaw, 23 December 1918, PAS-S, NR 3, box 1, file 21.
98 Bradshaw cited the account in the *Leader* as 19 January 1919, but I have not been able to locate this article between 18 and 30 January. See Bradshaw to Holmes, 30 January 1919, PAS-S, NR 3, box 1, file 21.
99 Letter to W.R. Motherwell, 22 August 1912, W.R. Motherwell Papers, PAS-R, R 2.712.
100 Ibid., letter, 27 July 1907.
101 Ibid., Nicolle to Motherwell, 4 May 1908.
102 Ibid., Motherwell to Wensley, April 1914.
103 T.F. Clarke to Bradshaw, 29 December 1920, PAS-S, NR 3, file 21, box 1, Game Guardian Files.
104 *Lethbridge News*, 29 August 1901.
105 Letter reprinted as "The Extinction of Game," *Lethbridge News*, 14 May 1903.
106 "High Cost of Munitions Might Save Ducks," *Lethbridge Daily Herald*, 28 August 1917: 3.
107 L.M. Lloyd Walters, Report of a Patrol from Fort Resolution, 1918, NAC, Indian Affairs Records, RG 10, vol. 4084, file 496,658.
108 Report on Cold Storage in Canada, *Sessional Paper 210 for the year 1917* (Ottawa: Government Printer, 1917), 8.
109 See John B. Burnham, "The War and Game," reprinted by the Commission of Conservation, CIHM 82388, 1-2.
110 *The Call of Canada* (Montreal: Dominion Cartridge Company, 1920), 1. For key changes in BC legislation, see the 1905 amendment; the 1920 amendment prohibited the sale and barter of all "big game" and birds, and hunters could store their meat only during open season in cold storage facilities with a special licence. In 1924, licensed merchants and storekeepers who sold meat were restricted to selling only the amount that they as individuals were allowed to hunt at that time. In Alberta, the 1907 ordinances licensed game dealers but only on the condition that they keep accounts of the animals they sold and the names of their hunters. By 1922, game dealers were restricted to certain game birds. Saskatchewan's ordinances prohibited game sales but allowed in 1916 for restaurateurs and hotel keepers to sell cooked game, a provision struck out in 1917. Manitoba's legislature outlawed the trade and sale of deer and some game birds in 1913.
111 See Bradshaw to Willett, 6 February 1919, PAS-S, NR 3, box 1, Big Game – General, file 21.
112 Willett to Bradshaw, 23 January 1919, PAS-S, NR 3, box 1, Big Game – General, file 21.
113 Ibid., Bradshaw to Schmitz, 9 January 1920, PAS-S.
114 Ibid., Bradshaw to Venn, 16 March 1920, PAS-S.
115 See ibid., letters of 1917 in this file and, particularly, Motherwell to Patrick, 5 March 1917.
116 Summary of Game Regulations, NAC, RG 10, vol. 6731, file 420-1.
117 Ibid.
118 See Gilbert Malcolm Sproat to Indian Superintendent, 16 July 1878, NAC, RG 10, vol. 3666, file 10,143.

119 Reed to Indian Agents, 5 November 1889, NAC, RG 10, vol. 6732, file 420-2.
120 Reed, letter, 27 April 1893, NAC, RG 10, vol. 6732, file 420-2.
121 J.A. Markle to Regina Indian Commissioner, 2 November 1893, NAC, RG 10, vol. 6732, file 420-2.
122 Dept. Supt. General to Regina Indian Commissioner, 13 November 1893, NAC, RG 10, vol. 6732, file 420-2.
123 Laird to T.J. Fleetham, 7 February 1907, NAC, Indian Affairs Letterbooks, RG 10, vol. 5155, file 271.
124 Indian Affairs Memorandum to Dr. Roche, 31 January 1917, NAC, RG 10, vol. 6731, file 420-1.
125 T.H. Carter to Bradbury, 17 January 1917, NAC, RG 10, vol. 6731, file 420-1.
·126 Sibbald to Padley, 23 December 1903, NAC, RG 10, vol. 6732, file 420-2.
127 Lawton to Scott, 4 March 1919, NAC, RG 10, vol. 6731, file 420-1.
128 W.E. Ditchburn, Inspector of Indian Agencies, Victoria, BC, to Duncan Campbell Scott, 19 May 1915, NAC, RG 10, vol. 6731, file 420-1. On Stoney Indian history, see Chief John Snow, *These Mountains Are Our Sacred Places: The Story of the Stoney Indians* (Toronto: S. Stevens, 1977).
129 Bradbury to W.J. Roche, Supt. Gen., 6 February 1917, NAC, RG 10, vol. 6731, file 420-1.
130 Chiefs Peter Wesley, Moses Bearspaw to Gov't of Canada, 9 April 1907, from Morley, NAC, RG 10, vol. 6732, file 420-2.
131 See account of the trial in NAC, RG 10, vol. 6732, file 420-2A.
132 *Macleod Gazette*, 2 October 1894.
133 Hewitt, *Conservation*, 12-13.
134 Minutes, 14 April 1925, J.H. Evans, Dep. Minister of Agriculture and Immigration in Manitoba, in Provincial/Dominion Wildlife Conferences notes and reports, NAC, RG 10, vol. 7631, file 420-1-2.
135 M.B. Williams, *Guardians of the Wild* (Toronto: Thomas Nelson and Sons, 1936), 58-62.
136 Brown to Premier Bracken, 27 October 1930, PAM, box 30, file 15.9.1, part 1.
137 Deputy Minister, Game Branch Files, RG 17, B1 box 20; G.H. Revell, Provincial Game Guardian, Report to Etter, 1931, SAS-S.
138 Ibid.; Walker, letter, 4 May 1931, Game Branch Files, NR 3, file 5. Miscellaneous Correspondence, box 1.

Chapter 4: Boosters, Wildlife, and Western Myths of Superabundance

1 For perspectives on the Laurier era, see Jean Barman, "The West beyond the West: The Demography of Settlement in British Columbia," *Journal of Canadian Studies* 25, 3 (1990): 5-18; Randy Widdis, *With Scarcely a Ripple: Anglo-Canadian Migration into the United States and Western Canada, 1880-1920* (Montreal: McGill-Queen's University Press, 1998); Kenneth Norrie and Doug Owram, *A History of the Canadian Economy* (Toronto: Harcourt Brace Jovanovich, 1991); and articles related to boosterism in *Town and City: Aspects of Western Canadian Urban Development*, ed. Alan F.J. Artibise (Regina: University of Regina, 1981).
2 For related themes, see E.J. Hart, *The Selling of Canada: The CPR and the Beginnings of Canadian Tourism* (Banff: Altitude Publishing, 1983); and Margery Tanner Hadley, "Photography, Tourism, and the CPR: Western Canada, 1884-1914," in *Essays on the Historical Geography of the Canadian West*, ed. L.A. Rosenvall and S.M. Evans (Calgary: Department of Geography, University of Calgary, 1987), 48-69. For tourism history, see Patricia Jasen, *Wild Things: Nature, Culture, and Tourism in Ontario, 1790-1914* (Toronto: University of Toronto Press, 1995); and Gerald L. Pocius, "Tourists, Health Seekers, and Sportsmen: Luring Americans to Newfoundland in the Early Twentieth Century," in *Twentieth-Century Newfoundland: Explorations*, ed. James Hiller and Peter Neary (St. John's: Breakwater, 1994), 47-77. The symbolic use of animals can be found in many social contexts; see Harriet Ritvo, *The Animal Estate: The English and Other Creatures in the Victorian Age* (Toronto: Penguin Books, 1990). John M. MacKenzie connects British interest in taxidermy to rising imperialism. John M. MacKenzie, *The Empire of Nature: Hunting, Conservation, and British Imperialism* (Manchester: Manchester University Press, 1988). James Turner, meanwhile, sees sensibilities toward animals changing with rising industrialism in Britain. James Turner, *Reckoning*

with the Beast: Animals, Pain, and Humanity in the Victorian Mind (Baltimore: Johns Hopkins University Press, 1980).

3 Janet Foster, *Working for Wildlife: The Beginnings of Preservation in Canada* (Toronto: University of Toronto Press, 1978). Michel F. Girard, *L'Écologisme retrouvé: Essor et déclin de la commission de la conservation du Canada* (Ottawa: Les Presses de l'Université d'Ottawa, 1994), 13-19; Paul-Louis Martin, *La Chasse au Québec* (Montreal: Éditions du Boréal, 1990), 72-74. PearlAnn Reichwein, *Beyond the Visionary Mountains: The Alpine Club of Canada and the Canadian National Park Idea, 1906-1969*, PhD dissertation, Carleton University, 1995; Frank Graham, Jr., *The Audubon Ark: A History of the National Audubon Society* (New York: Alfred A. Knopf, 1990); David Evans, *A History of Nature Conservation in Britain* (London: Routledge, 1994), 34-49; Karen Wonders, *Habitat Dioramas: Illusions of Wilderness in Museums of Natural History* (Uppsala, Sweden: Uppsala University Press, 1993), 114-43; Robert G. McCandless, *Yukon Wildlife: A Social History* (Edmonton: University of Alberta Press, 1985). I am suggesting here that some caveat should be placed on George Altmeyer's proposition that Canadian attitudes toward nature reflected those developing south of the border by the century's end. See George Altmeyer, "Three Ideas of Nature in Canada, 1893-1914," *Journal of Canadian Studies* 11, 3 (1976): 21-36.

4 Warren H. Elofson examines the implications of such ideas in "Adapting the Frontier Environment: Mixed and Dryland Farming Near Pincher Creek," *Prairie Forum* 19, 1 (1994): 44.

5 "Report of the Select Committee of the Senate Appointed to Inquire into the Resources of the Great Mackenzie Basin, 1888," in *Appendices to the Twenty-Second Volume of the Journals of the Senate of Canada* (Ottawa: Brown Chamberlain, 1888), 246; *Report of the Minister of Agriculture of the Province of Manitoba for the Year 1880* (Montreal: Gazette Printing, 1881). Later Department of the Interior brochures discussed wildlife as a food resource. See *The Lac La Biche District, Alberta: A Guide for Intending Settlers* and *The Last Best West*, the department's popular brochure, NAC, RG 76, vol. 389, file 541601.

6 Peter Corley-Smith, *White Bears and Other Curiosities: The First 100 Years of the Royal British Columbia Museum* (Victoria: Royal British Columbia Museum, 1989), 17.

7 Ibid., 17-36; see also *A Preliminary Catalogue of the Collections of Natural History and Ethnology in the Provincial Museum* (Victoria: Queen's Printer, 1898); *Visitor's Guidebook to the Museum* (Victoria: King's Printer, 1909), 5-20. Fannin's life is recounted in Kermode to Wade, 10 March 1925, PABC, box 3, file 12, GR 111.

8 John Fannin, "The Deer of British Columbia," *Victoria Daily Colonist*, 1 January 1892.

9 "History of the Provincial Museum of the Province of Saskatchewan," unpublished manuscript, PAS-R, R-E3374; "Report of the Provincial Taxidermist," included in the Report of the Chief Game Guardian, in *Saskatchewan Sessional Papers, 1912* (Regina: Government Printer, 1913), 255.

10 James Reilly, unpublished report of the Northwest Territories display at the World's Exposition in Chicago, October 1893, PAS-R, R.2.92.

11 See Richardson to Luxton regarding the stocking of a dominion exhibition, 3 January 1908, Whyte Museum of the Canadian Rockies Archives (hereafter WMCRA), Norman Luxton Files, file 2. For an overview of Luxton's tourist promotions, see Laurie Meijer Drees, *Making Banff a Wild West: Norman Luxton, Indians, and Banff Tourism, 1902-1945*, MA thesis, University of Calgary, 1991.

12 Scott and Luxton correspondence, 1907, NAC, RG 76, vol. 14, file 133. "It might induce a few hunters to visit that country if it were exhibited as a sample of the game to be found in British Columbia. It will certainly be an attraction if displayed as an ornament in your London office but as the Canadian Pacific cannot derive any advantage from that, we should not in my opinion be asked to give free transportation."

13 Bosworth to Scott, 7 July 1908, ibid.

14 George Colpitts, *Science, Streams, and Sport: Trout Conservation in Southern Alberta, 1907-1930*, MA thesis, University of Calgary, 1993, 66-74. See appendix listing associations and members. For an overview of association work in Alberta, see George Colpitts, "Fish and Game Conservation in Alberta, 1907-1930," *Alberta History* 42, 4 (1994): 16-26.

15 Correspondence, Calgary Good Roads Association, 1920, NAC, RG 84, vol. 107, file U125.

16   By 1908, three reserves had been set aside in British Columbia: the Yalakon Reserve in the Lillooet district, one in the East Kootenays, and one on Vancouver Island. See Arthur Bryan Williams, "4th Report of the Provincial Game and Forest Warden, 1908," *BC Sessional Papers, 1909* (Victoria: King's Printer, 1909), 511. The Cassiar district soon had a breeding reserve set aside to protect the area's big-game populations; Saskatchewan converted most of the former federal forest reserves into twelve game preserves. "Report of the Chief Game Guardian," in *Saskatchewan Sessional Papers, 1916* (Regina: Provincial Printer, 1916), 241. Manitoba had thirteen reserves by the end of the First World War; see "Section of Map Showing Areas Set Apart as Provincial Game Preserves in Manitoba," Manitoba Naturalist Society, PAM, PB 5066. On this antelope park, see *Lethbridge Daily Herald,* 14 and 25 March 1915. See City Clerk to Indian Agency and R.B. Bennett, 31 March 1914, NAC, Indian Affairs Correspondence, RG 10, vol. 4078, file 458,914. For a similar interest in placing buffalo on the Stoney reserve, see Mackie to Indian Agent, Morley, and related correspondence, 19 June 1917, NAC, RG 10, vol. 4086, file 501,858.

17   Peter C. Gould, *Green Politics: Back to Nature, Back to the Land, and Socialism in Britain: 1880-1900* (New York: St. Martin's Press, 1988), 19-20.

18   Banff's museum was called the "university of the hills" in *Prince of Playgrounds: Come Home by Canada and Revel in the Rockies,* Department of the Interior brochure (Ottawa: Department of the Interior, 1911), 25, GA.

19   Museum Reports files from 1903 onward, Sanson's inventories, and correspondence, NAC, RG 84, vol. 572. Also, Sanson's reports and correspondence in NAC, RG 84, vol. 977, file B318-1, parts 1 and 2. Dioramas in the Banff museum are described by J.B. Harkin, "A Development of the Diorama," *The Museum's Journal* 35, 8 (1935), offprint in RG 84, vol. 2155, file U318, part 2. Interior photographs taken in the 1940s can be seen in NAC, PA-135004 and PA-135006.

20   Harkin said that the museum completed a park visit, "rendering the place attractive to tourists during their stay" and encouraging repeat visits. J.B. Harkin letter, 1924, NAC, RG 84, vol. 977, file B318-1, part 2.

21   Incorporation of the Calgary Natural History Society, 27 January 1913, and the society's minutes book, City of Calgary Archives, Box 87-013. Correspondence of the society's members can be found in GA, "Calgary Museum," M2111, box 1, file 9; the *Calgary Herald* describes the museum in 24 April 1928.

22   Harlan Smith, "The Natural History Museums of British Columbia," *Science* 8, 201 (1898): 619-20.

23   Wonders, *Habitat Dioramas,* 19-20, 24.

24   "Arrange to Send Interesting Exhibit," *Medicine Hat Weekly News,* 13 August 1925.

25   Postcards of "The Museum, Provincial Parliament Buildings, Victoria, BC," PABC, box 41, file 4, GR 111, are reprinted in Corley-Smith, *White Bears,* frontispiece photo, 25, 38, and 46; diorama photos appear in *Visitor's Guidebook to the Museum.* Another good source for diorama photos is the yearly reports of the chief game guardian in *BC Sessional Papers.*

26   Postcard, "Calgary," ca. 1910, GA, N3884-24; postcard, "The Spoils of One Day at Pipestone, Man.," ca. 1910, PAM, Pipestone 2 File, N928.

27   R.T. Rodd to Found, 27 May 1924, NAC, RG 23, vol. 1001, 721-4-37.

28   "Takes Advertiser to Task," *Lethbridge Daily Herald,* 20 August 1910.

29   See Bradshaw's comments in Memo to Association, 5 March 1935, PAM, Deputy Minister, Game Branch Files, RG 17, box 32, file 29.2.1.

30   Emphasis added to "Report of the Chief Game Guardian," in *Saskatchewan Sessional Papers, 1912* (Regina: Government Printer, 1913), 247.

31   See Gordon Hewitt's edition of the proceedings, *Conservation of Wild Life in Canada in 1917: A Review* (Ottawa: Canadian Commission of Conservation, 1918).

32   He laments that "railways, ranchmen, and miners have taken possession of what was once the sportsman's paradise. Many parts of Montana, Wyoming, and Idaho are still worth visiting for the sake of sport, but the old glory of those States is gone never to return" (26). See also 37. William A. Baillie-Grohman, *Fifteen Years of Sport and Life in the Hunting Grounds of Western America and British Columbia* (London: Horace Cox, 1900), 36-40. Ironically,

H.W. Seton Karr's disappointment with the Canadian Rockies was published after Seton Karr travelled on one of the CPR's first excursions over the Great Divide. H.W. Seton Karr, *Shores and Alps of Alaska* (London: Sampson Low, Marston, Searle and Rivington, 1887), 5. T.R. Patillo described Calgary as a "sporting paradise" in 1890 and 1891; in 1902, he said that the same fields were overhunted, and the "fun has gone out of it." T.R. Patillo, *Moose-Hunting, Salmon-Fishing, and Other Sketches of Sport* (London: Sampson Low, Marston and Company, 1902), 138.

33 Robert A.J. McDonald, "Victoria, Vancouver, and the Economic Development of British Columbia, 1886-1914," in *British Columbia: Historical Readings,* ed. W. Peter Ward and Robert A.J. McDonald (Vancouver: Douglas and McIntyre, 1981), 384-88.

34 Clive Phillipps-Wolley, *Sport in the Crimea and Caucasus* (London: Richard Bentley and Sons, 1881); Clive Phillipps-Wolley, *A Sportsman's Eden* (London: Bentley and Sons, 1888), Letter 18, 191. His lecture to Victorians about aid to Russia was to the city's political elites; see *Victoria Daily Colonist,* 8 March 1892. For a biographical treatment of this "quintessential Englishman," see Peter Murray, *Home from the Hill: Three Gentlemen Adventurers* (Victoria: Horsdal and Schubart, 1994).

35 He describes the club in an article, "Big Game of North America," in Clive Phillipps-Wolley, *Big Game Shooting* (London: Longmans, Green, 1894), 346-85. For a general treatment of his booster spirit, see Murray, *Home from the Hill,* 84-86, 107. See the Victoria Gun Club's accusations against Union Club members who "asked for the law to be amended," "The Gun," *Victoria Daily Colonist,* 20 March 1892; Clive Phillipps-Wolley, "Big Game in the West: Famous Bags in British Columbia and Vancouver Island, Canada," 15 December 1906, PABC, pamphlet collection, 393, with description of the Union Club on 393-96.

36 Baillie-Grohman, *Fifteen Years,* 39, speaks of "an English resident of Victoria ... editor and chief contributor to a series of English books on sport." Baillie-Grohman was undoubtedly referring to the two-volume series *Big Game Shooting,* edited by Phillipps-Wolley.

37 In 1906, Williams believed that he had finally convinced the province's premier, previously "lukewarm" toward wildlife conservation, of "what could be made out of it." Williams to Herchmer, 23 February 1906, PABC, Game Guardian Files, Letterbook, box 5. *Visitor's Guidebook to the Museum,* 5.

38 Arthur Bryan Williams, *Game Trails in British Columbia: Big Game and Other Sport in the Wilds of British Columbia* (London: John Murray, 1925), viii.

39 Arthur Bryan Williams, *Game of British Columbia,* Bureau of Provincial Information, Bulletin 17 (Victoria: King's Printer, 1908), 5.

40 J.H. Hubbard, "Sport in the Canadian North-West: A Paper on the Game Birds and Animals of Manitoba and the North-West Territories," 29 July 1886, Peel Bibliography on Microfiche, no. 937, 33. Miller Christy mentions that Walter Hine prepared most of the trophies for the Colonial and Indian Exposition. Miller Christy, *Sport in Manitoba* (Liverpool: Turner and Dunnett, 1888), 6.

41 "The Game and Fur Trophy in the Canadian Court," *Illustrated London News,* 14 August 1886, 180.

42 Descriptions of the 1908 exhibition in *Rod and Gun and Motor Sports in Canada,* 9, 8 (January 1908): 1140-41.

43 *Canada – An Illustrated Weekly Journal,* 10, 122 (May 1908): 135.

44 CPR Staff Bulletin 72A, 1 January 1915, CPA.

45 CPR Staff Bulletin, July 1945, CPA, 10. Also, John Murray Gibbon's promotional activities are recounted in his unpublished biography, WMCRA, John Murray Gibbon Files.

46 Review of *Eyes of a Gypsy* in *Canadian Bookman,* ibid. In one novel, Gibbon described an American hunter who displayed wildlife taxidermy in his cabin and explained to a British visitor that America was overcrowded and overhunted and that all the animals came from Canada. John Murray Gibbon, *Drums Afar: An International Romance* (New York: J.J. Little and Ives, 1918), 281-83.

47 "What Our American Cousins Can Teach Us!" and editorial, *Rod and Gun,* 7, 5 (October, 1905): 520-22.

48 Ibid., 522.

49 Ibid., 523.

50 Frederic Irland, "Sport in an Untouched American Wilderness," an 1896 article reprinted in *Hunting and Fishing in Canada: A Turn-of-the-Century Treasury*, ed. Frank Oppel (Secaucus, NJ: Castle Books, 1988), 275.
51 Frederick Jackson Turner, *The Frontier in American History* (New York: Holt, 1950). Roderick Nash, *Wilderness and the American Mind*, rev. ed. (New Haven: Yale University Press, 1973), 131-47. *Fishing, Shooting, Canoe Trips, and Camping*, 29th ed. (Montreal: CPR, 1909).
52 "The Sportsman's Map of Canada and the Northwest Territory," 1908, CPA, X 186.
53 "Fishing, Shooting, Canoe Trips and Camping," 29th edition (Montreal: CPR, 1909), 5-6.
54 Ibid.
55 "Of all the North American continent, once a veritable 'Sportsman's Paradise,' [Canada's] picturesque wilds and noble waters have alone been spared the attacks of the game butchers and fish destroyers." *Fishing and Shooting on the Canadian Pacific Railway* (Montreal: CPR, 1890), 53; see also *Rod and Gun* 7, 5 (October 1905): 520-23.
56 *Wild Animals I Have Met in the Canadian Rockies*, Soo Line brochure (c. 1910), 3. Copy held in pamphlet collection of the PABC; see also CPR, *Fishing, Shooting*.
57 J.F. McFadden, *The Advantages of the Riding Mountain Forest Reserve*, brochure (Winnipeg: Riding Mountain National Park Committee, 1928), Manitoba Legislative Library Collection.
58 "The Buffalo Drive Is On," advertisement in *Moose Jaw Evening Times*, 6 March 1929.
59 See clipping and brochure file regarding Moose Jaw Wild Animal Park in the Moose Jaw Public Library Archives. *Moose Jaw Times Herald*, 23 July 1969; *Moose Jaw Times Herald*, 5 August 1939. The *Moose Jaw Times Herald* of 9 July 1966 recounted the last buffalo story related by Cree Chief Red Dog at the inauguration. I thank the staff at the Moose Jaw Public Library for making these files accessible.
60 Ibid.
61 Editorial, *Moose Jaw Times Herald*, 9 July 1966.
62 Ibid.
63 The book was published after his death. Gordon Hewitt, *The Conservation of Canadian Wildlife* (New York: Scribner's Sons, 1921), map illustration.

Chapter 5: Pioneer Society and Fish and Game Protection
1 John F. Reiger, *American Sportsmen and the Origins of Conservation* (Norman: University of Oklahoma Press, 1986); Keven Wamsley, "Good Clean Sport and a Deer Apiece: Game Legislation and State Formation in 19th Century Canada," *Canadian Journal of History of Sport* 25, 2 (1994): 1-20.
2 Reiger, *American Sportsmen*, 26-27; see Karen Wonders, "A Sportsman's Eden," *Beaver*, October-November 1999: 31.
3 R. Peter Gillis, "Rivers of Sawdust: The Battle over Industrial Pollution in Canada, 1865-1903," *Journal of Canadian Studies* 21, 1 (1986): 84-103. Margaret Beattie Bogue, "To Save Fish: Canada, the United States, the Great Lakes, and the Joint Commission of 1892," *Journal of American History* 79 (1993): 1429-54. A valuable contribution to the history of natural sciences and government remains Suzanne Zeller, *Inventing Canada: Early Victorian Science and the Idea of a Transcontinental Nation* (Toronto: University of Toronto Press, 1987).
4 W.B. Yeo, "W.F. Whitcher, Victorian Science in Canada's First National Park," *Research Links: A Forum for Natural, Cultural, and Social Studies* 2, 2 (1994): 5-6. Wilmot sent Lake Ontario ova to British Columbia because of their "superior colour." Wilmot to Litton, 16 May 1887, Royal Ontario Museum Archives (hereafter ROM), Wilmot Letterbooks. For a valuable contribution of primary materials and an analysis of the BC canning industry, see Dianne Newell, *The Development of the Pacific Salmon-Canning Industry* (Montreal: McGill-Queen's University Press, 1989). Wilmot's prominence at the International Fisheries Exhibition in London, 1883, and his debate with Huxley are recorded in the paper presented by Sir James Ramsay Gibson Maitland, *On the Culture of Salmonidae and the Acclimatization of Fish* (London: William Clowes, 1883), 19-23.
5 The Wentworth Society's meeting was reported in newspaper clippings included in ROM, Kerr Letterbook, 1860, vol. 2, SC 39.

6   A.B. McCullough, *The Commercial Fisheries of the Canadian Great Lakes* (Ottawa: Environment Canada, 1989), 83-85; on growing concerns about conservation, see Michel F. Girard, *L'Écologisme rétrouvé: Essor et déclin de la commission de la conservation du Canada* (Ottawa: Les Presses de l'Université d'Ottawa, 1994).
7   Vreeland's letter to Hornaday stressed the need for Canadians to enlarge Waterton National Park. Vreeland to Hornaday, 3 November 1910, NAC, RG 84, vol. 43, file W300. In this file, also see Vreeland's proposed resurvey of the park, undertaken with a Pincher Creek settler: H. Riviere to J. Herron, 24 April 1913. B.H. Chapman wanted to donate elk to Waterton, on the condition that the Parks Branch protect them. Harkin to Brown, 2 December 1912, ibid.
8   Colonel Henry Inman, *Buffalo Jones' Forty Years of Adventure* (London: Sampson Low, Marston and Company, 1899), 250-300.
9   Frank Gilbert Roe discusses Hornaday's often misleading natural history and his criticism of the Métis provisions hunt in *The North American Buffalo: A Critical Study of the Species in Its Wild State* (Toronto: University of Toronto Press, 1951), 12-24, 26-33, 75, 80-81.
10 Some of Hornaday's correspondence to the BC game office, and others from American conservationists, is found in PABC, Correspondence Files, GR 446, box 2, file 100-1.
11 H.V. Nelles addresses features of progressivism in his study of Crown natural resource planning, politics, and business in Ontario, *The Politics of Development: Forests, Mines, and Hydro-Electric Power in Ontario, 1849-1941* (Toronto: Macmillan of Canada, 1974). Samuel P. Hays, *Conservation and the Gospel of Efficiency: The Progressive Conservation Movement, 1890-1920* (Cambridge: Harvard University Press, 1959).
12 Rev. T.J. Crowley, "Fish and Game Protective Associations," paper delivered to the Conference on Wild Life, in *Commission of Conservation's 10th Annual Report* (Ottawa: J. de Labroquerie Tache, 1919), 43-44, 145.
13 See an impressive comparative analysis of first- and second-generation farmers in Lyle Dick, *Farmers Making Good: The Development of Abernethy District, Saskatchewan, 1880-1920* (Ottawa: Minister of Supply and Services, 1989).
14 Petitions in the correspondence of the Deputy Superintendent General to the Regina Indian Commissioner, 13 November 1893, NAC, RG 10, vol. 6732, file 420-2.
15 Baillie-Grohman quotation appears in Wonders, "A Sportsman's Eden," 31.
16 Inkster's testimony, "Report and Minutes of Evidence of the Select Committee of the Senate on the Existing Natural Food Products of the North-West Territories, and the Best Means of Conserving and Increasing Them," Appendix 1 of the *Journals of the Senate of Canada, 1887* (Ottawa: Maclean, Roger and Company, 1887), 169.
17 *Macleod Gazette*, 28 February 1889.
18 "Protection of Game," *Macleod Gazette*, 7 March 1889.
19 Ibid.
20 See Irgens to Winter, 11 December 1919, GA, Austin B. de Winter Files, M1327.
21 Petition to Lieutenant Governor ca. 1890, PAS-R, Northwest Territories, Bills and Unpublished Sessional Papers, R.2.92.
22 See Calgary, Edmonton, and Red Deer Petitions, ibid; and Motherwell Files, PAS-R, R 2.715.
23 Bradshaw to Schmitz, 9 January 1920, PAS-S, NR 3, box 1, Big Game – General, 1918-39, file 21.
24 "Report of the Chief Game Guardian," in *Saskatchewan Sessional Papers, 1912* (Regina: Government Printer, 1913), 248.
25 Ibid.
26 J.P. Turner, *The Prairie Chicken: Its Distribution and Need of Protection* (Winnipeg: Department of Agriculture and Immigration, 1917), Peel Bibliography Microforms Collection 2612.
27 Letter from the Fernie Game Protective Association, January 1906, PABC, GR 446, box 6, 1906 Letterbook.
28 Phillips to Williams, 13 May 1908, PABC, GR 446, box 6.
29 Resolutions of Fernie District Game Protection Association, 22 February 1907, ibid.
30 Dennis to Williams, 28 February 1907, PABC, GR 446, box 2, file 100-1.

31 Hornaday to Dennis, 16 February 1907, ibid.
32 *Forest and Stream* citation found in Williams's files in 1907, ibid.
33 Randall to Williams, 27 February 1907, ibid. Pennsylvania coal company president John Phillips pointed out the advantages of Hornaday's proposed reserve. It would not be located on coal leases, such as on the Fording River, and would be less convenient to the incursions of the Stoney Indians, whom he claimed were "the greatest hunters and big game killers on the Continent." John Phillips to Herchmer, President of the Fernie Game Protective Association, 15 March 1907; Hornaday to Williams, 24 February 1908, PABC, GR 446, box 16, file 3.
34 The meeting is described in Hornaday to Williams, 24 February 1908, PABC, GR 446, box 16, file 3.
35 Ibid.
36 "Goat Mountain Park" brochure found in ibid.
37 C.J. Lewis to Williams, 9 March 1908, ibid.
38 Hornaday to Williams, 6 February 1913, PABC, GR 446, box 3, file 5.
39 Statistics drawn from 1901, 1911, and 1921 Canada censuses; PABC, GR 446, box 3, file 3; GR 446, box 2, file 100-1.
40 See Kettle Valley letterhead in PABC, GR 446, box 3, file 3.
41 PABC, GR 446, box 35, file 2.
42 Gill to Luxton, 16 January 1908, WMCRA, Norman Luxton Files, file 2, M123.
43 Williams letter, 27 April 1906; Fulton to Hayward, 7 May 1906, PABC, Chief Game Guardian Files, GR 446, box 2, file 100-1; and Musgrove Correspondence, 1906, ibid., box 5.
44 Williams letter, 27 April 1906, ibid.
45 Fry allocations were to be made to the club since it was believed that "it would be impossible to hold the club together" without them. See Purvis to R.T. Rodd, and Rodd to Found, 18 and 20 April 1928, re Coleman Rod and Gun Club, NAC, RG 23, vol. 778, 718-11-1. See H. Wright to Department, 23 September 1919, NAC, RG 84, vol. 70, R296, part 1.
46 See Hunt to Secretary of the Interior, 31 March 1908.
47 Commission to W.D. Scott, 16 June 1913, NAC, RG 84, vol. 70, R296, part 1.
48 Boswell to Douglas, 31 March 1897, NAC, Game Preservation, NWT, vol. 747, file 469929.
49 Leopold to Layard, 14 June 1904, ibid.
50 Douglas to Smart, 17 October 1904, ibid.
51 Young to R.M. Venning, 18 February 1907, NAC, RG 23, vol. 344, file 2995, part 1.
52 A.T. Kinnaird to Garrett, 14 July 1910, GA, Austin B. de Winter Files, file 21; R.A. Darker to Department, 14 February 1907, NAC, RG 23, vol. 344, file 2995, part 1. The press played a role in creating perceptions that Native ways of hunting and, to a smaller extent, fishing were at odds with the ways of British Canadians. See W. Keith Regular, *"Red Backs and White Burdens": A Study of White Attitudes towards Indians in Southern Alberta: 1896-1911*, MA thesis, University of Calgary, 1985, 138. Chief John Snow, *These Mountains Are Our Sacred Places: The Story of the Stoney People* (Toronto: Samuel Stevens, 1977), 47.
53 "R.A. Darker: Manager for South Alberta," *Life* 1, 13 (1912): 5. I would like to thank John W. Darker for information on the Darker family, including this magazine reference.
54 For these activities, see GA, Austin B. de Winter Files, M1327.
55 See Young to Prince, 30 August 1906, NAC, RG 23, vol. 344, file 2995, part 1.
56 Hayden to Department, 20 June 1919, NAC, RG 23, vol. 999, 721-4-37.
57 Letterhead found in NAC, RG 23, vol. 778, file 16, 718-11-1.
58 Constitution of League, 1 January 1920, Alberta Provincial Archives, Acc 87.3271/1.
59 Their observations might have been correct since the actual number of angling permits sold by the Department of Marine and Fisheries in the 1920s did not correspond to the regional population increases. The sale of angling permits was growing but not as spectacularly as settlement populations. In 1912, the fishing overseer in southern Alberta reported 1,250 angling permits sold; in 1913, 3,500; and in 1914, 4,200. That number remained stable until 1926, when almost 6,000 were sold. It was not until the end of the decade that the number increased to 8,000. Based on reports from southern Alberta, in Annual Reports of Fisheries Branch of the Department of Marine and Fisheries, 1912-30, in *Sessional Papers* (Ottawa: Government Printers, 1913-31).

60 See NAC, RG 23, vol. 1002, 721-4-37.
61 Rodd to Found, 20 December 1926, ibid.
62 Gillespie to Hawkins, 22 June 1920, NAC, RG 23, vol. 999, 721-4-37; see also Ebbert to Shaw, 6 May 1921, ibid.
63 See Resolutions of Calgary Anglers Association, 24 January 1921, ibid.
64 See Graham to Harkin, 18 June 1917, NAC, RG 84, vol. 70, U3-1-1, part 1.
65 Richardson to Rodd, 7 November 1924, NAC, RG 23, vol. 1001, 721-4-37.
66 R.T. Rodd to Found, 27 May 1924, NAC, RG 23, vol. 1001, 721-4-37.
67 Eastwood to Desbarats, 24 March 1915, GA, Austin B. de Winter Files, M1327.
68 Kemish to Department, 26 February 1921, NAC, RG 23, vol. 999, 721-4-37.
69 The *Times* on 4 March 1909 reported that Darker "spent several days in High River, anxious to establish a branch of the above association in High River."
70 Ibid., 11 January 1906.
71 Ibid., 15 February 1906.
72 Ibid., 25 March 1909.
73 Ibid., 8 April 1909.
74 Petition, High River Anglers, 18 February 1919, NAC, RG 23, vol. 999, 721-4-37; High River Angling Protective Association, Meeting Minutes, 16 February 1920, NAC, RG 23, vol. 777, 781-11-1.
75 See my work on this association in *Science, Streams, and Sport: Trout Conservation in Southern Alberta, 1900-1930*, MA thesis, University of Calgary, 1993, 50-51.
76 See Highwood River Anglers and Protective Association to Assistant Minister, 27 April 1922, NAC, RG 23, vol. 1001, 721-4-37.
77 Rodd to A.M. Ballachey, 17 May 1928, NAC, RG 23, vol. 733, 715-12-1.
78 Emphasis added; see High River *Times* clipping in RG 23, vol. 1002, file 28, 721-4-37.
79 For samples of protest letters, see correspondence from April 1922, NAC, RG 23, vol. 999, 721-4-37; R.B. Miller, in 1953, noted a number of erroneous assumptions in tributary closure policy and pointed out that fish and game associations still requested closure as a conservation strategy. See R.B. Miller, "The Regulation of Trout Fishing in Alberta," *Canadian Fish Culturalist* 14 (1953): 22.
80 Newsletter materials found in Morlan to Watt, 26 October 1925, NAC, RG 23, vol. 1002, 721-4-37; ibid., file 26.
81 See petition, 1919, NAC, RG 23, vol. 999, 721-4-37.
82 Ibid., Frank Watt to G.C. Coote, 27 March 1922.
83 Langley report with petition, 20 August 1919, NAC, RG 23, vol. 999; Robi to Finlayson, July 1919, ibid.
84 Davidson to Found, 24 November 1919, ibid.
85 Elliot to Deputy Minister, 25 November 1922, NAC, RG 23, vol. 777, 781-11-1.
86 Frank Watt to G.C. Coote, 27 March 1922, NAC, RG 23, vol. 999, 721-4-37.
87 See R.T. Rodd's letters to Found, 21 July 1926, 20 November 1926, NAC, RG 23, vol. 1002; and 28 May 1924, vol. 777.
88 Ibid., Rodd to Found, 20 December 1926.
89 Dave Blacklock letter, *Calgary Herald*, 13 February 1928.
90 Departmental Memo, 5 September 1918, NAC, RG 23, vol. 777, 781-11-1.
91 See statistics provided by Elliot to Found, 19 February 1926, NAC, RG 23, vol. 1002. These observations were confirmed by the end of the decade by a Banff hatchery official who estimated that the Highwood River was the most heavily fished stream in the district. See J.E. Martin Report, 31 December 1928, NAC, RG 23, vol. 779.
92 Report of the Highwood River Angling Protective Association, 1924, NAC, RG 23, vol. 1001, file 26; *61st Annual Report, Fisheries Branch, Department of Marine and Fisheries: 1927-1928* (Ottawa: King's Printer, 1928), 185.
93 Clipping found in NAC, RG 23, vol. 733.
94 See correspondence between Richardson and R.T. Rodd, December 1929-January 1930, NAC, RG 23, vol. 733.
95 Ibid.
96 H.N. Sheppard, Vice President of the High River Association, to Minister, 10 April 1922, NAC, RG 23, vol. 1001, 721-4-37.

97   Rodd to Found, 16 May 1928, NAC, RG 23, vol. 733, 715-12-1.
98   W.A. Bigelow, *Forceps, Fins, and Feathers: The Memoirs of Dr. W.A. Bigelow* (Altona, MB: D.W. Friesen and Sons, 1969).
99   Wheeler to Secretary of Department of the Interior, 16 November 1904, NAC, RG 15, vol. 939, file 909378.
100 Wheeler to A.C. Reddie, Deputy Provincial Secretary, Victoria, 7 February 1905, NAC, RG 15, vol. 939, file 909378.
101 Colin Groff to J.B. Harkin, 8 January 1934, National Parks Publicity Files, NAC, RG 84, vol. 108, file U125-18.
102 Ibid.
103 Travis to Brewster, 20 June 1928, Brewster Files, WMCRA, M2, file 24.
104 Begg correspondence, 16 April 1887, NAC, RG 84, vol. 535, file 146313.
105 Ibid.
106 Graham to Williamson, memo, 19 September 1921, NAC, RG 84, vol. 74, file J296.
107 "Report of Rocky Mountains National Park," *Annual Report of the Department of Interior for the Year 1907* (Ottawa: Government Printer, 1908), part 4, 6.
108 "Indian Hunters Killing off Game," *Vancouver Daily Province*, 24 February 1905; see comments concerning Amerindian hunting in *Fishing, Shooting, Canoe Trips, and Camping* (Montreal: CPR, 1909), CPA.
109 New York *Sun* article from July 1932, WMCRA, Brewster Files, file M82/15.
110 The accounts are not clear whether these are outright head sales or if tourist hunters were having taxidermy arranged through the trading shop. WMCRA, Brewster Files, Stock Book, M82, file 18.
111 Lawton to Luxton, 14 January 1908, WMCRA, Norman Luxton Papers, M123, file 2.
112 On Luxton's work in Banff, see Laurie Meijer-Drees, *Norman Luxton: Mountain Man*, MA thesis, University of Calgary, 1990.
113 See Luxton Correspondence, WMCRA, M123. On the issue of head sales, see William Hornaday's correspondence with Luxton. Hornaday made the interesting observation that his New York Zoological Park had no success selling Luxton's sheep heads. "Strange as it may seem, there is no sale here for even the best Rocky Mountain sheep heads," Hornaday said to Luxton in a letter. "People will buy them when they are out West in the country where the animals live and grow up, and they find pleasure in bringing them home as souvenirs of a pleasant trip." But in New York, Hornaday said, the same head to a dealer "means nothing, and very few are sold." Hornaday to Luxton, 12 January 1908, WMCRA, Norman Luxton Papers, M123, file 2. See also general correspondence in this file.
114 Williams memo, 28 June 1906, PABC, GR 446, box 5, Letterbook.
115 Charles Barber, "Report of Game Department," in the Annual Report of the Department of Agriculture, in *Sessional Papers of the Legislature of Manitoba, 1902-1915* (Winnipeg: Government Printer, n.d.).
116 W.F. Lothian provides a history of parks and their often changing boundaries. In 1895, for instance, Waterton, or "Kootenay Lakes Forest Park," was created. With the Dominion Forest Reserve Act, Waterton was changed in 1906 to "Kootenay Lakes Forest Reserve." In 1911, the Dominion Forest Reserves and Parks Act created dominion parks such as Waterton within existing forest reserves. The originally tiny boundaries of Waterton were significantly enlarged in 1914. Most parks followed similar changes in boundaries and status as forest reserves or parks. Glacier, long a forest reserve, became a park in 1911; Elk Island Park was created from a forest reserve in 1913; and Jasper was established as "Jasper Forest Park of Canada" in 1907. Other national parks were Mount Revelstoke (1907), Kootenay (1920), Wood Buffalo (1922), Prince Albert (1927), and Riding Mountain (1929). W.F. Lothian, *A Brief History of Canada's National Parks* (Ottawa: Environment Canada, 1987).
117 See Leslie Bella, *Parks for Profit* (Montreal: Harvest House, 1987), 47.
118 *Regina Leader*, 22 November 1907.
119 See Gordon Hewitt's valuable picture of the Lloyd antelope enclosure in *The Conservation of Canadian Wildlife* (New York: Scribner's Sons, 1921), 136.

120 Ibid., 291.
121 *Calgary Herald,* 14 April 1927.
122 R.A. Darker, "Grouse in Alberta," *Rod and Gun in Canada* 11, 1 (1909): 23-25.
123 Oliver to Department, 10 July 1916, NAC, RG 23, vol. 999, 721-4-37.
124 "Game Increasing in Southern Alberta," *Lethbridge Daily Herald,* 16 June 1909; cf. "Alberta Crops Looking Good," ibid., 15 June 1909.
125 Desbarats to Eye Hill Schoolteacher, 9 April 1918; the request from the hotel owner is found in Fleming to Harkin, 18 March 1921, NAC, RG 22, vol. 777, 781-11-1.
126 Macleod Association's Application for Fry, NAC, RG 23, vol. 778, file 14, 718-11-1.
127 Samuel Wilmot, "On Fish Culture," Appendix H of "Report of the Department of Marine and Fisheries," *Sessional Papers* 4 (Ottawa: Government Printer, 1873), 106-9. For related issues, see Donald Worster's work on ideas of "nature's economy" in *Nature's Economy: The Roots of Ecology* (San Francisco: Sierra Club Books, 1977), 64-65; Edward E. Prince, "Methods of Coarse Fish Extermination," Report 2, in *Thirty-Seventh Annual Report of the Department of Marine and Fisheries for the Year 1904,* Sessional Papers 22 (Ottawa: King's Printer, 1905), xxi; "What Fish Culture Means" was one of the first press bulletins issued by the Fisheries Branch in June 1920. See Press/Publicity Files, 20 June 1920 Bulletin, NAC, RG 23, vol. 1558; "Banff Fish Hatchery: Angler's Best Friend," *Calgary Herald,* 18 June 1925.
128 J.A. Rodd to Gillespie, 14 November 1928, NAC, RG 23, vol. 779.
129 *Calgary Herald,* 24 November 1928.
130 George Colpitts, "Conservation, Science, and Canada's Fur Farming Industry, 1913-1945," *Social History/Histoire sociale* 30, 59 (1997): 77-108.
131 "Report of the Game Department for the Year 1913," in *Sessional Papers of the Legislative Assembly of Manitoba* (Winnipeg: Government Printer, 1913), 36.
132 "Report of the Superintendent of Jasper Park for the Year 1919," part 2 of *Annual Report of the Department of the Interior* (Ottawa: Government Printer, 1920), 24.
133 See George Bevan's report on Waterton Lakes Park, in ibid., 31.
134 See Harkin's report for the year 1921, in "Report of the Superintendent of Parks," part 2 of *Annual Report of the Department of the Interior* (Ottawa: Government Printer, 1922), 5.
135 See Harkin's report for the year 1923, in "Report of the Superintendent of Parks," part 2 of *Annual Report of the Department of the Interior* (Ottawa: Government Printer, 1924), 104.
136 Hewitt, *Conservation,* 238.
137 *Craig and Canyon,* 4 July 1935; see E. "Cougar" Lee Correspondence and Clippings, NAC, RG 84, vol. 138, file B261, A-2-a.
138 *Calgary Albertan,* 27 December 1935.
139 *Toronto Star Weekly,* 14 December 1935; see other coverage in *Craig and Canyon,* 14 February 1936; *Toronto Star Weekly,* 25 January 1935.
140 See Alan MacEachern's analysis of predator control in "Rationality and Rationalization in Canadian National Parks Predator Policy," in *Consuming Canada: Readings in Environmental History,* ed. Chad Gaffield and Pam Gaffield (Toronto: Copp Clark, 1995), 197-212.
141 *Calgary Herald,* 13 November 1923.
142 "New Trails Being Made through Rocky Mountain Scenic Routes," *Calgary Herald,* 13 November 1923.
143 Mabel B. Williams, *Kootenay National Park and the Banff-Windermere Highway* (Ottawa: Department of the Interior, 1928), 32.
144 "Report of the Superintendent of Jasper Park for the year 1920," part 2 of the *Annual Report of the Department of the Interior* (Ottawa: Government Printer, 1921), 26.
145 Hewitt, *Conservation,* 238.
146 "Elk Increasing So Rapidly as to Drive out Mountain Sheep," *Medicine Hat Weekly News,* 23 July 1925.
147 The photographer, W.J. Oliver, confirmed that the animals were shot without suffering. See "Camera-Man Has Thrilling Experience as Thousands of Buffalo Stampede Over Head," *Calgary Daily Herald,* 10 November 1923.
148 "Tourist Map of Alberta," in *Medicine Hat Weekly News,* 25 June 1925.

149 Of twenty-six convictions by guardians in southern Alberta in 1915, for instance, nineteen were "foreigners." *49th Annual Report, Fisheries Branch, Department of the Naval Service: 1915-1916* (Ottawa: King's Printer, 1916), 229.

Conclusion

1 This pioneer expression is cited by Lyle Dick, *Farmers Making Good: The Development of Abernethy District, Saskatchewan, 1880-1920* (Ottawa: Minister of Supply and Services, 1989).

2 See Gerald Killan, "Ontario's Provincial Parks and Changing Conceptions of 'Protected Places,'" in *Changing Parks: The History, Future, and Cultural Context of Parks and Heritage Landscapes*, ed. John Marsh and Bruce W. Hodgins (Toronto: Natural Heritage, 1998), 24-49.

3 Alan MacEachern, "Rationality and Rationalization in Canadian National Parks Predator Policy," in *Consuming Canada: Readings in Environmental History*, ed. Chad Gaffield and Pam Gaffield (Toronto: Copp Clark, 1995), 197-212.

4 See also C.W. Allin, *The Politics of Wilderness Preservation*, Contributions in Political Science 64 (Westport, CT: Greenwood Press, 1982); W. Ashworth, *The Late Great Lakes: An Environmental History* (New York: Alfred A. Knopf, 1986); R.Y. Edwards, "The Preservation of Wilderness: Is Man a Part of Nature – or a Thing Apart?" *Canadian Audubon*, January-February 1967: 1-7; Samuel P. Hays, *Beauty, Health, and Permanence: Environmental Politics in the United States, 1955-1985* (Cambridge: Cambridge University Press, 1987); and Gerald Killan, *Protected Places: A History of Ontario's Provincial Park System* (Toronto: Dundurn Press; Ontario Ministry of Natural Resources, 1993).

5 See correspondence and memos on the Wainwright closure in NAC, RG 22, vol. 48, file 286.

6 See Gary G. Gray, *Wildlife and People: The Human Dimensions of Wildlife Ecology* (Urbana: University of Illinois Press, 1993).

7 Colin Tudge, *Last Animals at the Zoo: How Mass Extinction Can Be Stopped* (Washington: Island Press, 1992), 5-28; Timothy M. Swanson, "Wildlife and Wildlands: Diversity and Development," in *Economics for the Wilds: Wildlife, Diversity, and Development*, ed. Timothy M. Swanson and Edward B. Barbier (Washington: Island Press, 1992), 1-14; see also the essays in Daniel J. Decker and Gary R. Goff, eds., *Valuing Wildlife: Economic and Social Perspectives* (Boulder: Westview Press, 1987).

Selected Bibliography

Allen, David Elliston. *The Naturalist in Britain: A Social History.* Princeton: Princeton University Press, 1994.

Altherr, Thomas L. "'Flesh Is the Paradise of a Man of Flesh': Cultural Conflict over Indian Hunting Beliefs and Rituals in New France as Recorded in the *Jesuit Relations.*" In "Notes and Comments." *Canadian Historical Review* 64, 2 (1983): 267-76.

Altmeyer, George. "Three Ideas of Nature in Canada, 1893-1914." *Journal of Canadian Studies* 11, 3 (1976): 21-36.

Bella, Leslie. *Parks for Profit.* Montreal: Harvest House, 1987.

Berger, Carl. *Science, God, and Nature in Victorian Canada.* Toronto: University of Toronto Press, 1982.

Black-Rogers, Mary. "Varieties of 'Starving': Semantics and Survival in the Subarctic Fur Trade, 1750-1850." *Ethnohistory* 33, 4 (1986): 353-83.

Bogue, Margaret Beattie. "To Save Fish: Canada, the United States, the Great Lakes, and the Joint Commission of 1892." *Journal of American History* 79 (1993): 1429-54.

Bordo, Jonathan. "Jack Pine: Wilderness Sublime or the Erasure of the Aboriginal Presence from the Landscape?" *Journal of Canadian Studies* 27, 4 (1992-93): 98-128.

Bramwell, Anna. *Ecology in the 20th Century.* New Haven: Yale University Press, 1989.

Callicott, J. Baird. "Traditional American Indian and Western European Attitudes toward Nature: An Overview." In *Defense of the Land Ethic: Essays in Environmental Philosophy.* Albany: State University of New York Press, 1989. 182-84.

Carlos, Ann, and Frank Lewis. "Indians, the Beaver, and the Bay: The Economics of Depletion in the Lands of the Hudson's Bay Company, 1700-1763." *Journal of Economic History* 53, 3 (1993): 465-94.

Carter, Sarah. *Lost Harvests: Prairie Indian Reserve Farmers and Government Policy.* Montreal: McGill-Queen's University Press, 1990.

Colpitts, George. "Conservation, Science, and Canada's Fur Farming Industry, 1913-1945." *Social History/Histoire sociale* 30, 59 (1997): 77-108.

–. "'Victuals to Put into Our Mouths': Environmental Perspectives on Fur Trade Provisioning Activities at Cumberland House, 1775-1782." *Prairie Forum* 22, 1 (1997): 1-22.

–. "Wildlife Promotions, Western Canadian Boosterism, and the Conservation Movement 1890-1914." *American Review of Canadian Studies* 2 (1998): 103-30.

Craig Brown, Robert. "The Doctrine of Usefulness: Natural Resource and National Park Policy in Canada, 1887-1914." In *Canadian Parks in Perspective.* Ed. J.G. Nelson. Calgary: The Canadian National Parks Today and Tomorrow Conference, 1968.

Crosby, Alfred W. *Ecological Imperialism: The Biological Expansion of Europe, 900-1900.* Cambridge: Cambridge University Press, 1991.

Dagg, Anne Innis. *Canadian Wildlife and Man.* Toronto: McClelland and Stewart, 1974.

Davis, Richard Clarke. *Voyages of Discovery: 20th Century Evolution of the Narratives of Wilderness Travel in the Canadian North.* PhD dissertation, University of New Brunswick, 1979.

Decker, Daniel J., and Gary R. Goff, eds. *Valuing Wildlife: Economic and Social Perspectives.* Boulder: Westview Press, 1987.

Dick, Lyle. *Farmers Making Good: The Development of Abernethy District, Saskatchewan, 1880-1920.* Ottawa: Minister of Supply and Services, 1989.

Dobak, William A. "Killing the Canadian Buffalo, 1821-1881." *Western Historical Quarterly* 27, 1 (1996): 33-52.

Doyle, James. "American Literary Images of the Canadian Prairies, 1860-1910." *Great Plains Quarterly* 3, 1 (1983): 30-38.

Ens, Gerhard J. *Homeland to Hinterland: The Changing Worlds of the Red River Métis in the Nineteenth Century.* Toronto: University of Toronto Press, 1996.

Evans, David. *A History of Nature Conservation in Britain.* London: Routledge, 1992.

Flores, Dan. "Bison Ecology and Bison Diplomacy: The Southern Plains from 1800 to 1850." *Journal of American History* 78, 2 (1991): 465-85.

Foster, Janet. *Working for Wildlife: The Beginning of Preservation in Canada.* Toronto: University of Toronto Press, 1978.

Foster, John. "The Métis and the End of the Plains Buffalo in Alberta." In *Buffalo.* Ed. John Foster, Dick Harrison, and I.S. MacLaren. Edmonton: University of Alberta Press, 1992. 61-78.

Fowke, Vernon C. *The National Policy and the Wheat Economy.* Toronto: University of Toronto Press, 1957.

Francis, R. Douglas. *Images of the West: Changing Perceptions of the Prairies, 1690-1960.* Saskatoon: Western Producer Prairie Books, 1989.

Fraser, Esther. *Wheeler.* Banff: Summerthought Publications, 1978.

Friesen, Gerald. *The Canadian Prairies: A History.* Toronto: University of Toronto Press, 1987.

Gaffield, Chad, and Pam Gaffield, eds. *Consuming Canada: Readings in Environmental History.* Toronto: Copp Clark, 1995.

Gayton, Don. *The Wheatgrass Mechanism: Science and Imagination in the Western Canadian Landscape.* Saskatoon: Fifth House Publishers, 1990.

Geist, Valerius. *Buffalo Nation: History and Legend of the North American Bison.* Saskatoon: Fifth House Publishers, 1996.

Gillis, R. Peter. "Rivers of Sawdust: The Battle over Industrial Pollution in Canada, 1865-1903." *Journal of Canadian Studies* 21, 1 (1986): 84-103.

Gillis, R. Peter, and Thomas R. Roach. "The American Influence on Conservation in Canada: 1899-1911." *Journal of Forest History* 30, 4 (1986): 160-74.

Girard, Michel F. "The Commission of Conservation as a Forerunner to the National Research Council 1909-1921." In *Building Canadian Science: The Role of the National Research Council.* Ed. Richard A. Jarrell and Yves Gingras. Ottawa: Canadian Science and Technology Historical Association, 1991.

–. *L'Écologisme retrouvé: Essor et déclin de la commission de la conservation du Canada.* Ottawa: Les Presses de l'Université d'Ottawa, 1994.

Gould, Peter C. *Green Politics: Back to Nature, Back to the Land, and Socialism in Britain: 1880-1900.* New York: St. Martin's Press, 1988.

Graham, Jr., Frank. *The Audubon Ark: A History of the National Audubon Society.* New York: Alfred A. Knopf, 1990.

Gray, Gary G. *Wildlife and People: The Human Dimensions of Wildlife Ecology.* Urbana: University of Illinois Press, 1993.

Hadley, Margery Tanner. "Photography, Tourism, and the CPR: Western Canada, 1884-1914." In *Essays on the Historical Geography of the Canadian West.* Ed. L.A. Rosenvall and S.M. Evans. Calgary: Department of Geography, University of Calgary, 1987. 48-69.

Hammond, Lorne. *"No Ordinary Degree of System": The Columbia Department of the Hudson's Bay Company and the Harvesting of Wildlife, 1825-1849.* MA thesis, University of Victoria, 1988.

Hart, E.J. *The Selling of Canada: The CPR and the Beginnings of Canadian Tourism.* Banff: Altitude Publishing, 1983.

Hartwig, Hermann. *Animals and Men.* Trans. Richard Winston and Clara Winston. New York: Natural History Press, 1965.

Harvey, David D. "The Lure of the North: American Approaches to the Canadian Wilderness." *Canadian Review of American Studies* 17, 1 (1986): 35-50.

Hays, Samuel P. *Conservation and the Gospel of Efficiency: The Progressive Conservation Movement, 1890-1920.* Cambridge: Harvard University Press, 1959.

Hewitt, C. Gordon. *The Conservation of Canadian Wildlife.* New York: Charles Scribner's Sons, 1921.

Huth, Hans. *Nature and the American: Three Centuries of Changing Attitudes.* Berkeley: University of California Press, 1957.

Isenberg, Andrew C. "The Returns of the Bison: Nostalgia, Profit, and Preservation." *Environmental History* 2, 2 (1997): 179-96.

–. "The Wild and the Tamed: The Destruction of the Bison." Paper presented at the Themes and Issues in North American Environmental History Conference, University of Toronto, May 1998.

Jasen, Patricia. *Wild Things: Nature, Culture, and Tourism in Ontario, 1790-1914.* Toronto: University of Toronto Press, 1995.

Killan, Gerald. "Ontario's Provincial Parks and Changing Conceptions of 'Protected Places.'" In *Changing Parks: The History, Future, and Cultural Context of Parks and Heritage Landscapes.* Ed. John Marsh and Bruce W. Hodgins. Toronto: Natural Heritage, 1998. 24-49.

–. *Protected Places: A History of Ontario's Provincial Park System.* Toronto: Dundurn Press; Ontario Ministry of Natural Resources, 1993.

Krech, Shepard, III. *The Ecological Indian: Myth and History.* New York: W.W. Norton, 1999.

–, ed. *The Subarctic Fur Trade: Native Social and Economic Adaptations.* Vancouver: UBC Press, 1984.

Lindsay, Debra. *Science in the Subarctic: Trappers, Traders, and the Smithsonian Institution.* Washington: Smithsonian Institution, 1993.

Livingston, John A. *The Fallacy of Wildlife Conservation.* Toronto: McClelland and Stewart, 1981.

Lothian, W.F. *A History of Canada's National Parks.* 4 vols. Ottawa: Parks Canada, 1981.

MacGregor, James G. *Vision of an Ordered Land: The Story of the Dominion Land Survey.* Saskatoon: Western Producer Prairie Books, 1981.

MacKenzie, John M. *The Empire of Nature: Hunting, Conservation, and British.* Manchester: Manchester University Press, 1988.

Martin, Calvin. *Keepers of the Game: Indian-Animal Relationships in the Fur Trade.* Berkeley: University of California Press, 1978.

–. "Subarctic Indians and Wildlife." In *Old Trails and New Directions.* Ed. Carol M. Judd and Arthur J. Ray. Toronto: University of Toronto Press, 1980. 73-81.

Martin, Chester. *"Dominion Lands" Policy.* Ottawa: Carleton Library, 1973.

Martin, Paul-Louis. *La Chasse au Québec.* Québec: Boréal, 1990.

McCandless, Robert G. *Yukon Wildlife: A Social History.* Edmonton: University of Alberta Press, 1985.

Merchant, Carolyn. *Major Problems in American Environmental History: Documents and Essays.* Lexington, MA: D.C. Heath, 1993.

Mighetto, Lisa. *Wild Animals and American Environmental Ethics.* Tucson: University of Arizona Press, 1991.

Milloy, John. "'Our Country': The Significance of the Buffalo Resource for a Plains Cree Sense of Territory." In *Aboriginal Resource Use in Canada: Historical and Legal Aspects.* Ed. Kerry Abel and Jean Friesen. Manitoba Studies in Native History 6. Winnipeg: University of Manitoba Press, 1991. 51-70.

Nash, Roderick. *Wilderness and the American Mind.* New Haven: Yale University Press, 1967.

Nelles, H.V. *The Politics of Development: Forests, Mines, and Hydro-Electric Power in Ontario, 1849-1941.* Toronto: University of Toronto Press, 1974.

Nelson, J.G. *The Last Refuge.* Montreal: Harvest House, 1973.

Novak, Milan, et al. *Furbearer Harvests in North America, 1600-1984.* Toronto: Ontario Ministry of Natural Resources, 1987.

Oelschlaeger, Max. *The Idea of Wilderness: From Prehistory to the Age of Ecology.* New Haven: Yale University Press, 1991.

Owram, Doug. *Promise of Eden: The Canadian Expansionist Movement and the Idea of the West 1856-1900*. Toronto: University of Toronto Press, 1980, 1992.

Penick, Jr., James. "The Progressives and the Environment." In *The Progressive Era*. Ed. Lewis L. Gould. Syracuse: Syracuse University Press, 1974. 115-31.

Pocius, Gerald L. "Tourists, Health Seekers, and Sportsmen: Luring Americans to Newfoundland in the Early Twentieth Century." In *Twentieth-Century Newfoundland: Explorations*. Ed. James Hiller and Peter Neary. St. John's: Breakwater, 1994. 47-77.

Potyondi, Barry. *In Palliser's Triangle: Living in the Grasslands, 1850-1930*. Saskatoon: Purich Publishing, 1995.

Ray, Arthur J. *The Canadian Fur Trade in the Industrial Age*. Toronto: University of Toronto Press, 1990.

–. *Indians in the Fur Trade: Their Role as Trappers, Hunters, and Middlemen in the Lands Southwest of Hudson Bay: 1660-1870*. Toronto: University of Toronto Press, 1974.

–. "Some Conservation Schemes of the Hudson's Bay Company, 1821-50: An Examination of the Problems of Resource Management in the Fur Trade." *Journal of Historical Geography* 1, 1 (1975): 49-68.

Reichwein, PearlAnn. *Beyond the Visionary Mountains: The Alpine Club of Canada and the Canadian National Park Idea, 1906-1969*. PhD dissertation, Carleton University, 1995.

Reiger, John F. *American Sportsmen and the Origins of Conservation*. Norman: University of Oklahoma Press, 1986.

Ritvo, Harriet. *The Animal Estate: The English and Other Creatures in the Victorian Age*. Toronto: Penguin Books, 1990.

Roe, Frank Gilbert. *The North American Buffalo: A Critical Study of the Species in Its Wild State*. Toronto: University of Toronto Press, 1951.

Runte, Alfred. *National Parks: The American Experience*. Lincoln: University of Nebraska Press, 1997.

Schmitt, Peter J. *Back to Nature: The Arcadian Myth in Urban America*. New York: Oxford University Press, 1969.

Smith, Brian J. "The Historical and Archaeological Evidence for the Use of Fish as an Alternative Subsistence Resource among Northern Plains Bison Hunters." In *Aboriginal Resource Use in Canada: Historical and Legal Aspects*. Ed. Kerry Abel and Jean Friesen. Manitoba Studies in Native History 6. Winnipeg: University of Manitoba Press, 1991. 35-49.

Spry, Irene. "The Great Transformation: The Disappearance of the Commons in Western Canada." In *Man and Nature on the Prairies*. Ed. Richard Allen. Regina: Canadian Plains Research Center, 1976. 21-45.

–. "The Tragedy of the Loss of the Commons in Western Canada." In *As Long as the Sun Shines and the Water Flows: A Reader in Canadian Native Studies*. Ed. Ian A.L. Getty and Antoine S. Lussier. Vancouver: UBC Press, 1983. 203-28.

Swanson, Timothy M. "Wildlife and Wildlands: Diversity and Development." In *Economics for the Wilds: Wildlife, Diversity, and Development*. Ed. Timothy M. Swanson and Edward B. Barbier. Washington: Island Press, 1992. 1-14.

Thomas, Keith. *Man and the Natural World: A History of the Modern Sensibility*. New York: Pantheon Books, 1983.

Tough, Frank. *"As Their Resources Fail": Native Peoples and the Economic History of Northern Manitoba, 1870-1930*. Vancouver: UBC Press, 1996.

Tudge, Colin. *Last Animals at the Zoo: How Mass Extinction Can Be Stopped*. Washington: Island Press, 1992.

Turner, James. *Reckoning with the Beast: Animals, Pain, and Humanity in the Victorian Mind*. Baltimore: Johns Hopkins University Press, 1980.

Vecsey, Christopher, and Robert W. Venables. *American Indian Environments: Ecological Issues in Native American History*. New York: Syracuse University Press, 1980.

Van Kirk, Sylvia. *The Development of National Park Policy in Canada's Mountain National Parks, 1885-1930*. MA thesis, University of Alberta, 1969.

Van West, John J. "Ojibwa Fisheries, Commercial Fishers Development, and Fisheries Administration, 1873-1915: An Examination of Conflicting Interest and the Collapse of the Sturgeon Fisheries of the Lake of the Woods." *Native Studies Review* 6, 1 (1980): 30-35.

Wadland, John. *Ernest Thompson Seton: Man in Nature and the Progressive Era 1880-1915*. New York: Arno Press, 1978.

Waiser, W.A. *The Field Naturalist: John Macoun, the Geological Survey, and Natural Science*. Toronto: University of Toronto Press, 1989.

Wamsley, Keven. "Good Clean Sport and a Deer Apiece: Game Legislation and State Formation in 19th Century Canada." *Canadian Journal of History of Sport* 25, 2 (1994): 1-20.

Wetherell, Donald Grant, with Irene Kmet. *Useful Pleasures: The Shaping of Leisure in Alberta 1896-1945*. Regina: Canadian Plains Research Center, University of Regina, 1990.

Wonders, Karen. *Habitat Dioramas: Illusions of Wilderness in Museums of Natural History*. Uppsala, Sweden: Uppsala University Press, 1993.

–. "A Sportsman's Eden." *Beaver*, 79, 5 (October-November 1999): 26-32; *Beaver*, 79, 6 (December 1999-January 2000): 30-35, 37.

Worster, Donald. *Nature's Economy: A History of Ecological Ideas*. Cambridge: Cambridge University Press, 1985.

Yerbury, J.C. *The Subarctic Indians and the Fur Trade, 1680-1860*. Vancouver: UBC Press, 1986.

Zeller, Suzanne. *Inventing Canada: Early Victorian Science and the Idea of a Transcontinental Nation*. Toronto: University of Toronto Press, 1987.

Index

Alberta Fish and Game Association, 143, 157
Alberta Gun Club (Lethbridge), 88
American Game Protection Association, 92
Amerindians: Assiniboine, 21, 23, 32; Blood, 26; Chipewyan, 20, 25, 66; Cree, 20, 23, 26, 28-29, 66, 84, 123; Dogrib, 16, 20; Ojibwa, 24; provisioning trade in general, 14-37; Slavey, 16, 20, 66; social customs around the exchange of provisions, 24, 26-28; Stoney, 98-99, 136, 153-54
Amerindians, and game legislation, 51, 87-88, 93-95
Antelope, 19, 68, 73-74, 98, 108, 163
Auto travel and conservation, 143, 147-48

Back-to-nature movement, 70-71
Banff, 140
Banff National Park. See Rocky Mountains National Park
Bear hunts, 68, 73
Bears: black, 3, 73, 151, 160; in fur trade, 20; grizzly, 5, 71, 74, 84, 89; as meat, 18; polar, 17; skins exported, 17
Bedson, Samuel, 49, 55-57, 57-60, 128
Beef famine, 75, 79-80
Begbie, Matthew Baillie, 35, 106
Begg, Alexander, 51, 152
Bell, Charles, 54, 60
Bighorn sheep. See Mountain sheep
Boosterism, 103-24
Bradshaw, Fred, 90, 93-94, 114, 133
Brewster, Jim, 152-53
Brewster family, 118
British Royal Society, 34
Brown, George, 40
Brown, Robert, 34-35

Buffalo, 9, 11, 19, 20, 27, 29, 44, 62, 64-65, 108, 111-12, 123, 128, 152, 162; bones, 64-65; domestication, 51-62; meat prices, 23, 49-51; popular stories about, 65; tamed, 57; tongues, 16; wool, 16
Bulletin (Edmonton), on Bedson buffalo, 60
Butler, William Francis, 62, 67

Calgary Anglers Association, 144, 148
Calgary conservation, 141, 148, 166
Calgary Herald, 137, 140, 143, 161
Calgary natural history museum, 69
Calgary Rod and Gun Club, 87
Canadian Commission of Conservation, 114, 129
Canadian National Parks Association, 118, 166
Canadian Pacific Railway, 6, 72, 108, 115, 117-21, 136, 139
Caribou, 71, 90; domestication, 60
Claresholm Fish and Game Protective Association, 143
Cocking, Matthew, 21
Coldstream Gun Club, 137
Coleman Rod and Gun Club, 143
Conservation, 93, 103-4, 108, 114, 123, 125-26, 129, 133; and boosterism, 10, 104; and First Nations, 10, 93-94, 96-98, 100-1; pioneer initiatives, 10, 86, 125-27, 129-63, 145-50, 155; and urban development, 10, 130
Conservation associations, 125-27, 131, 169-71; Calgary, 109, 132, 140-42, 144; Claresholm, 143; Coleman, 143, 148; Cranbrook, 137; Delta, 138; Edmonton, 109, 132, 140, 155; Fernie, 134-35; High River, 145-48; Macleod, 54, 65, 131, 158;

Printed and bound in Canada by Friesens
Set in Stone by Artegraphica Design Co. Ltd.
Copy editor: Dallas Harrison
Proofreader: Carina Blåfield